From the Bush to the Roots
The Story of
Good Samaritan Ministries
in Africa

By Bettie P. Mitchell

Copyright © 2014 Bettie P. Mitchell
All rights reserved. Written permission must be secured from the author to use or reproduce any portion of this book.

Published by Good Samaritan Ministries
7929 S.W. Cirrus Drive, Building 23
Beaverton, Oregon 97005 U.S.A.

First Printing 2014
Printed in the United States of America

Scripture quotations in this publication are taken from the New Jerusalem Bible.

About the Title: *From the Bush to the Roots*

This title is essential. This book is a guide from the bush back to the roots. Only then is it possible to keep the bush alive and healthy. When future generations look at Good Samaritan Ministries, they may see only the bush, the ministry in their time. If they do not see the roots of the bush, the bush will surely die. It is the story of the roots that will always provide the central direction for each generation of Samaritans.

Root: in botany, that part of a plant normally underground. Its primary functions are anchorage of the plant, absorption of water and dissolved minerals and conduction of these to the stem, and storage of reserve foods.

We must start at Nineveh (Mosul, Iraq) in 1976. God initiated a direct call and the authority of this ministry.
We became an act of obedience to
The Call—"Teach nothing but My
Kingdom."

We were warned at Irbil, three days later, never to lose focus of the ministry to one for the temptation of the crowds.

Clearly the Lord spoke at Irbil, "Do you see this child? This is who you will teach."

Dedication

I dedicate this book to the grass roots people who worked for the best in His Kingdom. Many are not named in this book, but they are remembered, appreciated and seen by the Lord Himself. This book is dedicated to all who had a little to give, and prayed fervently to give more.

I dedicate this book to the readers who will decide on the value of each story as it relates to their own lives, and their desire to help make a difference in Africa.

Good Samaritan Ministries deeply appreciates the people from around the world who have given to Africa. We realize we are one of many ministries. We know miracles are being done through many ministries. One thing that makes this Samaritan ministry different is the intimate, empowering relationships with the laborers laboring in the fields.

No leader in the field is more important than the words Jesus used, "In the least, I am."

This book was transcribed by Kim Hallberg. She has labored tirelessly month after month, not only with this book, but the other books that preceded it. She is a miracle to me: her gifts, her talents, and her purpose in this mission.

Also, I am profoundly grateful to Joan Baker who, several years ago, wrote a book of the biographies of many international Samaritan leaders, *Samaritans Along The Way*.

Good Samaritan Ministries here in the United States has made the Samaritan journey with the people of Africa. The people of Africa have made this journey with all of us. To this day, we continue moving together. God has blessed us all!

Bettie P. Mitchell
Founder and International Director (1976-2009)
Good Samaritan Ministries, International HQ Office
7929 SW Cirrus Dr., #23, Beaverton OR 97008
www.GoodSamaritanMinistries.org

Preface

The Call of the Lord is this: "You shall train nations and peoples to give up their woes and their victim mentalities. You shall fully train them to be lifetime Samaritans. The Christian faith must be a faith with action, not a faith of religion or just words and works. It must be alive!

Above all, we call others, train them and they bear fruit. Do not hesitate! This call is greater than we will ever know! It is the Lord who has given it and it came to us from the Walls of Ancient Nineveh.

Where are we? Are we called to this work for a lifetime? Will the Lord someday say to us, "Well done, my good and faithful servants"?

Recently, the Lord gave me a Word. I was asking Him about fasting and prayer. I said, "Lord, you have always given me a profound prayer life, but I only fast three days a year." He spoke to me very definitely and said, "You fasted your freedom. You gave everything to me. Therefore, I have given to you this Samaritan life."

The Introduction

When I started the work of Good Samaritan Ministries in the house, I had no master plan of development. Development occurred in miraculous ways. Doors opened and the unexpected happened. You must believe me, I never thought of going to Africa. I had no intention to go to Africa, but beginning in 1986, Africa opened its door and asked Good Samaritan Ministries to come in.

Africa is made up of 53 countries. 14 out of those countries are landlocked. One-third of the continent is desert, 25% is in the Sahara. The continent covers 11 million square miles, with a population of a little over one billion. Africa is the second largest continent in the world. Good Samaritan Ministries has done development work in 20 African countries.

Africa is a short and wide continent; therefore, the southern tip of Africa is much closer to the equator than the Southern tip of South America. Much of the continent is affected by the equator, which runs through the middle of Africa.

From 1987 through 2006, I made 10 trips to Africa. Many of those trips were with teams. I personally visited 15 countries, and called indigenous National Directors to lead the development of the work in each country. Good Samaritan Ministries provided training and development opportunities in each country. **Linkage with other countries in Africa, and other Good Samaritan countries throughout the world was and continues to be essential.** We called forth and trained many leaders, and those leaders achieved significant breakthroughs themselves. Most of them successfully built effective teams to train Samaritans and meet needs countrywide. **Thus, every country had many grass roots local centers.**

Three of our African countries' directors have received Ph.D.s: James Opiyo in Kenya received an Honorary Ph.D. in 2012, Osborn Muyanja, of Uganda, and Faraday Iwuchukwu, of Nigeria, received Ph.Ds. James and Osborn were high school graduates when they came into the work.

The Lord created His significance in many lives.

The key is full-time Samaritans through the influence and actions of the Holy Spirit. Each Samaritan is a fellow

Samaritan, free to change the face of Africa from poverty mentality to dynamic faith. My visits numbered: Kenya, nine; Nigeria, eight; Uganda, four; Tanzania, four; Malawi, one; Zambia, one; South Africa, three; Sierra Leone, three; Burundi, one; Liberia, one; Ghana, one; Cameroon, one; Senegal, one; Rwanda, one; and Congo, one.

As the ministry grew in significance in many of the countries, other teams were sent out on many journeys. **We all represented the work of the Lord Jesus.** The active work of faith brings about the explosion of significant action. **The places and peoples were free to develop! We empowered all to go and do likewise.**

The purpose of this book is to stimulate thought and discussion. How can Christianity be more vital to development? If we develop a person, a people, an attitude, and a spirit, can this vitalization change the world?

World Vision Magazine reported in 1991, "The number one problem in Africa is the starvation for leadership. Africa needs leaders who value people, see people with their dignity, and their resources, not as things that can be used, manipulated, and exploited."

In the first generation of Good Samaritan Ministries, passion, heroic discipline, and remarkable breakthroughs occurred here in America and in Africa. As the first generation received and heard the "Call," great leaders were created by the "Call" itself. The leaders were from the meek and lowly. Those that had almost nothing, those who were distanced from any influence became people of great influence, for they took the passion of the "Call" and chose to become lifetime Samaritans.

This book is written to the next generations. Will your passion be like the first century Samaritans, or waning? Will it become less because you desire to become more? The heroes in this book represent the challenges to the next generations of Samaritans.

The following words are from letters I wrote over the years. They are important enough to speak to all of us at this time.

What is Good Samaritan Ministries?

No matter what people tell you what Good Samaritans Ministries is about, it is about an extraordinary miracle done in the Name of the Lord. It is about our personal attitude toward the people we see suffering. It is about our own prejudice, our own coins, our own conscience, and our own life. **What is a Samaritan? It is not an organization. It is each unique, individual life.** Many Samaritans are helping one another, thus creating sufficient help for the ones that lie stuck and half-dead on the road. Sometimes a ministry is half-dead in the road. Look at that and be shaken of the Lord. Something new is about to quicken your spirit. The Spirit of the Lord will change the actions of our hearts.

Good Samaritan is not about works and projects. It is about spirit and truth. It is about life. It is about the life of one person who makes a difference in the lives of many.

Often, in Africa, there is a feeling that somehow or other, if they had more help, if they had more money, they would be better people. Africa is a great people and God has provided for them according to His riches and His glory. Your greater work in Africa will be to see after the elderly, tend the young, and be compassionate to the widow and to truly be a Samaritan, a genuine neighbor, a giving person, a lifting up person. When you see someone that others would completely hate or ignore, it will be to that person that you go and help. This is the purpose, the intent, and the holy calling. Most of us are counselors, friends of the poor, the lame, and the weak, paying enough for those that no one was willing to pay for at all. I am not speaking of money, I am speaking of time, mercy, and the things we can do with what we do have.

I have never found that God is in the 'silver and gold' business. He's in the 'stand up and walk in the Name of Jesus' business. When we begin to pray 'silver and gold' prayers, we often return with an empty hand. It has been my experience and it is so, that God is not training us in 'silver and gold' prayers. He's training us to 'stand up and walk in the Name of Jesus.' This is a lesson I've had to learn, and James

Opiyo had to learn. Every servant that follows Jesus must learn this or possibly fail and be in Satan's hands.

I do not have big expectations or big plans. I have a little salt, a widow's mite, and a firm and gentle heart. I believe that what is small is truly what becomes large. **And so, we will plant the mustard seed, the smallest of all possible seeds, to watch the bush grow.**

Table of Contents

Dedication		4
Preface		5
Introduction		6
Ch. 1	The Road to Avutu	13
Ch. 2	We Arrive in Avutu	21
Ch. 3	The Birth of the Samaritans, Kenya	27
Ch. 4	The Training	41
Ch. 5	Build Team Work	43
Ch. 6	The Door Opens in Uganda	55
Ch. 7	The Old Seniors	63
Ch. 8	The Return Home	71
Ch. 9	The Jenipher Oduor Story	75
Ch. 10.	Shock and Grief, 1992 Africa	107
Ch. 11	The Shock Continues – Tanzania and Nigeria	117
Ch. 12	I Must Be About My Father's Business	125
Ch. 13	Prayer Support Team/SATELLITES	145
Ch. 14	We Must See Both Sides	149
Ch. 15	Development! Development! Development!	167
Ch. 16	Miss April	177
Ch. 17	Building the Character of Teams	189
Ch. 18	We Went On	199
Ch. 19	Papa Jerry & Mama Bettie	205
Ch. 20	The Sacrifices	221
Ch. 21	Why Go?	237
Ch. 22	God's Business	249
Ch. 23	The Story of New Countries	255
Ch. 24	The Impossible is Begun	265
Ch. 25	The Rebirth of the Samaritan Community	275
Ch. 26	Test and Tragedy Builds the Whole	285
Ch. 27	Suffering, Leadership and Transitions	291
Ch. 28	The Vision of Jesus	299
Ch. 29	The West Africa Continental Training Center	311
Ch. 30	The Final Strength Given – Journey in 2006	321
Ch. 31	The Education Story	335
Ch. 32	The Final Word	353
Ch. 33	In Memory of Heroes of the Faith	371

CHAPTER 1

THE ROAD TO AVUTU

December 22, 1985, I asked my husband if we could go to Maranatha Church in Portland, Oregon. I was seeking spiritual growth and development. Yes, we had endurance and spiritual growth, but wasn't there more?

As we came into Maranatha Church, I learned that Wendell Wallace, a pastor and evangelist, was the speaker that night. Knowing of him, I was glad.

At the end of the service, there was an altar call. Many people lined the aisle. I decided to join them at the end of the line. Finally, the man in front of me went forward for Pastor Wallace to anoint him with oil and pray for him. Pastor Wallace asked him what it was he wanted from the Lord. The man replied instantly, "A triple portion of the Spirit of Elijah." Pastor Wallace had a large bottle of anointing oil in his hand. Shockingly, he poured the whole bottle of oil over him. The man's whole body dripped oil.

I was still waiting, but I was waiting on the floor. I was slain in the Spirit. Now, if one lies on the floor in the midst of an African American mixed race church, there is a huge amount of prayer going on around you, but for me, it was a time of eternal rest. Deep down inside, I chuckled wondering what I looked like spread out on my back. As people looked down from the balcony, I must have been a strange sight—this very white lady with black faces all around her.

I never did get to Pastor Wallace. I lay there a long time. When you're in that holy rest, you don't have any sense of need or request of things that have to be shared with God. God is sharing a time of eternity with you. In those moments on the floor, I had found the spiritual growth and development I was seeking.

This was a defining moment. In wonder, as I looked back on this time, here was the beginning of the Road to Avutu. I was spiritually slain, for the Africans who would soon unexpectedly visit and ask for help.

A time and a season went by and one day there was a Bishop named Tom Abungu from Kenya who was speaking at Tom's Pancake House in Beaverton. Now, it just so happened that two members from Good Samaritan Ministries had decided to have breakfast at Tom's Pancake House, Ellyn Anderson and Jean Brown. They overheard some of the enthusiasm coming from the other room, enthusiasm that pounded into the spirit and left imprint to save the souls of men.

After Bishop Tom had finished and was ready to leave, Ellyn and Jean approached him and asked him if he would visit Good Samaritan Ministries and come to see me. He took a card.

I knew nothing about this and several weeks passed. One day, Bishop Tom called me. He was back in Portland, and he wanted to come to the Good Samaritan Ministries office.

When this potent man of God walked into my office, the electricity of the Spirit had entered the room, an amount of electricity never experienced before in that office, or in my life.

Bishop Tom spent the whole day. We talked and prayed and laughed. I came to learn he was a man who would go out into the wilderness in Kenya to fast and pray for forty days. I marveled at this because I couldn't imagine fasting and praying for one day, let alone forty! Was this the definition of spiritual growth and development? What was happening? What was this?

Before Bishop Tom left, he prayed with the staff, and we made an agreement to help with a project in Kenya. He said goodbye. He didn't call again. I received no letter from him. About three months passed. One day, at my office, a telephone call came from a man who said his name was Pastor James Opiyo. Bishop Tom Abungu had sent him. He was in the San Francisco area. He said he was trying to get to Oregon to see me. He said he was in a tough position because he had no money and the couple who were allowing him to stay at their house had told him he had to leave.

I would like to inject a word here. Over the years, I could have made a mantra, a refrain to every request that came into Good Samaritan Ministries, "We have no money." Requests were overwhelming.

Spiritual growth and development did not respond well to the money we saw, but through heavenly invitations we learned to live and move and have our being by His Spirit. I said to this stranger on the phone, "James, it will be arranged for you to get to Oregon immediately, and we will keep you. You are to come. All will be provided."

Years later, James told me how astonished he was on the other end of the line. Yes, Bishop Tom had told him to make a call on Bettie Mitchell at Good Samaritan Ministries. Who was knocking on our door? Our invitation was immediate and remains always present in our relationship with this man, Pastor James Opiyo of Kenya.

When James came, he had little with him, but he was dressed in a suit, a tie, and a dress shirt. He was a pastor, and I learned that is the way African pastors dress.

During the initial meetings with James, the funniest thing happened. I could not believe that he had no money. I could not believe that anyone could be in the United States and have no money at all! So I said, "James, pull out and empty all of your pockets. I want to see if you have no money!" Each pocket was pulled and hanging from his clothes; indeed, he had no money. It was surely an audacious beginning for a relationship that has had lasting imprint on each of our lives.

I learned James Opiyo was from the Luo Tribe of Western Kenya. The Luo tribe had Semitic roots and had originally migrated from Iraq.

James was a Pastor under Bishop Tom. He had founded seven churches in his region. I learned he had been to a conference in Phoenix, and had sought to get to Oregon, but made it only to San Francisco. He was in a desperate situation because his host gave him a telephone and said, "You are to get out of here, and we mean it!"

James and I began to communicate and learn more about each other. I let James see for himself what the ministry was, and I looked into his soul to see what he was. I'm sure the Spirit looked into each of our souls to wonder: would this meeting bear fruit?

James spent almost two months in Oregon. On August 26, 1986, at our Board Meeting, an agreement was signed that James Opiyo would take Good Samaritan Ministries to Kenya. It was not to be just to his church, or Bishop Tom's church, but to Kenya, East Africa.

As a stipulation of the signing of this agreement, we asked James to come back to Oregon and bring his wife, Teresa. She needed to know exactly about the assignment and what this ministry was. On May 15, 1987, Teresa and James came from Kenya after a shocking circumstance.

We had purchased their tickets. At the last minute, the tickets were lost, and they thought for sure we would not be able to bring them. Satan's obstacles are God's opportunities. We brought them, and they stayed for three months of training.

We learned a great deal about each other. James was stubborn, and I am extraordinarily stubborn, but we were each willing to be broken to Christ. The Holy Spirit moved when we allowed it to change our minds and bring us into agreement. Some agreements were hard, some were easier.

It was important that James learn the ministry was not about "things." It was not about providing for the need of things in Africa. This Call is about the Spirit of the Samaritan, who sees the need and creates out of what is seen, a solution that will last and be eternal in its fruit. Thus, when James asked for clothing for people in Kenya, I said, "No James. I can only offer you training." That produced some of our stubborn moments, but training won, and later, James understood fully that the training had to conquer his list of needs and wants.

James Opiyo has an infectious laughter. When he smiled or laughed, the whole room became electrically charged with the Spirit of the Lord. He was an unusual man in that he was not so intensely locked into deeds, but realized that attitude has everything to do with victory.

Gradually, I asked James a lot of questions, and began to draw out some of his personal life story.

In November of 1967, James and Teresa were married. On the same day, they gave their lives to Christ Jesus, kneeling down in a park in Mombasa, Kenya. James told me that when he and Teresa were married, they had no money and one blanket. They were young, and really had no prospects of money. I am sure this experience drove them to their knees to accept that only God could help them survive.

That very day of their conversion to Christ, James found a large bill of Kenyan shillings in the street. They shared the blanket, they shared their lives, and they have given birth to three children: Jane, Hezron, and Jerry.

His parents' names were Hezron and Gaudesia. His father, Hezron, was born in 1922.

When James was born in 1952, it so-happened his father was in jail in Uganda. It was about politics and a season of the times rather than criminal activity, but the family was in dire straits.

James had a grandfather named William. He was a petrol attendant in a town in Kenya. A white man came to the station and asked for five liters of gas. William put in eight liters. The white man grabbed a whip from his vehicle, and beat William severely. Grandfather William was so traumatized that he went back to his birth village of Uranga and never left again. He would not look at a white person. He did not want to see a white person. A white person scared him. Many years later, I learned that Grandfather William and President Barack Obama's Grandfather, Hussein Onyango, were brothers of the same father. Hussein Onyango was Luo. For many years, they all lived in Uranga.

It is rather significant that Hussein Onyango, President Barack Obama's Grandfather, is buried in Uranga on the present site of the Bettie-Jerry School, but that is a long story, and a long time later when we will unfold how things came to pass. Even a school became an honorary degree among us all.

In 1986, when James Opiyo returned from his first visit to the United States, he went back to Nakuru, the fourth largest city in Kenya. Since he was under Bishop Tom's authority, he had to return to seek in prayer what was to be done.

His father, Hezron, came to Nakuru. He was the first person James introduced to the ministry of Good Samaritan. He said to his father, "This is a ministry, not a church." James asked the Mayor of Nakuru to give a plot to establish the ministry. During the night, they discussed plans with Teresa. She believed the plot was to be at home in the rural village of Uranga.

In one week, a pastor named Dixon came from Uranga to Nakuru. He said they would be able to get land in Uranga.

By 1987, after their second visit to Oregon, they had to make a decision where to start a building. They called Pastor Dixon when they were still in Oregon. Dixon got the land, and when they returned to Uranga, James immediately called 30 pastors into his very small house. (We're talking about a three-room house!) He immediately began to teach and train them. In a short time, it came to be that there were too many to fit into the house, so they moved under the trees. We provided enough funds to repair the Opiyo house, giving them a water tank and some better roofing. They began to build a Good Samaritan Ministries center on the donated land.

My mother died in 1986, leaving me with some inheritance, and I decided one of the first things I would do with that inheritance was build the first Good Samaritan Ministries center in Africa. The building cost $5,000. It was dedicated to my parents and to all mothers and fathers who sent forth their children.

James reported, during that period of time, things developed very rapidly. People kept coming. He put Peter, James and John, three members of the community, in charge of the construction. Later, when Jerry and I, and the Bakers went to Kenya, we saw these three great builders working. Wow! What an experience! The Samaritans met daily from 4:00 to 6:00 a.m., and formed a prayer support team of twelve. Every Saturday and Wednesday, the team met and prayed at least six hours.

James reported to me that the hardest idea to convince the people of was that Good Samaritan Ministries was not a new religion. James said someone came and found me talking with a drunkard of Uranga. We sponsored his child to go to school. Church people did not usually talk to drunkards, but Samaritans do.

One of the strongest commitments of Good Samaritan Ministries is to the power of personal relationships. In some ways, I see this as unique. For, in my experience, in other situations, particularly in churches, relationships are temporal. If a person leaves, the relationship is over. It has no lasting substance, and it is easy to forget the people who left.

For me, it was impossible to forget a relationship. It was impossible for it to be over. It may be stalled a little, but it definitely would not be over. This is the substance of and profound commitment to the Word of our Lord, who said, *"Lo, I will be with you always, even unto the end of the world."* (Matthew 28:20) He established permanency in relationships that is not often seen in the ways we connect, even in our own families. I repeat the words, "Lo, I am with you always, even unto the end of the world." I repeat the words, "Lo I am with you always, even unto the end of the world." This is the definition of permanent relationship.

Evarestus

Patty and Paul Stevens were members of Good Samaritan Ministries, and in 1986, they brought a young Nigerian man named Evarestus to my office. Evarestus was like a scared little kid. I could see in his face, absolute terror.

His story was that he had been sponsored to go to college in Oregon, and his sponsor had agreed to pay the fees his dad had provided through the sale of some land in Avutu. Suddenly, the man was arrested in the United Kingdom, and was unable to sponsor Evarestus in school. Only three months in America, from a village named Avutu in Nigeria, Evarestus had no hope of a sponsor and no place to turn. As he came to my office, I sat him on my lap as he sobbed. I sensed it was not self-pity in Evarestus, but a sincere desire to do what was right in the Lord's eyes. Evarestus and I bonded. We came to know each other, and Good Samaritan Ministries began to help him. We took over some of the sponsorship problems, and provided him with housing and food.

I found in Evarestus a rare kindness and profound gratitude. He became important in our decision to journey to Africa. I have always believed, in a relationship, you pay the whole price, not just part of it. You whole-heartedly support, you whole-heartedly give, and you whole-heartedly encourage.

As November 1987 was approaching, Joan Baker and I, and Joan's husband, Ted, and my husband, Jerry, decided to make a trip to Kenya. This was a very big decision, and in many ways a decision that terrified me.

My understanding that Africa might be primitive reached the level of believing that I could be sleeping on the floor and perhaps snakes would crawl across my body. Now, this sounds very foolish, but fear is fear, and it can only be conquered if it is addressed directly. We made the decision to go. **Once faith begins, action must follow.**

Ted and Jerry were to fly directly to Nairobi. Joan and I flew to Lagos, Nigeria. You see we had to visit Evarestus' family. We had to talk over with them the problems he was having. We had to report in to them. Did they ask us to do this? No. We did this because this is part of the cost of bonding that comes to all of us when we do it together. It was a tremendous decision to fly into Lagos, Nigeria, to find the road to Avutu.

Of course, the Nigerians had something they wanted us to take, and so a big box was packed and put on the plane with us. We were told Peter, Evarestus' brother, would meet us at the airport in Lagos. Coming into the Lagos Airport is a shocking experience. In those days, you experienced tremendous intimidation. As we were trying to get our luggage, and looking for Peter, my solution to the problem was to shout out, "Peter, Peter!" How funny this must have sounded in the airport in Lagos, this white woman, in a sea of black faces, shouting out, "Peter, Peter!" Little did they know it was a shout from my terror. It was a good thing Peter arrived because many people had begun to manipulate us and asked for fees to do this and fees to do that. They were trying to charge us to get into Nigeria. Without Peter, I don't know where the story would have ended. From Peter's side, we were the only two white women at the airport, and it was easy to spot us. We made it safely out of Lagos Airport and stayed over-night with Nigerians. Lagos was a sprawling city of millions.

The journey to Avutu would be many hours. We had to fly to Port Harcourt and then drive to Avutu in a rented car. On the journey, as we were stopped by the Nigerian Police along a dark stretch of road, the police asked us to unload our entire luggage and all of our belongings from the vehicle. When they saw the box, they were very excited and threw everything out of it, taking what they wanted. They let us pass. We were on the Road to Avutu.

CHAPTER 2

WE ARRIVE IN AVUTU

Finally, later that night, we arrived at Avutu. The mother of Evarestus was waiting with a lantern. They had been waiting, expecting us hours earlier. We missed a great celebration, but here we were! Joan and I had finally arrived! Evarestus' mother, Victoria, began to dance with me, and hug me. As she grabbed us, she showed love and shocking recognition of the cherished gift we were giving to honor their family.

I could write a whole book on the heat and humidity of Nigeria. It is so oppressive you feel like you are living in a bath of sweat. As we were not used to this, it was difficult for us.

Joan and I fell into the bed assigned to us and slept restlessly for a short length of time, when we began to hear singing.

It was our first experience with morning prayers in Africa. We went out of our room, barely covered with our nightclothes, and sat with Evarestus' extended family. The singing continued. Clapping, dancing, praise, and prayer touched our weary bodies with new life! We soon learned that the first order of family life was the worship of God. As each day dawned, the family would be daily found in His worship and praise. When it was over, people quickly dressed for the day. They began to put the house and grounds in order and prepare the food.

For me, this was a life-changing event, and oh dear God I wish it had changed my life. A memory was created in me of what is important and what is not. Worship and praise first, and work follows. All priorities to God are given unto the beginning of the day.

When we went outside, we were able to look around at our surroundings. We saw the great beauty around us, and we began to realize we were in a large village. The people of Avutu all knew one another. Every child was every other person's child. Everyone knew we had come to meet Evarestus' parents, and that we were helping him through school. We were honored guests, for in the Lord's eyes, we had done what was honorable.

After breakfast, the celebration planned for the day before began. Enthusiastic children welcomed us with songs and dancing. The simplicity of this home in Avutu touched our hearts deeply. Here was living faith!

Later in the day, a car drove up. An unexpected visitor named Faraday Iwuchukwu, from Port Harcourt, arrived to see us and to spend the night. Evarestus' family in Avutu did not know him. Living in America, Evarestus' sister, Eunice, had informed Faraday that we were going to be in Avutu and that he should come and meet with us. (She and Faraday had gone to the same Bible College in Nigeria.) Now, this was an unexpected turn of events for all of us!

Faraday had a good reputation among the Christians in Nigeria. He was respected for his abilities and his commitment to Christ Jesus.

Faraday had been National Secretary of the Council of Churches of Nigeria. He had been on many committees, and served in many capacities, both in education and church pastoral ministry.

Pastor Faraday and I met and discussed Good Samaritan Ministries. I shared the things I saw that needed to happen in Christianity, and he was seeking what could happen. He was at a turning point in the direction he wanted to go in ministry.

Faraday found himself spiritually dissatisfied. The needs of the people were not being met. There was a huge competitive spirit in Nigeria. Often people climbed on top of others to get where they wanted to go. There were very few who had the courage to look directly in the face of the genuine needs of the people. Few paid the price for the guardianship of Christ among the poor, the lame and the weak. Faraday had tried ambition and he was dissatisfied with it.

We made a tentative agreement, at the meeting at Avutu, that he would sponsor the development of Good Samaritan Ministries in Nigeria. We did some training. We looked at his idea of helping people, and our idea of helping people. Often, in Africa, helping is materialistic, and definitely, there is a place for this. However, the greatest need is for integrity, and spiritual maturity. The fullness of Christ is the fullness of the person. This was a gaping hole. Could Good Samaritan Ministries make a dent in the moral suffering of competition and the religious spirit that never had time for the needs of the people?

Nigeria is considered a wealthy nation in Africa, which means more than half of its people live in abject poverty. There is oil, and there is potential for development. It has the largest population of any African country. The population in 2009 was 154,729,000. The size of Nigeria is slightly more than twice the size of California. There is a huge divide between the Muslims and the Christians. The Northern half of Nigeria is 95% Muslim. Southern Nigeria is largely Christian. The divide between the two is absolute. The government was oppressive.

Faraday spoke of the event of the meeting between himself and Mama Bettie, "God spoke prophetically and we resolved there and then to work together. Mama Bettie came with a profound, in depth, conceptually practical, prophetic teaching I had never known in all of my theological education. She has been my greatest teacher after the Lord Jesus."

Because our time in Avutu was short, we saw only a limited part, but the event I remember most was attending the Catholic Church. On Sunday morning, we told Peter we would like to go to church, so he took us into the local commercial area and brought us to a church. In my spirit, I thought this must be an Episcopal church, because I knew Evarestus was a Protestant. Now, you can't imagine what Joan Baker and I felt as two simple white women sitting in an all-African church. You wouldn't believe the clothing and headdresses. Nigeria is famous for its color and outlandishly styled headdresses.

When the pastor called the congregation to come up for communion, Joan Baker and I got in the line to take communion. When we reached the priest, he said, "Are you Catholic?" I said, "No. I thought we were in an Episcopal Church." He said, "You may not take communion," and sent us back to our seats. This was rather unsettling, as we already felt very awkward. Years later, the Lord redeemed that memory with two experiences.

The Lord brought me to New York to help perform a Catholic wedding. The Priest asked me to give the homily. He talked to me, and related to me as a person. Later, one of our young adult members of Good Samaritan Ministries committed suicide. The funeral service was Catholic, and we all received communion.

I've always considered it strange that if you are not a member, you aren't invited to eat at the table. Perhaps the issue in my heart and spirit is, was this the way of Jesus? Was this hospitality? Would we say to a guest, you may not come to the table because you don't agree with us? It is a strange archaic leftover custom to hold communion separated, but there will come a day in the Catholic Church, and in all of our churches, that the separation will be over.

Now let me speak about Evarestus' family, particularly his father, Theophilus. I liked Theophilus so much. He was a good host. He tried hard to understand us (of course Peter had to translate everything.) I talked to Theophilus and Victoria at length about Evarestus' problems with his sponsor, about the problems he was having in America, and about the hardships that he was experiencing in trying to go to school. I assured them that this was a community project, and they, with us, were part of the project to educate Evarestus.

I had learned from Evarestus before I left America that his father had sold a piece of land in order to provide the funds for Evarestus to come to the U.S. for schooling. However, due to political problems, he could not send funds to the United States himself. As Evarestus needed a sponsor, a friend, who had a bank account in another country, agreed to take the funds and become his sponsor. He would send the funds, as needed, to Evarestus for school. After the first three months in Oregon, Evarestus was informed that his sponsor had been incarcerated for political reasons, and that his father's funds were gone.

It was important for us to reassure the family that their son would be all right, and that we would watch over him lovingly, as parents would, honoring their parenthood with him.

I will always remember Evarestus' father sitting outdoors with his man friends, eating the cacao. They offered us some. It was very bitter, but when ingested it produced euphoria.

Peter told me thirty years later of his parents' first impression of me. They called me "The Stubborn One."

Before we left Avutu, we presented an olive wood gift from the Holy Land to the family. It was a carving of the Parable of the Good Samaritan. Peter recently shared with me it was still above the door to his father's room. It had never been taken down.

Years later, Evarestus' mother, Victoria, came to America and had dinner at our house. We embraced and danced. When we left Avutu something had happened to us. Avutu had become a symbol for a new beginning in Africa. Nigeria would become fertile soil for Samaritans.
We must remember this ministry is to individuals. As the church is corporate and collective, the Samaritan recognizes the need of a single individual, and walks with that person through whatever grief and tragedy has profoundly touched their life.

Avutu symbolizes all that we are and all that we could be to one another. We are all people of a village, living in the shadow of our Mighty God. With a Father's hand, a Father's encouragement, we can become protectors of the Father's creation.

CHAPTER 3

THE BIRTH OF THE SAMARITANS, KENYA

Joan and I flew into Nairobi, Kenya, and met our husbands who had spent the night at a hotel. We were all very weary. We headed out for the city of Nakuru in the Rift Valley. It is the fourth largest city in Kenya. We stayed in the Kenya City Mission housing. Of course, Bishop Tom Abungu was there, but we were being hosted and led by Reverend James Opiyo.

It was a hard adjustment to get used to an environment where everything is dark. Most of the houses were dark, the walls were dark, the lighting was not very light, if there was lighting, and every face was so dark. In a photo, the people could barely be recognized.

There was one harder adjustment—toilets—a hole in the floor! I've never been very muscular in the legs, and squatting, almost impossible! Maneuvering a small hole and then a big job, I had a history of constipation. If I would say there was one thing that was hard about Kenya, it would be toilets. Sometimes I think I could write a doctoral thesis on toilets.

What was wonderful about Kenya was the Spirit of Hospitality, a spirit I never see in America. We're so reserved, so formal, and, perhaps, withdrawn from the astonishing explosion of the Spirit of Hospitality that could welcome the stranger and immediately change spirits of abandonment, hopelessness, and rejection.

Big smiles, singing and dancing, keep the beat of the music and praise God. There is enormous African understanding that children are the key greeters of all guests. The grown-ups prepare the house and put out the food, but the children, when they dance and sing looking at you, give the meaning to life.

The first Sunday in Nakuru, I was asked to preach. There seemed to be about 300 people in the church. By this time, I had an African dress. Women's heads had to be covered. I remember very well the sermon that day, my first sermon in Africa, *"Not by Might, Not by Power, But by My Spirit."* (Zechariah 4:6)

I already sensed that Pentecostal religion in Kenya could have a lot of human might and power. It was to this that these words

"By His Spirit" were addressed. I didn't stand up front and preach. I walked around the room. I touched the people. I paid attention to them. I was talking to them, not talking at them. For that hour, relationship was movement, eyes meeting, touching the needs of many.

Joan, Ted, Jerry, and all of the pastors of the church, sat on formal chairs at the back of the altar. I sat with the people. Many knew this moment had come from God.

Papa Jerry, my husband, has a remarkable calling to children. He shows them love by his playfulness. He reaches out using puppets. The puppet talks to the children, teases them, and encourages them. This was his role in Kenya, and this became a large part of his role in Africa.

There was a widow in the front of the room. She had many children around her. I was told her name was Jenipher Oduor. She had nine children, and her husband had died three months before. She was a special woman from the very first time I laid eyes on her. We were invited to many homes for lunch, and then others for dinner. But, Jennifer Oduor invited us for breakfast. This was unique.

Before we left the United States, Julie Stevens, 7 years old, had given me a gold cross on a gold chain. I believe there was a gold heart and key on the chain as well. She said, "You will be called out by the Spirit to give this to someone." Jane Dijkslag, a long-time member of Good Samaritan Ministries, had given me $100 for a widow in need.

We arrived at Mama Jenipher's house, and met some of her children. She had a simple one-room apartment. We all gathered in the one room. Some had to stand. Of course, we had the borrowed chairs of honor. As I looked at Jenipher, I saw her face was unique in all of the faces I have met in Africa. She did not show her grief to get people's attention. She had a quiet grief, and her eyes shone like the Glory of God. During the morning, I put the chain around Jennifer's neck, carefully fastening it. I spoke to her of the importance of the gift, and that it was from the Lord Himself.

There came upon Jenipher, a look seldom seen in any country among any people.

At that moment, Jenipher became a saint. We left the $100. Later, I found out this paid all of her months of back rent.

Many houses had us for one meal, but only at Jenipher's did she insist that we also stay for lunch. This was from God alone. There was immediate love between Jenipher and myself. There was nothing that could stop this relationship from being permanent. Jenipher Oduor was a Woman of God.

After a few days in Nakuru, we headed to Uranga near Lake Victoria. They had been waiting a long time, and by the time we got there, it was dark. Africans have a special time system. They call it African Time. It means sometime within a day or two, I will arrive. In the Western world, time is more punctual. Africans measure time by the quality of time spent and the needs around them. We measure time by our schedules. Perhaps they are right. We could improve our measure of time.

As we came, there was, of course, the great Luo Song of Welcome. Many faces greeted us. Many faces eagerly looked at these Mzungu (white people). James and Teresa Opiyo lived in a three-room house with an outdoor kitchen. Joan and Ted shared one twin bed in one of the rooms. We had a double bed in the other room. Both beds had mosquito netting. There was a small closet room built to put our bath water in so we could bathe indoors. Bath water consisted of a basin of water that was heated for the white people, and a cup to pour and rinse. Normally, several had to take a bath in the same basin, but we were encouraged to each have fresh water.

We drank water from a jug that had a filtering system, and we had brought water purification tablets. I want to add to this story that Ted and Joan found it somehow possible to sleep in that single bed. We were there for almost three weeks.

James immediately asked us to begin training, and people came into the main room of the Opiyo house: pastors, a few women, and a lot of men. Joan and I were there to train. We immediately began to talk about listening, encouraging, and about the value of wise counsel that could come out of their lives shared in the holy balance of communication.

I decided to demonstrate a counseling session with my first client in Africa, Pastor Dixon. Pastor Dixon was not a young man. He and his wife had given birth to eleven children. Three died in infancy. I found Dixon to be a difficult person, because when he preached, he shouted. When he preached, the widows sat on the ground with their hands folded. As the outdoor service progressed, I wondered. Why was he shouting? What was he screaming?

As part of our training sessions, I decided to take a case study on Pastor Dixon's life. I found that his firstborn daughter died at 19 years of age. She could have been saved by medical intervention, but the Lord had not provided the funds for her medical care.

Pastor Dixon had done God's work faithfully, but when it was his child, there was no provision. He had profound grief, lasting grief. The grief of the shouter could not quiet his inside pain. We became lifetime friends.

We met James Opiyo's first client in Africa. His name was Peter. Peter was mentally ill. Often, he would tear his clothes off and walk around naked. He was extremely disturbed. When James returned from Oregon, he decided to choose Peter for his first client; therefore, I decided to choose Peter also. Peter was appointed the first caregiver of the new center. Peter was the only person I sent a Christmas gift of money to for many years. He received medication he needed, thanks to Good Samaritan Ministries, and Peter began to be a person who could help the ministry. He wore an old leather jacket that was severely worn out. James explained to me it was his old jacket Peter was wearing, and he would not take it off.

We were taken to the new center where the construction was taking place. It was about two-thirds complete. James and I decided to work together to purchase some of the materials still needed, and we would together supervise the completion of the building. We went shopping two or three times and brought the materials back to the builders. By God's grace, although we had arrived in November, by December 15th, the building was complete and ready for the dedication.

An interesting miracle happened before the dedication. I preached in a church near Uranga, and as I looked out over the audience, I saw two people I knew. Jenipher Oduor had come 200 miles with her nine children, and John Oundo was there. Now, who was John Oundo? I must tell this story.

Teresa Opiyo's brother and sisters and her mother lived on the family homestead in Uranga. They were all alcoholics. James decided to take us to the homestead for dinner so I might try to lead them to Christ. I could see they were all drunk, so after dinner I spoke only for a few minutes, and then said I was coming back in the morning at 10:00 a.m., as I wanted to talk to them. The next morning at 10:00, chairs were set up under the trees, and the people who had been drunk, were sober enough for me to talk to them. I was told that none of them yet were Christians, and so it would have been natural for me to bring a message of Christ to them. Wouldn't any Christian visitor bring Christ to the people? Hadn't many come to do just that?

I, instead, decided to talk to them about alcoholism, and how serious it was. I explained to them what their death would be like, what would happen to their bodies if they died of alcoholism, and that alcoholism always caused death unless the alcoholic stopped drinking.

Then I looked at Teresa Opiyo's brother sitting in the front row. John was dressed in an undershirt and a pair of pants. I doubt if he had on shoes. I spoke directly to John and his friend, whom I didn't know at all. I said, "I would like for you to go with Pastor Joshua Agola, behind that building over there, and I want you to decide whether you would be willing to develop and lead a program to bring alcoholics out of alcoholism and into life." They were gone about ten minutes, and when John returned, I said, "John, what have you decided?" His answer was, "Yes, I will do it." John never had another drink. He had been an alcoholic for twenty years.

So, when John showed up at church the following Sunday, I knew something big had happened.

John accepted Christ. He was not led to the Lord. He was led to an identity that would give him new life. This, indeed, was the Lord. This was Jesus, himself, giving John purpose and substance.

It was decided that we would baptize in the Nzaia River near Uranga. A certain time was set for the baptisms. For those walking, it was a long walk. For those riding in our vehicle, it was a short distance.

Now, it is rather dangerous to get into an African river, and I had read that we should never do it. I fastened my pants tight, pulled socks up over them, and got in the river. There were two baptism teams with two Africans, and Jerry, Ted and myself. Joan Baker recorded fifty-nine people who were baptized that day. One of them was John Oundo. We baptized Teresa's mother, Mama Benta, and all of her sisters. Jennifer Oduor came and brought baby Bettie to be dedicated. Oh yes, I forgot to tell you, the day of that Sunday service near Uranga, Jennifer Oduor declared that she had renamed her three-month-old daughter, Bettie. I talked about Jesus and the Jordan River. I renamed the Nzaia River the Jordan River, as I poured into it a small vial of water from the Jordan River.

As we looked around Uranga, we were told we were in "The Bush." It is important for us to explain what the "bush" means. It means that each family has a section of land and they plant many bushes around it that become the bush, because it protects the whole of the homestead.

In the homestead itself, there are houses for various family members, cattle, sometimes a burial ground, and a kind of smoke-cook house. There could be up to five or six different buildings on the compound. At the homestead, you will find chickens running all over. Added to the bush are two difficult visitors, flies twelve hours a day, and mosquitoes twelve hours a night. We were at the equator so the hours were evenly divided between day and night.

Uranga was a community largely of seniors, but also many children, as family systems would live together in the homestead. If family members moved to the city, it was encouraged and rather culturally imperative to also build a small home in the bush, the place of their birth and their heritage.

Downtown Uranga had about five stores, somewhat of a hotel, and a place for a weekly market. There was no gas station, but there were several churches in Uranga. Many denominations claimed a spot in this region.

Health conditions were dire. Almost no one had a water tank of any kind. They drank out of stagnant ponds. There was seldom boiling of the water before they drank it, although some of them used a filtering system. Cattle and man drank from the same waterhole. The people were suffering from mouth disease, eye disease, injuries that had not been treated, severe malaria that made its regular rounds among all of the age groups, sometimes typhoid. It was a medical disaster area, and there was no medical care available, except 18 miles away. A person coming in who needed medical care for the birth of a baby had to be put on a bicycle and taken over an extremely rough road to the town of Siaya.

A decision was made by Good Samaritan Ministries in Oregon to ship a container, including a donated camping Volkswagen van, which would become an ambulance. The vehicle and the container were filled with a tent, medical supplies, bedding, towels, and all sorts of necessities. After it was shipped, it took months, and considerable bribes, for the container to be released, as Mombasa, at that time, was not a very ethical port of entry. Finally, the ambulance came to Uranga. It came about two years after our first visit.

The things sent in the ambulance produced a breakthrough for the children in school. They had a Boy Scout group, but in order to fulfill the requirements of Boy Scouts, they had to have equipment that no one in the region had. When the container arrived with scouting requirements such as a tent, they became the number one Scout Troop in the whole of the district, and everyone talked about the Boy Scout Troop from Uranga.

I asked James how many people lived in the region. He estimated 10,000, but you had trouble seeing them because they were all behind their bushes. You would go down very rough paths, not realizing at all, by the visual eye, how many families lived in the area.

Joshua Agola and James decided to take us to see Simon Halonda. Simon was becoming elderly. He had been the witch doctor of the region for many years. Of course, he wasn't a Christian. I knew in my spirit the pastors were taking me to his house to test me. In my spirit, I knew the pastors had decided to put Simon Halonda in front of me as a test of where I had come from and what I was about.

As a witch doctor, Simon was respected as the most powerful man in the region.

We had dinner at Simon's, and then we went out after the meal to sit under the trees in a large circle. I began to talk to Simon Halonda. Although there were at least fifty people present, I talked to none of them. I talked to Simon Halonda directly. I explained to him the only person bigger than the witch doctor in God's eyes was Jesus Christ. I explained to him that in order to come into this eternal life, into His Kingdom, he needed to accept Jesus Christ, and the power of His Call on Simon Halonda's life. I said, "Simon Halonda, you and I are going to kneel down right now and we, together, are going to accept Jesus Christ as our Lord." After our prayer, five of Simon's twenty wives, including his oldest wife, came forward and asked if they could accept Jesus too.

Simon Halonda and I became lifetime friends. Recently, Simon passed away, but every time I went to Kenya, there was a connection and occasionally we wrote letters to one another. Simon had dozens of children, and he was a little worried about how he was going to make a living if he wasn't a witch doctor anymore. I said, "Simon, you're an old man and your children will support you. You must follow Jesus."

I must add here a funny story. Ten years later, I came again on another trip to Kenya, and I asked James and Joshua if Simon Halonda had been baptized and they said, "No. He's an old man and he can't walk to the river." I said, "We're going to go get him right now and we're going to baptize him!" They said he was at a wedding. I said, "Nevertheless, we're going to go get him, and he's going to be baptized right now!" We showed up at the wedding, found Simon and his oldest wife there, loaded them in the vehicle, and took them to a nearby empty church. I said, "Simon Halonda, you have never been baptized. Do you know what I have in this bag I'm carrying? I have a small amount of Jordan River water, the water that was used to baptize Jesus. I believe that you want to be baptized." His wife chimed in, "I do too." So, I got the little vial out that was supposed to contain the water and oh my goodness, it contained olive oil from the Holy Land, but no Jordan River water in my bag!

What could I do, but take that oil, pour it all over Simon and his wife's head, and baptize them in the Name of the Father, the Son, and the Holy Spirit.

I never told anyone in Kenya about the oil. In fact, it was a secret for many years. But, I know that one thing clearly happened: Simon and his oldest wife received baptism.

One day, James Opiyo said, "You know, there has been a problem in our family for 20 years. My grandfather, Hezron's father, had four wives. His third wife was Hezron's mother. The other wives were jealous, so they made Grandfather William send that wife and Hezron away from the family homestead. This left Hezron and his mother landless to fend for themselves. Eventually, Hezron's family was able to build a homestead, but it was with great difficulty, and with the greatest of grief. Grandfather William had not spoken to his son, Hezron, for 20 years.

James said we're going to visit the homestead of William, and we will see what can be done. This was a big move, as even James himself had little or no contact with William. As we went past an archaeological site of the region dating back 100's of years, we came into the homestead of William and his family system. Of course, Kenyan hospitality caused us to receive great greetings, but as we came, I had a purpose and a mission: the reconciliation of William and Hezron. After a time, it came to the point of me saying, "You know I am your sister and you are my family. We are here for you and Hezron's family to be reunited and healed." William laughed and thought it was a great idea. Hezron and William were reconciled. They even prayed together.

Now, the fruit of that event was Grandfather William decided to become a Christian, and he was among those whom we baptized at the river.

From that day on, Grandfather William had a very special relationship of great love and affection for me. He said he often dreamed of me. Remember, I was a Mzungu (white), and he had hated all white people since the beating many years before.

I found that people could receive the Christ of action more than the Christ of religion. Is Jesus in the actions of faith, or is He only in the religion and the denominations of Christianity?

The whole purpose of our work in Africa, the core value, was to develop the people's actions of faith. Jesus' name had power and assignment.

Jerry decided to assess the health needs in the region. He found them so severe that he accumulated every item we had brought to help ourselves, and let the Luo's form lines to receive help. Later, he became known as Dr. Jerry. Jerry was a trained medic in the Army during the Korean War. We started with first aid, some assessment and whatever medical intervention possible. This brought great breakthroughs of comfort to the people. We also brought massive doses of prayer.

When the day of the dedication of the new Good Samaritan Ministries Center came, the whole of Uranga came to see what was up. There was crowding, singing, looking, touching. There was enthusiasm. I had brought a plaque which read, "Honor Thy Father and Thy Mother." The death of my parents had provided the funds for the building.

I desired not to have my name on this building. I desired not to be the center of the people's attention. However, they had put my name on a plaque outside of the building. At the dedication, I was to pull the curtain and dedicate the building. I picked up baby Bettie from Jenipher's arms, and holding baby Bettie in my arms, I spoke to the crowd, "Today we are dedicating this building for the use of the people of Kenya, for the use of Good Samaritan Ministries. No one will ever know if Bettie Mitchell was black or Bettie Mitchell was white. Three month-old Baby Bettie and I pulled the cord together, and the building was dedicated!

I want to note that in the years ahead, on December 15th, every year, there has always been a special ceremony, and that story has been told again and again. As Baby Bettie grew, she herself told the story. Here was the first building in Africa, the birthplace of Africa Good Samaritan Ministries.

Great stories, great people emerged in the development of Kenya as a ministry of Samaritans. Most of the pastors of the region worked six days a week in the field as Samaritans, and on Sunday as preachers in their church.

I must describe that first Good Samaritan Ministries building in Africa. It is still there at Uranga. The new center had two small rooms and a hallway. This center became the cradle of Africa Good Samaritan Ministries. In this cradle, 19 countries in Africa would follow the pattern to train and develop Samaritan laborers and provide Samaritan ministry and development to the people.

While we were in Kenya, we arranged for two gifts to be made. One gift was a toy box that all the children in Uranga would share at the center, and the other gift was a special box to hold the funds that the people of Uranga would donate to Good Samaritan Ministries. When we dedicated the funds box, immediately, people began to run from the large circle around the box and put their money in the box. **The people of Uranga were anxious to support this ministry, for they understood the ministry came from God and it belonged to all of the people.**

Volunteer jobs were available for everyone, not paying jobs, but full-time volunteer jobs. Naboth had sickle cell anemia and extreme hearing problems. James Opiyo was a creative genius. Naboth was appointed the Red Cross Training Program Director for the region. James and Teresa had graduated from Red Cross Training in Oregon. They knew it was important to graduate the people in that region from the same training. We had brought the books for them to use in the training program. James did give Naboth one encouragement. He said, "Naboth, if you will do this, Good Samaritan will educate your brother." From this decision, the sponsorship program for education grew in meaning and significance. Education became a permanent part of Good Samaritan Ministries—Africa.

James had vision. The vision was local centers throughout Kenya. The vision was not empty words. It was not said to impress anyone. It was the truth. The truth manifested great breakthroughs throughout Kenya. James would go into a local area, meet with the people, talk about the ministry, talk about the mission, talk about The Call, and if they agreed, they could develop the ministry in their area. In the years ahead, many of those areas would develop their own counseling offices. In the years ahead, it was my policy to write a personal letter three times a year to each one of those local centers' directors, and later, when the ministry was in Africa at large, I remained faithful to the same plan. Out of that, sometimes I would write 300 to 400 letters a month. A typist typed eight hours a day, five days a week, to keep up with the letters. The letters were to be received by people who, perhaps, would never receive mail. They were to be received as training and development. They were sent personally, not as form letters that all said the same thing, but as real letters, that spoke deep into the lives of the people in that region.

After December 15th, we immediately headed to Nairobi to catch a plane for the United States.

After a short night's sleep in Nairobi, we took the airplane home. We were suddenly thrust back into the white world. I want to say that this is the truth. I could almost not bear to look at the white world. The white world felt it was developed. What I saw was that the African world was developed. They had teachable spirits. They were open to learn and change. They had vision. They had community. They had integrity. Is the white world developed, or have we lost the development of the most essential things that make us part of the divine creation? It was hard because Christmas decorations were all over the airplane.

Before I left, I asked James what he gave Teresa for Christmas. He said, "I usually give her six eggs." That's development. That is what love is. Something small becomes very great.

This was the first of many trips to Kenya, and many trips to other countries of Africa. This first journey was the most significant journey of all because it was the seed of developing the great leaders, the seed of that first generation who received The Call, the generation that came to live it and to pass it down to the generations. This first generation was sorely tested, and this generation stood that test.

As we returned to the United States, sorted out all of the mail and reported to all of the people here, there was great enthusiasm. A generation of people here began to see the potent witness that this story could give to the whole Christian world, and indeed to governments and to all who were willing to develop their own sense of Christian action through the unity created by the Spirit. Here was the compassion, the life, the breath of the Holy Spirit, alive among us all. There was full agreement that this ministry would freely go forth.

Letter from me to Peter (first client of Good Samaritan Ministries in Africa):

July 2, 1988
Dear Peter:

You are my very special friend and every day you are in my heart in a way that is different. It is written deep within me that you need me to be your friend, to believe in you and to continue to pray for you. I know it is hard for you, and that your sickness sometimes is very heavy upon your mind. I want you to take hold of my hand in the spirit and I want you to trust me, Peter. You can be well. You will be well. James needs you. I need you to give your very, very best, and to be trustworthy. I need you to be James' best friend. Believe the Lord Jesus is your best friend, Peter.

I am going to say something that is true. The thing that touched me most in my heart during the entire trip to Africa was baptizing you in the new River Jordan. Baptizing you in this river and giving you to the Lord was like giving my very own son, my precious child, out of my own body. I take your life to be so precious to me and I look forward to seeing you so much in 1990. Peter, hang on. Trust the Lord. Look up at the heavens and say, "Jesus I trust you." Would you write me a letter Peter? You can dictate it to somebody who will write it in English. I want to know what you need. Will you tell me? Will you talk to me? Will you open your heart to me? Will you remember how much I trust you Peter?

Papa Jerry got the baptism of the Holy Spirit and the gift of tongues. How I am praising the Lord for this. I know the Lord has given me many gifts, but mainly the gift of His faithfulness. God is so good. What did James do with the brown sheep? What is news of the center? Write and tell me about it.

Your special Samaritan friend,
Bettie Mitchell
International Executive Director
Good Samaritan Ministries

Whenever I came to Kenya, I always looked for Peter. We always knew when we saw each other, how real our relationship was.

There was one telephone line into Uranga. I mean, literally, one telephone line. In order to call Uranga from the United States, I had to put in a call to Nairobi, and then the Nairobi operator had to wait until the telephone line was clear, to get me through, if at all possible, to James Opiyo in Uranga. Now, do you think that was easy? Often, in the middle of the night, I was sitting three or four hours, waiting for the telephone line to clear. During the heavy, rainy season, the telephone lines were often down.

However, it has always been my belief, and will continue to be the belief of Good Samaritan Ministries, that personal contact is the lifeline of this work. It was my personal policy, as the leader of Good Samaritan Ministries, to be available 24 hours a day, seven days a week, to all international calls, and then when they came, I returned the call, so that from our end, we paid for it. It did not matter how many times they called. **It mattered that they mattered. If the ministry is the ministry of Christ Jesus, then the value of face-to-face, letter writing, profound communication gives our faith the power to survive the attacks of Satan, the discomfort of years, the persecutions that come. This gives us encouragement, and gives us an incredible prayer life together. This is the root and power of Good Samaritan Ministries in Africa.**

CHAPTER 4

THE TRAINING

In 1988, Hezron, the father of James Opiyo, was dying of cancer. Hezron was a man of God and tremendously encouraging to others. He died a skeleton because his liver completely ceased to function. Three days before he died, Grandfather William came to Hezron and prayed for reconciliation. Grandfather William said, "I give you as a tithe to the Lord." That was a profound miracle of healing between father and son.

James was torn because he was due to go to Jerusalem in 1988 for our first International Conference. His father spoke to him firmly, "James, if I have not yet died, you are not to stay behind, but you are to go on that journey."

Just before James was to leave for Jerusalem, Hezron died and his funeral was finished. James came to the Holy Land a very broken man, grieving, but willing to learn.

At the International Conference in Jerusalem, there were several people from the United States, leaders in our work here; Sadiq, Chairman of the Board from Pakistan; Majed Alloush, Yassin, and others directing the "Call" in Palestine; and James Opiyo, representing our work in Africa.

Sadiq was able to come into the Holy Land by a great miracle. I had told him he had to meet us in Egypt on top of Mt. Sinai. He and James Opiyo met each other for the first time on top of Mt. Sinai. When we came to the Israeli border, he had no visa, and Israel had never, under any circumstances, allowed any Pakistani into the country. By God's grace and peace, Sam Bar-El, the tour guide for Israel, is a great personal friend. He had the border guards call Jerusalem and speak to the head of Israeli tourism. Permission was given, and a Pakistani entered Israel for the first time. It was a miracle.

During the 1988 conference, we studied the Palestinian refugee camps. There were 30 of us, plus seven Palestinians participating. When the group went home, I stayed on with James Opiyo at Yassin Hamdan's family house in Bethany, East Jerusalem. We stayed for several days. This was a key place to train James to be more concerned about others than his own religious spirit of fasting.

In the small four-room house of Yassin's family, James took over the living room and wanted to stay in there for three days of fasting and prayer. Outside, the family was hauling stones up and down a very steep hill to build the new house for part of the family. As I watched James completely absorbed in his grief and his prayer life, I spoke to him firmly and I said, "James, this is the kind of fast that the Lord would require of you. You will go outside and you will work to help build the new house. You will push the wheel barrel back and forth, for it is truly in working with your hands to help your neighbors, that you will find the Lord comforting you and healing you."

Years later, James shared with me that from that point on, he had all trainees go through similar experiences of working, building, participating, and it was this whole experience that got him out of the classroom mentality and into the spirit of Good Samaritan Ministries. James was baptized in the Jordan River, as was Sadiq. It was in this manner that Kenya and Pakistan became bonded in the ministry. The first generation was called to unite in their efforts to know one another, and to pay the price of genuine community.

CHAPTER 5

BUILD TEAM WORK

We made a journey to Nigeria, Kenya, and Uganda, Africa, from October 31st to December 17, 1990. The following team members were included: Bettie P. Mitchell, International Executive Director; Gerald Mitchell, Medical and Education Advisor; Arabelle Fliniau, GSM Board Member; Chip Lake, Video and Film Producer, who filmed the GSM African Story; Maqbool Kamal Masih, National Executive Director, GSM—Pakistan; Reverend Dr. Faraday Iwuchukwu, National Executive Director, Nigeria; Reverend James Opiyo, National Executive Director, Kenya; Reverend Stanley Muwanga, Director of GSM—Uganda; Judith Sellangah, Kenya Board Member.

Bettie, Jerry and Arabelle spent eight days in Nigeria at the beginning of this journey. We visited Evarestus' family, and confirmed that GSM was founded in their home. We visited the birthplace and family home of Reverend Dr. Faraday Iwuchukwu at Mbano, and met under the ancient tree with the Chief and Elders of the community. They were primitive people, but highly developed in their sense of trust and community. We immediately liked this area and felt bonded to its people.

Mbano is famous in African literature. It is an area where Christianity birthed, went through great loss and rebirthed. Mbano is a significant region of the Iboh Tribe.

Faraday was highly trained in administration, church, and a recognized leader in the Christian community. He saw a need for Samaritans, but there was a great need to be trained from the bottom up in the grass roots way. His wife, Angela, had a Master's Degree in Counseling.

We did training while we were there, meeting with a large group of pastors and lay leaders.

Our goal was not only to train others and develop a network of laborers, but to become deeply acquainted with Faraday as a person, a family man, and a Samaritan. We developed a deep trust relationship and prayer life together. We spent seven weeks together in Africa as Faraday went on with us to Kenya and

Uganda. We found deep spiritual and practical balance in our relationship.

GSM required all National Directors to write a comprehensive annual report. This required, in many of them, the development of needed administrative skills. We developed goals and priorities for GSM in 1991. We provided funds for Nigeria GSM legalization. We set up a scholarship fund for two students, and identified the need for eight others.

Our greatest goal was to establish a solid relationship with all in-country GSM centers, and a deep understanding and respect for the holy work of each of us. We learned to pray together as fellow laborers in the Kingdom of God.

It is hard to train a leader in new concepts of relationship balance. It is hard to establish the priority of relationships that last for the generations. These may sound like lofty goals. They are passionate goals, the desire of the Lord through the Holy Spirit. Over the years, we slowly learned to work in one accord.

On November 10th, we flew to Kenya. Faraday flew with us, and this brought together the team as a whole, except Stanley Muwanga, who would only be with us in Uganda.

My goal in going to any country was for us to learn the culture and to have an in-depth appreciation and understanding of its importance to the people. I came to know that the elders of any African community are highly valued, treated with respect, and their advice is always sought. This would be very important in the development of Good Samaritan Ministries—Africa.

We must never enter into a country and rigidly think we know what we are coming to do. Samaritans have to join with us, and discover what we have to do together. Often, their ideas were greater than ours. Their understanding could reach great depths. We needed a tremendous amount of education from the Africans. I believe more education was needed from them than they needed from us. The African culture is to be respected. Each country needed to be free to develop its own initiatives, and use its creativity to make the training happen for the people there. Our relationships must have integrity and hold together in the season of our leadership. **We must never forget the least in**

any country. Our leadership must never think too much of itself!

While we were in Kenya, we met with the Kenyan Board of Directors and reviewed policies and accomplishments. We met a Kenyan government official in charge of non-profit charitable organizations to straighten out a legal problem. We established and dedicated a GSM Center in an extremely poverty stricken area of Nairobi. We met with Board Members individually to discuss their views on our work in Kenya, and to give them feedback and training. We met with Dr. William Odinga at the Medical School. We evaluated the possible status of our medical programs. He made a formal request for some desperately needed medical equipment for the medical school. We are talking about a blood pressure kit and a microscope. I was very impressed with the caliber of Dr. Odinga's work for us. He had a keen interest in our program.

We spent a whole day in the Uranga region making 13 home visits to the severely needy or handicapped. I used this time to do extensive counselor training, and emphasized the need to delegate The Call to the needy themselves. We set up several key ministries: food, clothing, physical therapy, and an Addiction Recovery Program (ARP). I taught about the major importance of calling Samaritans into action everywhere we go.

We began to seriously convince pastors that the Christian religion cannot be based on loud words, but must be developed by actions of mercy visible among all of the people. This is the key to the argument between the lawyer and Jesus in the parable of the Good Samaritan.

We met with a District Commissioner and the Chiefs of many regions of Kenya to make our program clear to the government officials who needed to give their sanction and blessings to the activities in their region.

Each of us spent significant time teaching and sharing from our own perspectives, the Samaritan story. This also enabled me to do a lot of teacher training with the whole of our team, as well as the local Kenyans. This was particularly important to the fieldwork of our directors. The thirst for training was almost an absolute.

Of course, we met with Mama Jenipher Odour, and Baby Bettie. They joined our team and went in the vehicle with us for two weeks in Kenya. **I insisted we needed widows and orphans in the front lines, as they are called to be the grass roots of the Samaritan spirit.** I learned Jenipher had a third grade education and she became a widow at 39 years of age with the total responsibility for the survival of her nine children. We sponsored three of her children in school, and I paid her rent, which was $10 a month. Jenipher was a profound and important member of GSM International. She was one of the key intercessors for this ministry and the world. She and Joshua Agola of Uranga were the permanent intercessors from Kenya. Jenipher was willing to help build GSM in Nakuru with Pastor Dan Oloo. (Do not forget his name.)

We spent a week with George Okendo, the Chairman of the GSM Kenya Board of Directors in Nairobi and Uranga. We were impressed with his commitment, administrative skill, and his ability to get things done. He was an administrator for all of the Kenyan Government pension funds, and he worked in the office of the Vice President of Kenya. He handled a lot of work for James, and he was an uncompromising support at all levels of the ministry.

We met with pastors from many parts of the country and from many denominations. Out of these meetings, many became supportive of our work. Some of these pastors were heads of whole denominations.

We all were involved in Sunday church services, and in Uranga, we divided the team and spoke at three different churches.

We went to a "harambee" fundraiser for the roof of the Seventh Day Adventist Church in Uranga. We learned they had built their church, but had been unable to put the roof on for nearly 20 years. One of the ideas of the community as a whole was to support that one church, and begin the practical funding of putting that roof on with them. The "harambee" was successful. All of the African Samaritans gave, and we added from our side as well. The roof was completed through the Samaritan Spirit on the Seventh Day Adventist Church in Uranga.

At this point, I should define harambee. Harambee is a Kenyan method of raising funds for a needed community project. The meeting would be held under the trees and there was a prize. The prize might be a live chicken, or a basket, always something simple. The rule of harambee is that every time you bid, you pay what you bid. If you bid three times, you pay all three times, raising the bid each time. This is a lot different than an American auction. This is sacrifice! This is the spirit of harambee. This is the whole-hearted, generous spirit, the definition of African community.

In visiting various regions of Kenya, we came to a village called Minya. There, we spent two days with 25 Samaritans and Pastor Isaya, who was the director of our programs in that region. We met with the school deputy about education needs, which were obviously severe, as the students were in tattered clothing. We selected needy students for scholarships. We visited several homes. We learned of the assets of Minya that could provide strength in the ministry: a good director, one acre of land owned by GSM, and one large garden planted for GSM on Lake Victoria. This garden provided food for the needy, and as they sold food, funds were then provided for much needed medical supplies.

The workers were committed. They met twice a month and worked hard in between. **Children are members of Good Samaritan Ministries.** We gave 1,600 Kenyan schillings to provide a plow that would be owned by GSM, and we provided emergency medical aid for a boy with eye problems. We evaluated the need for income generation and saw that a GSM fishing boat and a water pump were important to expand the farm program.

John Oundo, now a recovering alcoholic, was given a Samaritan Award for the greatest creative innovation in his work for the past three years. He was an excellent counselor, and had 52 alcoholics involved in the Addictions Recovery Program at Uranga. He worked daily with alcoholics all over the region. His work centered in Christ. He became chairman of a local school committee, and raised money to build a decent three-room school. He had the best fundraising program we saw in Africa, and he worked from good long-range planning.

Later, when we built the larger center at Uranga, John humbly said, "I will build the toilets." And he did!

As I saw the work of John and his dedication, I appointed him to be an Addictions Recovery Program Director trainer for all of Kenya. ARP Directors were selected from three regions of Kenya, and we brought them to Uranga for immediate training. All were former alcoholics, and one drug addict. They accepted without hesitation, and each began their programs in their local areas. John regularly visited each of their programs and supervised their work.

John and I led two severe alcoholics to the Lord, and they were baptized. I was able to observe John in their counseling program, and in his method of follow-through. The ARP is one of our greatest accomplishments in Africa. All who left alcohol on our visit in 1987 participated in this program, and none returned to drinking.

There is a funny story about John Oundo. He and his wife, Dorcas, were childless, but when we came in 1987, Dorcas conceived and later gave birth to baby Bettie. When we came in 1990, shortly thereafter Dorcas conceived and she gave birth to baby Jerry. Eventually, Dorcas had baby Arabelle and baby Eric. This is how things are in Kenya. If someone is significant to the life of the family, the child receives the name of that significant person. It is an honor to the family and an honor to us.

I inventoried our assets in Kenya, and evaluated the vehicle we had sent. It was in good condition and had just been overhauled. The vehicle was labeled GSM Ambulance, and had saved the lives of many.

In Africa, the school year begins in January. December is a one-month school holiday. We visited eight elementary schools in two regions of Kenya. Children, parents, teachers, and school committees were present. Our team members gave major addresses and we helped raise funds for textbooks. In the Uranga area, four or five children have to share one textbook due to lack of funds. Our organization in Uranga donates to four schools for textbooks. The school will take the elementary children who have no money in exchange for the textbooks. This gives GSM, Kenya, more opportunity to bring children into the program.

Sidok School was 374th out of 485 schools in the district in 1987. Because of our work with Good Samaritan Ministries, Kenya, by 1990, Sidok was first out of 485 schools, and 48th out of 13,000 schools. Jerry and Beaverton School District #48 helped us send school supplies and Kenya GSM paid for one-quarter of the books for the school. Sidok had 11 teachers and 310 pupils. They had only two teacher's chairs and one table for the whole school.

The children had no toys or creative outlets other than music. We wanted to develop their creativity. In 1989, we began a toy program at the Uranga Center. In 1990, we brought many new toys. The Tualatin Hills Park and Recreation District donated 50 softballs. We left one at each school after playing with the children. Because of our toy program, our children began to make toys and Sidok School led in this program. Their arts and crafts program helped them to become No. 1. The toy designs were a major part of their curriculum.

Jerry and Arabelle examined, and, if possible, in Uranga, treated 180 people with first aid. We visited our First Aid Training Course at the center. This course was given to all high school students in the region. The classes were always full. Many whole families took the class. There were no doctors and no medicine available for 20 kilometers. There were few bicycles and only one owned car in the entire area. There were over 150 elderly shut-ins living in abominable conditions. Whatever medical supplies we sent or brought were the provision for the general medical treatment for the area. Almost no one in the region had money or income.

Medicine was very scarce in Kenya. For example, Pastor Gordon, a full-time Samaritan and Pastor of the Pentecostal Church in Uranga had diabetes and needed insulin shots to live. He went to the medical center at Kisimu, the third largest city in Kenya. No insulin was available. He could not afford the diet requirements, and insulin was scarce. The hospitals could be unsafe and proper medical supplies rare.

Because we learned of Pastor Gordon's medical condition in 1987, we put him on a monthly funding for his insulin needs that could be bought through private medical facilities. Pastor

Gordon lived for six more years, and died in 1993. This gave him six extra years to raise his children.

We visited a small medical center built by the government in another small town. Although the building was mostly finished, only a staff was available in the eight-room facility. There were very few medical supplies and nothing else for at least one more year. There was no money. We saw eight empty rooms and had breakfast with them.

At the Minya Center, James Adoyo, got an eye infection in 1983. He could not see a doctor. He had been blind since 1983. In 1990, now 34 years old, he had a wife and baby. Minya GSM built his house.

We began a library program at the Uranga Center. We donated money for the construction of a large bookcase, and Jerry and Arabelle set up the checkout system with Rose Alloush who would be the director of the program. We inventoried the Bible pictures sent in 1988 by Denton, Kansas, and we divided the pictures among Nigeria, Kenya and Pakistan. Each country received at least 50 large Biblical Story pictures. We divided the library books we took between Kenya and Pakistan, as we were starting a library program in Pakistan as well.

As a result of our home visits to the desperate, we initiated a Senior Citizens Program as a permanent part of our work.

Two of our home visits were especially significant to our work in Africa. The first was Old Lucy. Old Lucy had been paralyzed for 25 years. She was lying naked on the floor with a blanket thrown over her, and a dish with scraps of food by her side. There was a certain twinkle in Old Lucy that I particularly liked and, you see, I had been led to bring one dress to Africa, a long cotton dress with a hood. Since Old Lucy was naked, she, of course, would become the owner and proudly wear her new dress. It was obvious she was receiving very little care and that her situation was dire. We arranged for her to have a better mattress, with a plastic over it so it would not get wet, a pillow, and a caregiver. We appointed Rose Alloush, who also ran the library, to be Old Lucy's caregiver. We arranged for both Lucy and Samuel to receive wheelchairs that would be brought by other teams coming to Kenya.

Now, I want you to imagine this. We've come into the church. It is Sunday morning, and low and behold, Lucy is lying on the front pew in her colorful new garment. As everyone is praising God and singing, Lucy is moving her hands back and forth, joining in the praise. Finally, she is not naked and she can go to church! We carried her in the vehicle.

I learned something significant through Old Lucy. She could have good care. She could have improved conditions. For instance, we left cream for her to soften her skin, **but would she have a purpose? That is one of the great questions in working with anyone in Africa**. This question was ignored or lost. I took the pastors to see Lucy in 1992 when she had her wheelchair, and I said to all of them, "Lucy is to be the intercessor for all of you. When you come from a trip, you are to come to Lucy and have her lay hands on you and pray. When you are about to leave, you are to come to Lucy and she is to pray over you. This will be her purpose and you are to honor this old one who has come so far to be well among you."

We visited the old man, Samuel Okoth Akunya, who, as a quadriplegic, had lain on the floor for 20 years with hardly any clothes. He had never had physical therapy. We got a drum and began to help him move his fists on the drum to gain some energy and strength. His appreciation of our visit became a permanent part of the story of the heroes of the first generation of GSM Kenya. When Samuel died, he left in his will that a portion of his land was to be used by Good Samaritan Ministries, Kenya. The center built on that land is known as the Senior Citizens' Center. Kenya GSM also dug a small well there, providing people with water for drinking and domestic use.

We had two baptism days in two regions of Kenya. We trained the pastors and the candidates so that each individual baptism would have in-depth meaning. Baptism would not be just words and water, but healing, the raising from the dead in the spiritual realm, the fear of death departing. Great changes took place because we took quality time with each baptism. Our team baptized 64. Grandfather William and paralyzed Old Lucy were baptized. When we came home, GSM—Beaverton sent baptism certificates for each person baptized.

While on this journey, I was able to do Biblical and conceptual training with our team, and key Samaritan leaders in Kenya. I was able to closely observe the strengths and weaknesses of each of our directors, and make major contributions to their training. They learned a lot from each other. We had several counselor training sessions, and I did some counseling with each of the directors. I was able to train the directors in administrative skills. **Communication was to be highly valued among us all.** They learned what was expected in their reports to us. I trained them in what I expected when we visited their country, and why we would come. We were able to establish common practices and agreements among us.

As we travelled and worked together, we were all exposed to the rough edges of living together under stressful conditions. Each of us was honed. Maturing spiritual development had to take place. We came to truly know each other. We had major influence on each other. We developed deep trust for and a committed prayer life with each other. We saw the wisdom of God in choosing each of us. We seemed long ago prepared for this very work.

We put the African Training Center and James Opiyo to a hard test for competency and broad fitness for the larger work in Africa. He learned much as he was stretched to the max. I recommended that James be considered for the team to Pakistan the next year. He was a highly skilled and competent National Director who could offer much assistance and encouragement to the development of our work in Pakistan. It would give me an opportunity to continue to refine James' administrative, communication and teaching skills.

We were greatly able to encourage our Samaritan laborers. I personally gave small financial gratitude gifts to several of them. Their contributions are remarkable. Pastor Dixon received $200 for the floor of his house. He is the Director of the Uranga program. We gave $100 to John Oundo for his Addictions Recovery Program. You see, one of his new members needed glasses for cataracts.

We established a permanent widows and orphans fund in Nairobi to be administered by Judith Sellangah. The widows and orphans funds are a sacred part of all of our work in Africa continuing today.

CHAPTER 6

THE DOOR OPENS IN UGANDA

On November 26, 1990, our team left Kenya to spend a week in Uganda. We were driven to the border between Kenya and Uganda where we were met by Stanley Muwanga who had agreed to develop our work in Uganda. He was a man I had never met and a man whom I knew little about. He desired to encourage this work. Stanley had developed a small team of GSM workers in Kampala. He rented an empty house for us on the outskirts of Kampala.

When we reached Kampala, we had to immediately go to the bank to exchange money, buy mattresses and bedding for ourselves, cooking and eating utensils and food.

The inflation level in Uganda was horrific. Often people took a basket to the bank to carry the money out. Many bills must be carried. Each bill had the least value imaginable.

When coming into Uganda, we were very tired. We had been living out in the bush in some primitive conditions. Our bathing facilities had been quite limited. That first night in Uganda, we felt dusty, and ready to settle in for rest. However, Stanley said we were going to the home of the Minister of State of Uganda that very night where we would have dinner. Balaki Kirya was a strong Christian. He was a key minister in the Ugandan government. He and his wife, Grace, always wanted to welcome significant visitors to their home. As tired as we were, we put on fresh clothes and went.

Stanley had promised us dinner at Balaki Kirya's home. It was soon obvious that no dinner was going to be served. We were given small dishes of peanuts and some soda pop. But, the visit to this house was personally one of the most remarkable and significant events in my lifetime, and to the greater story of Good Samaritan Ministries, Uganda.

Balaki Kirya (B.K.) and Grace were the most memorable Christians I met in Africa. B.K. was the longest surviving politician in Uganda, having lived through the periods of murder and the horrors of dictatorship, genocide, and civil war. B.K. was in and out of prison in Uganda for a total of nine years. Before that B.K. and Grace had escaped to Kenya. Uganda paid a ransom to Kenya to get B.K. back to Uganda. The plan was to kill him. Kenya returned B.K. to the border, but the guards became drunk and did not kill him. He had many narrow escapes from death.

How B.K. became a Christian is an interesting story. He was in prison and about to go on trial. It was assured that he was guilty and would be executed. He was preparing to die.

In the middle of the night, in 1969, ready to be executed, B.K. awakened from sound sleep. He heard a voice calling, "Balaki Kirya, what about Me?" This moved him deeply, but the incredible part of the story is the voice called his name three times and promised to deliver him.

Miraculously, the next day, the court found no reason to keep him, and released him. This was an unheard of event. For all who went to prison, never left it. Indeed, truly, Balaki Kirya was a man called out by the Lord.

Back to the living room in the Kirya home, it was warm and comfortable, but the most dramatic part for us was they had electricity. We could hardly believe we were in lights again!

B.K. was a very intense questioner. He was in charge of the security for all of Uganda and it was his job to question anyone who entered Uganda when the reasons for them being there were not clear.

Therefore, he went around the room asking each member of our team their name, where they were from, and why they were in Uganda. They were not friendly questions; they were questions of security, questions that demanded an accounting be given.

Finally, B.K. came to me. He asked the same questions. During the course of our conversation that followed, he found out I had written a book called *Who Is My Neighbor?* He became very excited about this. He turned to his wife, Grace, and said, "She's written a book and it's called *Who Is My Neighbor?*" The President and I have just been to Zambia where President Museveni gave a speech, "Who is my Neighbor?" to the elected Zambian government officials. He asked me if I had a copy of the book with me. I said, "Yes, I have one with me." He said, 'May I have it?" I said, "Of course."

Later in the week, I would find out that B.K. broke a rule of sleep that was absolute to his morning routine. After his prison experience with Jesus, for 20 years, he had nightly gone to bed at 8:00 p.m. and awakened consistently at 3:00 a.m. The first hour he spent reading the Word, the second hour he spent in prayer, and the third hour he spent reading the newspapers. Grace informed me that he made no exception to this. That night, B.K. made an exception, and spent the whole night reading my book. He told me later, he finished it that night.

Towards the end of our no-dinner visit, B.K. informed us that he had made a decision to take my husband and me to see President Museveni later in the week. He said, "I will send a vehicle for you, and this will include lunch. " We set the appointment. I could hardly believe what I was hearing. We had no dinner that night, but we were all full of the miracle that had just happened.

Before we left that evening to return to our humble abode to sleep on the floors, I asked B.K. if he would be willing to be my father in Africa. It was that personal, our conversation riveting to each of us. I explained to him that my father had died and I was greatly in need of a father in Africa. B.K. agreed and he kept that agreement the rest of his life.

During the week that we were in Uganda, we visited three significant areas.

The first area was called the Kisenji District in Kampala. It was an area of prostitutes, alcoholics, a large abandoned church, and 1,200 children. We surveyed the area with the Chief, an angry, broken man, trying to help in a hopeless situation. Streetlights were destroyed, sewers destroyed, water systems destroyed, sanitation zero, homes devastated, sin everywhere. The Chief said he was tired of Christians visiting and doing nothing. The power of the meeting was such that he began to believe we would not walk away.

The Masaka District was 120 kilometers from Kampala. It was an area of one of Uganda's most decimated regions from AIDS. Indeed, HIV AIDS was first seen in that region of Africa. We met a pastor in a small, partially built church.

Pastor Osborn received Jesus in 1985, and spent the next two years as an evangelist. When he came to this area as an evangelist, he realized he needed to stay to teach and encourage the people. For the next two and a half years, Osborn slept on the floor of a Muslim man's store in rural Masaka District, ministering in the partial church structure to a community of 300 Christians. By the time we arrived, half of his church had died from AIDS. There were almost no men left. Grandparents and orphans sat before us. They were now the whole church. At night, when Osborn went to sleep, 16 to 18 people crowded next to him in the Muslim man's store. They needed comfort and reassurance. They were young orphans and those dying of AIDS, too afraid to stay alone.

Today, the Muslim man is the Chief of the whole area. He became a Samaritan. His daughter teaches at the Good Samaritan School. He attends all meetings of Good Samaritan Ministries.

We made visits to three homes of AIDS' victims, surveyed the general area, visited graves, and had lunch with the Chief. Anger and frustration were close to boiling over points.

From the beginning, I could see in Osborn, a man of unusual character, a man of integrity and love for his people, a man so broken by grief that I wondered whether he could continue at all. In the back of a shuttered home we visited the graves of a family of six. We stood near one of the graves. Osborn and I looked into one another's eyes and I said, "What can we do for you Osborn?"

It was an eternal moment. What would we have answered in these circumstances? Here was a man with a pair of pants, a shirt, a Bible and a pair of shoes; a pastor who was broken and burying, hanging on and caring on for the family members that remained. His answer was so profound that I will never forget that moment and neither will he. He said, "You can educate the children."

Within a short length of time, we were ready to get into the vehicle and return to Kampala. I spoke firmly to Osborn and said, "You must come with us. You do not have enough training and you desperately need help to know how to handle the disease and the people of this region. You are to come to Kampala. You will get a passport and come to meet us in Uranga, Kenya, in a few days." He hesitated a few moments, spoke to a woman named Betty, who was assisting him with the work, left her in charge, and we all left together for Kampala. Now, suddenly, Osborn was a member of the team.

Before Osborn left Kiwangala, Masaka, and made the journey to Kenya to meet us, he returned to Kiwangala, trained Betty all night in Samaritan work, handed out condoms and rubber gloves with instructions, met with the Chief and elders, and obtained permission to immediately open one of the locked houses where all had died, to use as an orphanage. They had never thought of this. Hope was being born. It was a new hope for a weary people.

It was agreed Osborn would train in Kenya for several weeks. James would take him to Nairobi Medical University for special training in AIDS research, and medical care.

The third area of significance we visited in Uganda was an area called Wobulenzi, about 40 kilometers from Kampala. This was an area of severe war devastation, an area of widows and orphans. Many of the widows had been raped, including Flora. Flora Mutaka was the appointed GSM Director of the region. Flora was a widow for six years, and she had raised four children alone. She had been a pastor's wife. Her husband had been imprisoned. Osborn's father was released, but Flora's husband was murdered by the Obote regime. Flora had just remarried two years prior to our visit and she had a baby. When Osborn brought the GSM Call, she came to Kampala with baby Pauline for training with us. She opened the work and continued to be a key leader in Uganda until her death.

We spent 12 hours total with B.K. at his urging, on four different days of our six-day stay. He agreed to not only be my father in Africa, but to become the patron sponsor of GSM, Uganda. He had travelled in almost all countries of this world, spoken at churches around the world, and was one of the most outwardly declared Christian political leaders in the world.

B.K. had made arrangements for a car to pick us up. We went to lunch at the Nile Hotel. After lunch, in a hotel suite, we waited to be called to meet with the President of Uganda.

B.K. shared with me he had sought the Lord for healing of severe asthma for years, to no avail, and that he was also fighting high blood pressure. He asked if I could help. In prayer, during the next two hours, I was given a profound word for him, and we powerfully prayed together later that afternoon: "Turn the security of all of Uganda over to Me," said the Lord, "I will make this country secure and bring it peace." B.K. did just this and was immediately greatly improved.

While we waited in the hotel room to meet with the President, B.K. told me to go take a nap in a king-sized bed while he and Jerry talked in the sitting room. Finally, we were called to the meeting with President Museveni. The meeting lasted one hour, with only Minister Kirya, a secretary, Jerry, and me present. The President interviewed me extensively about The Call at Nineveh, the work, and our views of the developing work in Uganda. I interviewed him about his faith in Christ and his prayer needs. I highly recommended that he pray with Minister B.K. on a regular basis, as B.K. was a man who could be highly trusted. Later, B.K. told me that President Museveni was shocked to see my husband and me in traditional Ugandan dress. B.K. said that Museveni was shocked and attracted when we informed him that we had been to Kisenji and the Masaka area. He was shocked to see "whites," only a few days in his country, already had become Ugandans.

We negotiated together the critical needs we had seen. I asked for 49 blankets for Kiwangala, Masaka. I do not know why these words came out of my mouth, but the AIDS victims needed them. I asked for a water conduit and sewer pipes for the Kisenji District of Kampala, where 1,200 children were greatly endangered. It was unheard of for us to have gone to Kisenji. He asked if we would pay for the work if the government supplied the material. It was agreed upon. The blankets were delivered the following January, and all parts of this agreement were set in motion and fulfilled. Before we left the President's office, B.K. also requested that public toilets be built in Kisenji, as there was only one toilet for the whole area. B.K. informed me later that the President kept that agreement too.

At the end of the session, we had photos taken. I was allowed to lay hands on the President and pray with him. Faraday of Nigeria had given me a prophecy to deliver, "You are called to be a light for your people." I was given the words of our Lord, "He who asks for a little, more will be given." It is important to note that Museveni is still President of Uganda in 2013. He is not a president as a dictator, but a president as one who loves and wisely leads his people.

After years of complete and total devastation, war upon war, battle upon battle, he has encouraged and rebuilt his country, empowered the people, and passionately fought for their needs to be met. Yes, President Museveni became a Christian and in a recent year, he called for all of the pastors and Christian leaders to come together at the stadium where they would pray all night together. In a speech he gave, he asked them to become Samaritans.

Before we left, we met with an attorney, Peter Nyombi, to finalize legalization of GSM in Uganda. This also required an affidavit from the U.S. Embassy, which Jerry and I obtained. Arabelle, as an official Board member, and I signed all of the documents and legalization was filed with the government.

Pastor Osborn and Stanley Muwanga signed for Uganda. This meant we were able to operate legally and open a bank account.

For our enlarging team, we had training sessions covering counseling, group therapy, alcoholic recovery programs, AIDS, and sexual training. We did a lot of group problem solving. Judith Sellangah of Nairobi and Flora Mutaka had joined the team and were present at the training. The team was growing. **This was the first generation of Samaritans.**

Our most dramatic shared event of all took place on Sunday morning before we left Uganda. We had a final half-day training session in the place where we stayed—a place with almost no furniture, no electricity, and no conveniences. All of a sudden, a vehicle drove up in this rural part of Kampala, and out emerged B.K. and Grace Kirya. They had come for the training! It was Sunday morning. Was it a church service? No, it was a living sermon. "Go and do likewise." We did not sing or dance, but we kept ourselves focused on the work that lay ahead and the profound needs of the people to regain their lives.

Osborn was not able to go immediately with us to Kenya as his name was in a computer, and the glitch was that he was not to be given a passport. At one point, he had run away from the military with his commanding officer's knowledge and agreement that he was to go back to minister, as this was his calling. That event went in the computer. He appealed to B.K., who cleared the situation, and Osborn did arrive in Kenya before we left for the United States.

CHAPTER 7

THE OLD SENIORS

On December 2nd, the international team returned to Kenya, where we continued our work and training to December 17th, when everyone flew back to their homeland.

Maqbool Kamal Masih of Pakistan experienced a profound miracle from this journey. He became the Executive Director of Pakistan, learning firsthand what that meant. He made very valuable contributions to the African program. He was a giving person in a personal way, and not afraid to make financial gifts here and there. We celebrated his 40th birthday while we were in Uranga. He and I made detailed plans for the trip to Pakistan in 1991. We agreed to bring James Opiyo with the team to Pakistan. He began to really understand the development of this work in Pakistan, and location and training of Samaritans would be the priority for 1991. Bishop Tom Abungu recognized Maqbool's spiritual gifts and his contributions to Africa. He ordained Maqbool as a pastor on December 15th at 11:30 p.m., after a final dinner we had at Tom and Rhoda's house in Nakuru.

Chip Lake, our video producer, produced incredibly valuable photographic imagery that would turn into a great video about Africa. He worked extremely hard and when he came home, he worked even harder. The video, Mission to Africa, was produced. He was a great team player and a real asset to the program. His fare to Africa was paid by a Japanese friend who lived in Tokyo. We paid all of his expenses in Africa. He was with us for the entire journey. He shot 1,200 minutes of film and did a lot of writing. He interviewed all four National Directors and other key people on the film.

During these next few days, we continued to visit various centers of Good Samaritan Ministries and worked extensively in the Uranga area developing the whole people of the region to be wholly dedicated to the lifetime development of Good Samaritan Ministries, a development not only at Uranga, but in all of Kenya and other nations as well. For the first time, the people of Uranga experienced the International. Who were these people who could come to their region and spend this quality time with them? What was Uranga to experience such a story? It was an incredible miracle to each of us.

From our visits with so many seniors, we decided to initiate a senior citizens program as a permanent part of our work. We used the Pentecostal church across from the center in Uranga. We had a four-hour Christmas party for more than 100 elderly and handicapped individuals. They came from a 20-kilometer radius. We used our car to pick up all of the shut-ins. GSM—Beaverton provided the food for GSM--Kenya to cook. Everyone was given a delicious, hot meal and a bottle of pop. Many tasted soda pop for the first time.

I was brought to tears when a girl, whose legs were totally unable to make any movement, was carried a considerable distance on the back of a bicycle to be at the party. We encouraged each of the people there to tell stories from their lives to the whole crowd. Many of them had not seen each other for years. Four were paralyzed. Samuel, the quadriplegic, had seldom been off the mud hut floor for 20 years.

I told the Christmas story, using the people for the characters. I chose the quadriplegic man, who was propped up in front of all of them, to be the baby Jesus. We ended with carols, dancing, and our team laid hands on each person and individually prayed for them. The pastors of Uranga served them all day. None of us ate, as the food went to the guests. We served rice, vegetables, meat, bread and butter, and bananas. It was a feast greater than many had ever seen.

At the end, Samuel, the quadriplegic, was singing with all of us. Everyone on the team agreed that this day was a revolution in the pastor's work in the Christian ministry. They saw the story of the uninvited guests being received into the banquet hall. They had only read the Bible. They had never seen it take place.

That day, there was another miracle. We were anxiously awaiting the arrival of Osborn Muyanga from Uganda, and had expected him several days earlier. In the midst of the banquet, Osborn arrived and our team was complete.

The senior citizens program became a permanent part of the history of Good Samaritan Ministries. The passion of this ministry will include those who are unable to experience inclusion anywhere else. **These were, indeed, the greatest days of Good Samaritan Ministries. This was the first generation.** School scholarships became an important part of the story in Africa. You see, school fees were needed for children in all African centers. Our team learned a great deal from James about the careful handling of this program. By January 1991, we were sponsoring 35 students. There was a great need for high school scholarships, as most of the children in the region never went to high school. In fact, we sponsored the first person in the region that had ever gone to high school and graduated. A country cannot develop if it denies their children the basic education to work for the best interests of the family and the nation.

Arabelle and I were very pleased with the students who were selected. 200 students came to the center every Saturday afternoon. They were registered in our programs by name. At the end of each school year, the first, second, and third students in standings for each class in each school was given a special award from the center. In 1989, it was mostly clothing. In 1990, mostly school supplies were given. If they were first, they got three awards. The second got two awards, and the third received one award. 45 children received the awards and the congratulations from Arabelle, who had worked hard to document and begin the accounting for our people at home who were going to have to come through and sponsor these children.

Good Samaritan Ministries would have to make a moral decision: was this the right thing to do? Did we have the courage to do it, and to do it well?

One of the key words that I learned from B.K., from the first to the last of the time we ever spent together, was his emphasis on "moral fiber." He considered "moral fiber" to be the essence of the gospel. He taught "moral fiber," He used "moral fiber" in his relationships. He was a man of tremendous courage that influenced all of the development of Good Samaritan Ministries in Africa.

This is the story of 1990, when we began to work together as teams from nations. Our goal was to know each other, to understand each other's nation, and to support each other in a profound level of prayer. We had to reach across the world to have the divine blessing for this work. You see God had called this into His plan for the people of His Kingdom.

Osborn Muyanga stayed on in Kenya for six months. He, Nicholas Okungu, and a pastor named George Kadega, were the first trainees in the continental training program. Together, with James Opiyo, they were developing the training program that would eventually spread across nations of Africa, and; indeed, influence other nations of the world.

Pastor Osborn wrote me a letter May 23, 1991, called "Along the Training Program." The quotes from that letter are as follows:

The true action speaks louder than words. I have read about love and many people have taught me about love, but love has never manifested in my life as at this time, when I met people who DO love.

The two years I have spent in Masaka, I saw preachers coming, preaching and praying for the victims, and feeling sympathetic with me, but not touched and moved as Good Samaritans did.

My coming to Kenya is the time, which I was coming as a time of difficulties again because of the new people and of different tribes and characters. But what I have seen leads me to sit down with you and talk for days.

On February 4th, Osborn had an accident on the way to Nairobi. He said that one important thing that he learned is that there are good Samaritans and there are also bad Samaritans. How? After the accident had taken place at around 8:30 p.m., many people came to help in three types. The first is the people who came to watch. They looked sorry, but they were not moved to help. The second, the policemen who were on patrol, came to help as Samaritans, but instead, the first thing they did, was to help themselves to our luggage and bags. When they saw someone who managed to go out with his bag, there they applied force, even trying to threaten him with a pistol so that they may take his things. When they saw others coming also to help, you see, we have been helping these people, but they didn't even give us anything or say thanks. The third were the security men who came along in a vehicle, seeming to be taking them to their duty that night. They seemed to be late, but because of the incident, *they immediately stopped and started helping pulling out the victims, and putting us in their vehicle. They drove us up to the hospital. After making sure we were in the safe hands of the doctors, they drove off to work without asking for anything, not even a thank-you from us. I want to call these ones the true good Samaritans we need in our times.*

The time I spent in training with Nicholas, I learned to be an actor, dramatist, and to do things without excuse.

I met James Osewe from the Lake Region. I spent a whole month with this brother. What touched me mostly was his testimony being delivered from alcohol, which was his problem for more than 20 years. James Osewe is one of the remarkable Samaritans of the first generation. He had presence with the people and was tremendously gifted at making a difference in their lives. James Osewe called hundreds to be Samaritans and paid the price of training them.

The house of Reverend James Opiyo is my home. James is my Kenyan father, I found later. He showed me a great love and much concern before teaching me to love and be concerned for others. First, he did it to me. This was a great lesson to my life. He cared as much about me as he did for his son.

I was eating in the same place with him. The love I saw in James' house, created in me a big ministry of loving and caring for others.

I managed to visit Samuel, the quadriplegic. What made me happy was still recalling the day of December 14th, when he saw many people and heard a play in which he was included. Samuel, with a smile on his chin, managed to remember that on that day, he heard someone coming from Uganda.

I watched GSM, not only participate in a funeral, but make the coffin and give it to the family. We trainees went to all Kenyan centers. We learned the first aid program and had very quality time with children. We were instructed about the addictions recovery program.

I did not know before what kind of training I am going to take. First, I thought, I'm going to have a sit-in-class time, and have a lot of writing and book reading, but to my surprise, it wasn't so. I thank God very much in the way He trained me. I believe it is the same way Jesus trained His disciples, practically, in the field. Many people in our days are full of theory, but empty of practicals.

Photo -- James Opiyo of Kenya

James Opiyo was, and is, a visionary. He was not afraid to tackle the hard things.

It had been hard to convince Nicholas Okungu to stay in Uranga and be a trainee. You see, Nicholas loved being an evangelist and he travelled around doing his evangelistic work and leading people to Christ, always fasting and praying before a great crusade. The Lord had different plans, because Nicholas was needed at Uranga, this very poor rural region.

I know, personally, that James Opiyo put Nicholas to many tests that were extraordinarily difficult. One of his first assignments was to become the driver of the ambulance. He had to learn to take directions. Being told what to do, and coming into a spirit of obedience and agreement, these were hard tests. Nicholas Okungu went on to be a significant Samaritan laborer and National Director of GSM--Kenya. Later, we sent Nicholas to Pakistan. He was a man who could be respected by the ministry as a whole.

Nicholas started his life with alcoholic parents, and went on to be an alcoholic himself. He lacked confidence and developed abilities; but, one day, the Lord, through a divine miracle, brought him to Christ and delivered Him from alcohol. Even today, as I write this, Nicholas continues to be a fellow Samaritan. He is suffering now from cancer and has to have dialysis twice a week, but the light will never go out of his eyes as his life will continue to be an intercession from heaven on the day he goes home.

CHAPTER 8

TO RETURN HOME

I was hungry
And you formed a debate team
And debated the pros and cons of
World hunger.

I was imprisoned
And you crept away busily
Hoping someone would
Somehow find time to visit me.

I was poorly clothed
And in your mind you disapproved
Of my lack of style.

I was sick
And you thanked God
For your health.

I was homeless
And you preached
About spiritual shelter of the
Church.

I was lonely
And you left me alone
To pray for me.

You seem so content
So pleased with your Christianity
But I am still hungry and
Lonely and Cold.

~By Beatrice Amondi Obiero and Mary Onego
(Trainees in the Kenya GSM)

To return home is a shock to the system. Again, it is almost Christmas. The ministry is filled with correspondence to be answered; my desk buried! But the greatest question I carried in my soul; the question persisted and it would not let me go.

Could the ministry achieve a certain level of maturity that would recognize the needs of others so often more important than their own? This led to another question, could the clients, who often came in whining for long periods of time, become unselfish? Could they develop a strong heart and spirit for others? I decided these questions had to be answered.

We began an extensive training program and with the African video on the way, I added stories from the photo slides. Sometimes I would teach for two or three hours, showing slides, telling stories, using the names that had created our compassion in the journey to Africa. When you saw Old Lucy, there was a difference between seeing her and just hearing her story.

It was always tough with the Board of Directors. They came to a meeting every month or two, sat, and often knew little of the passion, which undergirded this ministry. The passion of Christ demanded that we know our world and not only seek their conversion to Christianity, but convert them deeply and permanently to unselfishness. What could it mean if we all loved our neighbors as ourselves?

I set a course of training the Board and the board members that followed in the years ahead. I read them letters from overseas. I talked to them. I made them listen to the stories and see the pictures. To business people, these must have been strange Board meetings, but it was unacceptable to the Kingdom of our Lord to ignore The Call and stick to the realities of the facts we created here. I was willing to die to break through the spirit of mediocrity, of business mind, and into the spirit of faith and community that would make a difference along the road, no matter where this ministry was called to travel.

Gradually, I told the clients the stories. I did not weigh them down with this, because they had their problems, and they came to see us for the building and healing of their own lives, but I wasn't afraid to speak to clients about the bigger picture. Many of the clients needed us to talk to them too if they were to grow healthy. They became interested, perhaps for the first time, in something beyond themselves and their immediate environment.

I trained the counselors to pray and to choose an expanded visual field that included the whole picture.

We lived in a time of transition. The people here became passionate themselves. We made agreements among us that we would meet the moral obligations of the bigger picture. Moral fiber was required to change the structure of our work. We were moving beyond feeding self to feed the many. **We set loose that roar of faith in action, faith to feed the many!**

Today, I am as passionate as I was then. I have retired and left stories and information behind, but the passion continues. Are we prepared for the reality of who is hungry, when we did not feed them, and who would never be educated because we didn't respond? **Who is our neighbor? Dear Lord God in heaven, who are we?**

In 1991, after much communication from Uganda, which gave us a picture of serious problems with the mental health of Stanley Muwanga, I made a decision that James Opiyo needed to be appointed Continental Director of Africa, and, as such, he could go to Uganda and personally take responsibility for the decision to transition the leadership of the ministry. He chose Osborn Muyanja to be the new National Director of Uganda. I was learning and came to know Africa needs to address Africa's problems.

This was the beginning of a new Call to empower Africa. The appointment of James was part of our faith that the Lord would have us operate with a new sense of order, one step at a time. James Opiyo's leadership would settle issues when explosions broke out when I was not available. James would go as a peacemaker, intercessor, and leader among all of the people.

CHAPTER 9

THE JENIPHER ODUOR STORY

Jenipher was known in the streets as St. Jenipher, a woman of rare courage and spirit, who was a lightning bolt to challenge the spirit, the faith, and the integrity of men who are claiming the word of God.

You have already met Jenipher Oduor in the story of 1987 and the story of 1990 when she traveled with the team throughout Kenya. (Her photo is on the cover of this book.) In early January of 1992, I received a telephone call from James Opiyo, our Continental Director of Good Samaritan Ministries in Africa. I could tell by James' voice that he was in shock and deep grief. He called to report to me that Mama Jenipher had died during the night surrounded by her nine children.

James then asked me, "What shall we do with the nine children?" Immediately, we began to make plans for those children.

James and Teresa Opiyo took baby Bettie and Jenipher's older daughter, Rose, into their own home. Members of Good Samaritan Ministries took the other children: Pastor Dixon, Nicholas Okungu, Moses Odero, and Bishop Tom Abungu.

Jenipher would be missed by many. I missed her fiercely. I wrote a personal letter to each of her children. They ranged in age from four to twenty. These nine little letters to her children tore my heart out.

James and I decided that George, the oldest, could stay in the room of their housing for one year. This would enable George to find work to support himself. It would also give the children a home base when they all came together. They would come to the home where they lived as a family with Mama Jenipher. I said, "James, we will take care of the rent for one year. George will make it. It is important that we provide for their unity as a family, as well as for their individual needs."

Jenipher's funeral was delayed until February 9th. At Uranga she had a mud hut with a straw roof. Uranga was her tribal home. When I came to Uranga the fall of 1992, I visited her home and grave. Most significantly, I found in Jenipher's hut, written on the wall and easily discernible, "God Love You."

I was told that Jenipher's funeral was attended by nearly 5,000 people. They killed two cows to feed the people. I told James they had to put a cement marker over the grave and put her name on it. If you go to Uranga, you can still visit the home and grave of Mama Jenipher today.

Personal Letters from the Oduor Story:

November 23, 1988

Dear sister Bettie,

The greatest thing I have ever discovered is love. For it has brought people of different race to come together and live like one person. Truly God's love is the great and high above human understanding

Much love in Christ Jesus,
Jenipher

August 5, 1989

Dear sister Bettie,

I also pray to God to help you arrive in Kenya without any problem. My heart is missing you or rather my heart is expecting your arrival next year. Unless I see you, I don't know how I can express my emotions to you.

Jenipher

March 4, 1990

Dear sister Bettie,

I still have faith that you still consider me through praying and that you are with me spiritually. We here also have meetings on Fridays and Wednesdays. The meetings held on Fridays have been directed to me to pray for Bettie. The times that are expected for the meetings, we pray for Bettie because of the work ahead of her. It is usually the first and respected prayer, and we pray first before doing anything at the meeting.

We also do not forget you, Mother. In my house, Little Bettie keeps quiet at the moment she hears that we are praying especially for you. My whole family loves and respects you. Bettie, herself makes fun that she is a white."

Bye Bye, Jenipher

July 1, 1990
Dear Bettie P. Mitchell,
Holy Sister Bettie, I hope it's well. My hoping that you are well makes my heartbeat more than expected. Here in Kenya, we are all sober through our Savior Jesus Christ. I still believe that Christ has the power and is able to do everything both here on earth and in Heaven.

Bettie, I cannot forget praying for you when I remember how you've helped me. I have all the reasons of praying for you when I remember the biggest burden you are facing. I pray that may God be your comrade in all the work that you are doing. This is always visioned to me through dreams by God that it's His will that you face the work. And I thank God for that.
Jenipher

March 20, 1990
To Friends of Good Samaritan Ministries:
We support a widow in Nakuru, who has nine children. She has no source of income. The youngest child is 3 years old. We also support Rose Alloush who is divorced due to tragic circumstances with her husband. She has three children in school. We put Rose through secretarial training and she works full-time for the ministry at Uranga, in Kenya. Each of these people has serious need for basic aid. One of the hard parts of my work is not only to travel and meet with people, but also to teach them. It is to raise them up to a greater work than just the beginning stages of basic Christian evangelism. It's also to follow through. Every night, when I go to bed, I'm aware of the needs of hundreds of people throughout the world who are fellow Samaritans, personal friends, suffering ones. This is indeed a call for your mercy, and for God's grace. If you know anyone who can help us with the school fees, notify me immediately at the Good Samaritan office, 503-644-2339.
Your sister in Christ Jesus our Lord,
Bettie P. Mitchell
International Executive Director

September 10, 1990
My dear sister Jenipher,

It is not very long now before we will be leaving for Africa. My husband Jerry is coming, and my sister Arabelle. I look forward to seeing you so much, Jenipher. In the meantime, as I prepare and carry such heavy burdens for the work all over the world, please keep me in prayer, particularly my health and my emotions. Ask the Lord for my patience to endure. I miss you, and I think daily of the humble prayers of your family for our lives. I'm not worthy of those prayers, Jenipher. I'm not worthy at all of your friendship, for who am I to know one such as you?

I love you, Jenipher, and there are no words to tell you how much I miss you and Little Bettie. Teach her how to play with me that she might be a joy and a blessing. I pray that I'll be a grandma to her in the heart.

Your sister in Christ Jesus our Lord,
Bettie P. Mitchell
International Executive Director

December 18, 1990
Dear Bettie P. Mitchell,

My sister, I can't hesitate to say that you actually went with my heart coz I felt and believed that both your heart and mine were strongly bonded together. Even up to this moment, I'm just feeling your presence in my house. I'm afraid to say that even I can't vibrate any word but thinking of you only. I don't know when I'll nurse my thoughts on you. The ridiculous part of it is that even when the dish has been served on the table, I entirely remember how we used to sit around the table with you at that time. I appreciate your visit in Kenya, particularly in my house, and I don't know how to thank you. Your presence has actually aided me a lot. Those genuine teachings which you used to give us, in real meaning, has benefited me a lot. I think too of gathering courage to teach others in the same format as you did. I once more thank you for your determinations and the fruitful facts, which cannot only build our physical body but also spiritually.

Mum, I won't forget praying for you. The moment I flash back my mind on you, only tears accompany my thoughts. I don't think if I'll ever have a comrade of your kind. Mum, you have taken my heart with you completely. Please pray for me, and may the almighty Father of all that live bless you.

Your sister in Christ Jesus our Lord,
Jenipher Oduor

January 17, 1991

My dear and beloved sister, Jenipher, Baby Bettie, and all of the children in your house and the neighbors in your neighborhood,

I can't wait any longer to write you a letter, precious sister, and to let you know that my heart is as satisfied as yours with the relationship Christ has lain before us. Our future seems to lie in the ministry. Our prayers, our spiritual level of understanding each other and the gift of our friendship will sustain us through incredible difficulties that others would find too hard.

I have received your first letter, Jenipher, and I understood everything that you said in the letter. When one has shared so deeply at the divine level of love, it is as if Christ was crucified and removed from us once again when we say goodbye. We have a "crucified" relationship that is sacrificial and deeply understanding of the genuine need within our souls.

First I want to tell you that I am very happy with the way you are as a mother of Baby Bettie. I watched over that very closely and deeply to see how your hand would guide and direct her life. I saw love, wisdom and great teaching in that hand. I believe the way you guide her will affect the way that you guide all of your children. The Lord will use each of your nine children in ways that are far beyond our eyes to see. I want you to know, Jenipher, that in my heart I will always see Baby Bettie as one of nine children. For it is unfair and beyond what your other children could bear if they were not all a part of my heart and this ministry. I want your children to know this and I want them to know me as friend and comforter through the Holy Spirit.

I particularly will always remember the wonderful afternoon at your house with your neighbors and family members. It was one of those times when joy overtakes us and we just had fun. There was beauty and I believe there was wisdom in the message of our relationship.

I miss you. As this war breaks out, my heart is deeply troubled. Last week I had a chance to go to Iraq and I wanted to go. I felt The Call and the sense of belonging in Iraq. It would have been easy for me to go. But I could not leave behind the work begun in Africa and it was a decision to stay behind and send Pastor Dan Simmons, a friend who went with our blessings and financial aide, including some Iraqi Dinar that I had stored away ($300 worth). He is in a Peace Camp now on the Iraq side of the Iraq-Saudi border. Our prayers are that he will get out when it is time. He hopes to leave that camp the 25th of January and work his way to Jordan and the West Bank. I am deeply in prayer for a breakthrough in mercy and understanding to come, and I am deeply in prayer that the bombs will not speak for who we really are. **It is a great tragedy to see bombs talk and men shout in pride.** How wonderful if I could spend 6 weeks in training those leaders to be world Samaritans. I think it would change the course of the history of man if everyone could go through 6 to 7 weeks of Samaritan training as we did as one group.

On our journey in Kenya, our days weren't so easy, were they Jenipher? You lost the precious things that were special to you and some days I thought that my bones were going to shake apart in that van. The weariness did take over my soul and spirit. But, ah, Jenipher, we have a life that almost no one has and we saw the incredible coming of the Kingdom of our Lord. It is coming!

Do I miss you? Do I think about you? First of all, I remember you tugging on my skirt. It makes me laugh and I just absolutely hilariously love our relationship. You are my mother, my sister, my friend, my confidant, and my deeply secret prayer partner who shares in the real knowledge of who I am. Yes, I miss you and I will pass everyday with the knowledge that we don't have to miss each other for we are always present, always alive and always with our Lord and His work.

Baby Bettie, I have some wonderful pictures of you and I am deeply missing you. I wonder how "dolly" is and did you ever find your blanket and all of the shoes and things that you lost? Don't forget that Bettie Mitchell is your special friend and that if God is willing and all things go well, in 1992, when you are five years old, well maybe almost 6, I'm coming back to see you and hold your hand and go on an important walk with you. At that time, I will probably have to bring another dolly, but since you take care of your dolly so well, it may be just fine. Tell your brothers and sisters "hello," and please take good care of Mother—she needs you a lot. I love you.

Jenipher, peace be unto you my sister. You did all that was needed and even more to sustain us and to be with us to keep this work in God's will and God's grace. I am incredibly proud to know you and to call you my close and personal friend.

Your sister in Christ Jesus our Lord,
Mama Bettie

February 1, 1991
Dear Jenipher and your children, especially Baby Bettie,

I had several things to send you, so I decided to write you another letter. I pray that this letter comes to you and brings you joy and peace. I am still having a very hard time dealing with this war in Iraq, sister. I spent a lot of time weeping, so hard, this week, and then I spent the rest of the week showing slides of the Iraqi children who are dear and precious friends of mine, and I talked about the effects of the war on children.

War has had a devastating effect on my life. I was a child all during WW II and I still feel the suffering from that war on my soul. In the Korean War, my husband went overseas for two years. The first two years we were married he was gone, and during this whole two years, I only spoke to him 15 minutes on the telephone, and saw him not at all. War kills many people and others are still alive, but they can feel dead. I am ashamed that the world has not recognized the devastation and destruction on the lives of children. Why do we continue to think that greed and power are more important than the development of a child?

I enclose with this letter, a check and I hope you can cash it. I will be sending a check every month, Jenipher, for this amount. I miss you, sister, deeply, and know that you are there. You are one of the two most important women to minister deep down in my spirit. The other woman is Joan Baker who watches over both of us. May the Lord Jesus tenderly bless our relationship and may I be there for you, sister, when you really don't know

what to do. I pray that Baby Bettie likes school and that she misses Mama Bettie. I pray that she knows that I am with her.
God Bless you,
Your sister Bettie

February 22, 1991
Dear Mummy Bettie Mitchell,
Praise the Lord. I am sure the Lord is with you. I would like to inform you that I received the letter, which you sent me. I was very happy to hear from you. My happiness to you has touched every member of my family. Before I got your letter, I thought of what happened to you. The way you wrote to me that your letter indicated to me that I am much nearer to you. I am very happy in my soul. Just after I read your letter, I wept in joy. I did not weep because of sadness but because of the great joy I had in getting your letter. In 1989, you advised me not to beg and truly I have heeded your advice and up to now, the Lord is guiding me.

Just as I write to you now, I have a burden of praying the Lord for you. I used to pray for you on Wednesdays and Fridays. And this is due to the nature of the job you do. If we don't pray for you, you won't have courage to do your work properly. And that is why I have a burden to pray for you to the Lord so that you may get strength to minister His word without any fear.
Your loving daughter,
Jenipher Oduor

March 15, 1991
Dear Jenipher and Baby Bettie,
I think of your other children, and I pray that the Lord will meet all of your needs, Jenipher. I know that poverty is ugly, but somewhere inside you is one of the richest women I have ever known. Your riches come from the spirit that dwells within you. May that spirit enrich the lives of each one of your children.

My sister, Mr. Jerry, Chip Lake, all of us every day, we think about that van, and the wonderfully bumpy, dirt roads, and the terrific time we had traveling together. I'm planning for sure to come in 1992. It won't be for very long, but it will be very important, Jenipher. I love you. The whole earth will someday know that Jenipher Oduor and Bettie Mitchell are genuine, absolute, final sisters in Christ Jesus our Lord. May the Lord give you a blessed Easter.

Mama Bettie, your sister

April 10, 1991

Dear sister Jenipher,

I am missing you terribly and writing you a note today to encourage you. I know that you need lifting up as much as I do and the more you pray for me the more I pray for you. You're getting increasingly greater prayer benefits from this ministry as well as we are from yours.

I talked to James and we were so excited about the opening of the center in Nakuru. This makes official the fact that you are in a major responsibility to direct a program and to help. I know there will be many miracles as you meet with Dan Oolo and those who are really deeply committed Samaritans. We are going to be surprised in 1992 when I come. We will not see human miracles, as we know, Jenipher. Only God can give us the grace to love as Christ loved and to break down the evil and bring the good as He did. The church in Nakuru has often been deeply steeped in competition and evil. This is God's opportunity to knock on the door and change the hearts of these believers. I deeply pray, sister, for great changes to occur in this area and for this church to become different than all of the other churches, by its spirit, not by its works of the flesh.

How are your babies, all of them? Are you well? I miss you. You, with James, are the dearest and most precious friends I have in Africa.

Mama Bettie, your sister

Mama Bettie to Baby Bettie:

P.S. Baby Bettie, you'd better listen to this letter, I have plenty to say to you. I want you to grow, to do well in school and to always remember that you are a special girl and a great friend of mine. I'm proud of you. Stand up and walk.

Dear Mama Bettie,

The dolly is okay. It is in good condition. Only the napkins were spoiled when she dipped the dolly in the water. Bettie is doing well and she likes school very much. She keeps on asking me all the time where is Bettie? And she calls her dolly Alvira

Ema. She appreciated very much your praise that she is pretty, and she is going to grow up to be a very special lady.

Thank you very much for the revelation you got about me that I am a richer woman than you have ever known. Indeed, I am exceedingly overjoyed about my riches that only come from the Spirit that dwells in me. Mama, I want you to pray for me so that God may provide for the seats or the chairs, because the ones you sat on when you came in my house were borrowed from the neighbors. This time it is my desire that when you come you may sit on our seats.

Your sister in Christ,
Jenipher Oduor

June 3, 1991
Dear Jenipher,
I didn't know that your husband had no brothers and sisters. Tell me your family history. Tell me about your mother, father, brothers and sisters. Where is your family? What's going on with them? In your next letter, I would also like for you to give me the names of each of your children, how old they are, whether they're in school, and a little about each one of them.

Tell Baby Bettie that she's no longer a baby, but she is Little Bettie, and I'm looking at her picture, which is right in front of my face every single day. Every single day I talk to her and laugh a little. And every day I give Bettie's mother, Jenipher, a big hug in my heart. I trust you so deeply. May Christ keep us, and may we not fail Him.

Your holy sister,
Bettie P. Mitchell
International Executive Director

June 10, 1991
My dear sister Bettie,
Mummy, I really love your house and especially you. This love to you is extended to wherever you are. I often forego my meals only to strengthen my prayers for you. I shed my tears to God because of you. Sometimes when I call Little Bettie, her response just soothes my heart that I'm with you. I mean when

she responds to my call. I just feel that it's you who has responded. It's my great joy to have a girl by the name Bettie!
Your sister in Christ Jesus,
Jenipher Oduor

June 24, 1991
My dear and precious friend Jenipher,
Mr. Jerry and I are going on vacation with our 7 year-old granddaughter, April, from July 1st to 15th. We are going to go into other states. We will see a passion play of the crucifixion and resurrection of Jesus in South Dakota, which is another state in the United States. We are really happy to make this trip with April, because she is a very special little girl in our lives. I was there when she was born. Her little life is one of God's graces to me and Mr. Jerry likes that too.
Every day I weep for a while. Today I wept a lot. There was joy, there was sorrow, and it was that deep suffering that comes from a compassionate soul. I get so tired sometimes Jenipher, but I have such joy. I don't know very many people in this world that know such joy.
Mama Bettie

July 2, 1991
My sister in Christ Mama Bettie,
I would like to relate to you about my family background. My late husband was born with brothers, but they all died, so he remained alone up to the time he also died. His mother and father also died so I am just alone in the family with my children. The mother of my late husband died in 1988 and the father died in 1972. So in the whole family, everybody died.
As regards to my parents, my late father died in 1968, and by that time, I had not got married yet to my late husband. My mother is still alive. She had children, but unfortunately most of them died. So we remained two girls who are not quite able to look after her properly.
I ask you to pray for me so that I may be able to get my own house in Uranga. The one I have now is a grass-thatched hut and it is leaking terribly so that I cannot stay in it.
Your sister in Christ Jesus, Jenipher Oduor

July 31, 1991

My dear sister in Christ Jesus, Jenipher,

I received your two wonderful letters and they cheered me up greatly just to touch that which is holy ground in divine friendship. Among the women at the cross, Jenipher, we stood. The Lord has taken much from us and given us more joy than anyone I know. He's taught us centrally that we are His. I firmly believe that you are the living sister of Christ Jesus and that I am His living sister also. I believe that this generation has been given to us for His work and that we have only seen the beginning of what He'll do through our faithfulness.

I deeply appreciated the story of your life Jenipher. I need to know those things about you. We need to know each other from the depths and the heights of our suffering and our joy. It will help to develop both of us and it will keep us faithful at the cross.

I had a wonderful letter from Rhoda and soon I will answer it. I wrote to her to give her encouragement for she is a great woman and I love her. I also send greetings in this letter to Dan Oolo. I know that many, many things are going to occur as you stay simple, real, honest, deep-faced Samaritans. Christ wants this work. He did this work. He fed 5,000 in one day when the apostles wanted to send them away hungry because preaching was more important than food. He did it, so shall you and I. I love you Jenipher and this morning I touch the hem of your garment to comfort you and to pray with you. I got up at 5:00 this morning to write you this letter.

Mama Bettie

October 18, 1991

Dear Beloved Bettie,

Please, Mama Bettie, never give up from the work that God has charged with you. I would like to remind you, with all my children, we love you very much. I want you to know that this is love from above that has joined us together even though we come from places that are far apart. Please, sister, read these two verses that are my deepest feelings about you: III John 1:2-3.

Yours in Christ,
Jenipher

Before Jenipher's death:
Dear Little Bettie,

Every day I watch over you while you go to school, while you pray, while you sing and while you dance. Is it okay that I'm white? Will you not be scared? It's not so bad to be white. After you get used to me, you'll like it some. I'm so glad you're brown. I like it a lot. Help Mama. Mama Jenipher is the best mother in the world. You are beautiful, Little Bettie, and you are my friend.
Mama Bettie

Dear sister Bettie,
I had a strong sympathy with you when I heard that your husband had suffered injuries in a bicycle accident. My emotions were so strong and powerful that I had to pray and fast, two consecutive days, asking God to help with you both. I have decided (including other family members) to have Wednesday as a specific day that is now my holy day for praying with my children for you, asking God to uplift you and the house. The prayers start at 9:00 p.m. and end at 10:00 p.m.
What I would like to inform you is that Baby Bettie is much different from the other children because when we are about to start off our prayers, she usually sits calmly and waits for the prayers to start.
Your sister in Jesus Christ,
Jenipher Oduor

The last letter I wrote to Jenipher:
January 6, 1992
Dear Jenipher,
I received your wonderful letter and it was an encouragement to my soul as I faced the oncoming year. I know that my letters encourage you too, and we are most fortunate, by God's grace, to have the ability to speak to each other in the mail.
I'm sending $50.00 this month. It will be $25.00 again next month. This is to cover the extra emergencies that you had. You must understand, Jenipher, I support many and I must be careful with the funds. I know you are careful. Don't build for Baby Bettie something that is better than the people around her. We

must not let her surge ahead and her spirit become better than others; we want to build in her a character of humility and acceptance of the fact that she's not above her people, she's like them.

Do you miss me, Jenipher? Well, James and I set the dates for coming and it will be soon. We will be leaving Oregon October 29, 1992, and returning to Oregon December 19th. The first part of the journey will be spent in Kenya. I will have very little time, as I must go to several other countries as well. We will have to do everything that we're going to do faster than we expected, but it will be enough, because we'll make it enough. I hunger and thirst to see your eyes and to have a good laugh with you, Jenipher. I'll even let you tug on my skirt. I love you.

Mama Bettie

Letters to the Children and the Development of Baby Bettie:

After Jenipher's death in early January 1992, I wrote a personal letter on January 13th to each of her children.

January 13, 1992

Dear George, (Age 20)

What can I say to you? You were so special to your mother. You will never have to be ashamed, as you were a great help to your mother. She was very proud of you, George. Even on your naughtiest days, you were a comfort to her soul and to the whole family. I know how deeply your spirit is wounded by this loss and how you look up at God and try to understand where Mama is. We know by faith that Mama is now a great prayer warrior for us, because that's what she wanted more than anything to be able to help the whole world. I know that's the reward that she's been given. Mama's going to help the whole world and her prayers are going to make a difference in the Kingdom of Heaven and on earth.

Mama Jenipher was beautiful. We loved her so much. George, she was my very best friend in the whole world and she was such a comfort to me. She hasn't left at all; she's still comforting us in a new way. I'm so proud of you, of all the children, and that I can be your best friend in the family. We won't abandon you and things will turn out well. Don't be afraid, son. You're going to make it. Don't worry about the children, but keep them together in your heart. Gather them anytime you can. Don't be a scatterer, be a gatherer of the fruits of your mother's labor. I expect great things from you now, for you are the head of a very special family.

George, you might say that you were raised poor and that you knew hunger. I might say that you were raised rich, for you received more love in this world than many will ever know about. That love will continue and we're going to be really close. Please write me a letter and talk to me, George, about anything in the whole world. I'll always put your letters aside as first in my heart.

Your Mama in Christ Jesus,
Bettie P. Mitchell

My dear sister and daughter and friend, Rose, (Age 18)

Honey, I am so sorry about the death of your mother. I want to take you in my arms and comfort you, sing you lullabies and talk to your spirit. It's one of the greatest losses of my lifetime and yet I can only count it as gain because your mother was such a great woman of God. She had a vision and she knew how to keep her family in one spirit. I know that she stands right in front of the throne of God and that her place is special. She will be a great intercessor for your life. She will not be gone. The importance of her prayer work and her mothering of you will increase year by year. You have not lost your mother you have gained the power of a healed mother. You are going to see great miracles in your life, Rose, and you're going to rise among your people as a woman of great faith. I entrust the life of Baby Bettie to your care. I want you to know that I will support you in everything that you decide to do and that I will be your friend, even as I was the friend to your mother. It is with great joy that I look forward to seeing you this year, and in the meantime, I want you to have peace. Your mother is with you. And, lo we are with you always even as Christ Jesus our Lord, unto the end of the world.

In Jesus name, your precious friend,
Mama Bettie

Dear Enuice, (Age 16)

I speak to you today, with tears in my eyes, comforting you on the death of your mother. She was my very greatest friend, someone that was so close to me that when we would breathe, in different nations, we were of one breath and one heart. I pray that you can find someone to translate this letter for you, that you will understand my great compassion for all of you and the presence of my faith in the life of your family. Your mother was a great Samaritan. She was honored among all people as a woman of great faith. How proud we are that Jesus has taken her home to do even greater work in His Kingdom. Don't be afraid. Your needs will be met, Eunice, and your comforting will be very great from the Lord Himself. Stand as a great woman of God all the days of your life. I stand with you!

In Jesus name, your precious friend,
Bettie Mitchell, Mama Bettie to you

Dear Anna, (Age 14)

How can I say how I feel about the death of your mother? I feel the same as you do. I sit with you, I ponder it, and I miss her fiercely. She was our friend. She was the mother of even Mama Bettie. I want you to know that you are going to be comforted, that your family will stay together in one spirit, and that you are going to find many miracles coming into your life as a result of the Lord's mercy, and your mother's greatness in the eyes of Jesus. Do not be afraid of the days to come and do not fall, but if you do the Lord will pick you up and hold you until you make it. I'm very proud of you. I'm not only the friend of Baby Bettie and Jenipher; I'm the personal friend of Anna. I'm here. I'll see you (in November) when I come.

Your Mama in Christ Jesus,
Mama Bettie

Dear Milicent, (Age 12)

I like your name. I would like to see you. I'd like to put my arms out to you and say come, run into them, be comforted. Your mother is close. Do not be afraid, she has not left but she has increased her work for your family. You will have more to eat

now. You will have greater mercy from many, and although your loss is as great as mine, you're going to find the songs of your mother deep in your heart forever and ever. Milicent, do well in school. Think of the friends that you have and understand that Mama Bettie is one of them. I will see you in November and we will sit and pray.
In Jesus' name,
Mama Bettie

Dear Benjamin, (Age 11)
I understand that you are 11 years old. We're going to miss your mother so much. It isn't going to be very easy for you, Benjamin, but I know that you are very, very brave. I am proud of you and I hope that you do well. It's hard to be a boy and have to go to school and do all the things that you are going to have to do. I know that you'll make it, Benjamin. Never forget Jesus and don't forget Mama Bettie either. We are with you.
In Jesus,
Mama Bettie

Dear Ester, (Age 8)
I miss your Mama. You miss her too. I sit with you and I want to cry. I'm going to smile up at her instead and let your Mama see my face with tears in my eyes. I'm going to smile at her and tell her that I love her. Will you do that too every day? Don't be afraid, Ester. Mama Bettie will not desert your family. You are all family now to me. You are my children. You are my heart. You will be okay. I will see you when I come in November. Do well in school and be comforted. You are loved always.
Your mom in Christ Jesus,
Mama Bettie

Dear Moses, (Age 6)
Mama is not dead. She is with Jesus and she's very happy. She likes Him a lot. Mama can see you and she can hear you and she can send lots of help with her prayers when you have needs. She's smiling. She's proud of you, Moses. You're her son, her special boy.

I'm Mama Bettie to you too and I'm going to comfort you deep in my heart. You'll be surprised how your family is going to do well. Everybody in your family is going to do well. I love you and I speak to you and encourage you to do well in school. Don't get mad. God is with you. He likes you a lot, Moses.

Your Mama in Jesus,
Bettie

Dear Baby (Big) Bettie, (Age 4)

I am so happy to write you a letter this morning and tell you that I love you. I pray for you all day long and I sing you little songs. I think about how you're going to do out at James' house and how much you are going to love being at the Center with your name on it.

It's going to be hard for you to not see your mommy, Jenipher, and it's hard for me too because she was my best friend, but when we look up at the sky, we're going to know for sure that she's looking at us and that she's big enough, really, to help us.

Don't be afraid, Bettie. I'll always be there with you and so will Mama and so will Daddy. Jesus is our protector and our very best friend. I love you and I'm very proud to call you, my namesake, and my best friend too.

In Jesus' name, Amen.
Mama Bettie

Later letters to the children:
August 2, 1992
My dear, dear Little Bettie,

I miss you so much. I've been looking around trying to decide what to bring and I have thought of the perfect thing. Are you doing well in school? How do you and Hezron play? What is your favorite thing to do?

I want to sit with you and we're going to run and we're going to dance a little and we're going to sing a song together. You and I also need to visit the grave of your mother. We need to point to the sign on the Good Samaritan Ministries Center that has our name on it. I want to lift you up and have a picture of the

sign with our names. I love you, honey, and I'm deeply proud of you.
Mama Bettie

June 10, 1992
Dear George,
As you gather the children and you meet from time to time, I want you to tell them that Mama Bettie loves them very much and that they are deep in her heart forever and ever. Tell them that I think that they are wonderful children and I am very proud of each one. I am concerned about your grades. I want to hear who is doing what in school. I would like, in the years ahead, to have little notes from each one. I want each child to learn English and be well educated. I want several of the children to go to the University. I want all of you children to do well, because you come from a great family, a great nation, and you all represent the Samaritan spirit in the Kingdom.
Love in Christ,
Mama Bettie

(Note: The accident during our visit caused George to have a badly broken arm.)
November 23, 1992 (after my visit)
My dear son George,
Despite the great tragedy after the accident, we had tender moments, George that no one can ever take away from us. I am instructing James Opiyo that your mother's grave is to be covered with cement and her name is to be put on it. It is to be done well. I want her grave to be marked permanently, for the world to someday visit. There is much to learn from the people and there is more to learn from your mother than many.
Always remember I am your special Mama Bettie

1993
Dear Mama Bettie,
I owe you this letter, I think, my sister. So I'm going to write tonight, a letter of great encouragement to you. How much I miss you!

I sit down tonight, and I think of you, and I want to report that your intercession bore much fruit in my life. About five people intercede for me in prayer so prayer always reaches me day or night. You're one of the five. I know that your prayers have increased for me, and the more needs you have, the more the Lord drives you to your knees to pray for me.
 Greet my brother Jerry. Tell him that God loves him very much. May God bless you. I never forget you.
 George

April 7, 1993
Dear Little Bettie,
 I pray that you are doing well in school. I pray that you know that I sit very, very close to you. Maybe you can't see me, but, oh, my heart is there with you.
 Jesus is very big and yet He is your brother. He is your big, big brother and He is in charge. He has great interest in you, Bettie, and He watches you so much to help you.
 I think that you are special and so are Hezron and all of your friends. God bless you on the opening of the Training Center. I am there with you. Put your finger on the sign on your name. It is our name, together.
 Your Mama,
 Bettie

October 11, 1993
My dear son George,
 How do you feel about your secret? I feel that you have much to do to repair from some of the harm, but that you must begin to grow up and face your responsibilities as a man. I am glad that you have had a healthy little baby boy. Papa Jerry and I are glad that you named him Jerry Mitchell. We will expect you to be able to take care of him and to do what is right for his mother.
 I know, George, that you are lonely and that you are struggling for your strength in this world. You are on the road and now, with a family, must become self-supporting. I pray for you, son. I am now a grandma and your baby is our grandson. I pray for you to take responsibility and prove yourself as a worthy father and a man of God. It is a serious business. It is the

business of your Father in Heaven and you must be faithful to it. Your mother and I are great intercessors for your life and for all of the family.

While I am in Egypt and Pakistan, I will be starting the Jenipher Oduor's Widows' and Orphans' Fund in all Samaritan parts of these countries. Soon there will be many nations in the world that will know your mother and know about this fund. They will keep it and not let it fall to the ground. Any man who cheats in any way with God's money will fall to the ground, as did Ananias and Sapphira in the Book of Acts. "What God has started must be completed."

You are my precious son, George, and a precious friend. Never feel that you have to keep a secret. What troubles your life, what agonies you face, what questions you have you may bring to me any time of the day or night. I may give you advice that you don't like, and you may not take it, but I will never judge you or forsake you.

I am your Mama and your fellow Samaritan,
Bettie P. Mitchell

January 24, 1994
My dear son George, and your new family,
On this recent journey we began more than 15 new Jenipher Oduor Widows' and Orphans' Funds in Pakistan, Egypt and Israel. It has also been started in Ukraine. How far your mother's life and work went. I pray, son, you learn through your close experience with death and your many experiences with tragedy, to be strong and to work each day as if it were your last, spreading good and giving much to the needs of others.

I am a great intercessor for your life and I continue to be your close personal friend.
Mama Bettie P. Mitchell

May 26, 1994
Dear Little Bettie,
I miss you a lot, and often. I stand and look at your pictures, which are right by my face, every day all day long, and I marvel that you are such a wonderful girl and how much you are growing. I pray that you always know, Bettie, the great

importance I place on your life. It is an important gift that you have been given, to have a home with James Opiyo, the Continental Director of Good Samaritan Ministries in Africa. There is no other child in all of Africa that has received such a blessing as you have. Use it well, study hard and grow deep in your inside in the love of Jesus.

I am your guardian and a part of your life.
Mama Bettie
P.S. Are you getting ready to write me a letter? Surely, you can draw me a picture. I will expect to hear from you this time. You are old enough to do this.

June 8, 1994
Dear George,
I know that building your house at home is important. I pray that you will move into your mother's house, which is on the homestead. It is livable. All that was needed were some furnishings and a new roof. I have found, in my life, that if I have integrity, it is more important than what I have in terms of earthly things. Your mother had integrity, George, and it was counted by God as the greatest part of her.

I continue to miss your mother a great deal. We continue to raise funds for the Jenipher Oduor Widows' and Orphans' Fund and some money came in—enough to ship 100 boxes of clothing, books, and medicine to Africa; enough to put a roof on a school for AIDS orphans; enough to send a container to Nigeria of much needed clothing and supplies; enough to have a Children's Camp for the sponsored children in Uganda. I pray, enough, to put a roof on a poor widow's house. You see, George, there are many things to be done, and I want you, son, to press into sharing funds with James and helping with Good Samaritan Ministries. As you give James a coin, now and again, he will always find a way to help you when you are in trouble.

I love you and I respect you as the oldest son, the pride of your mother and father. But, most of all, I must respect you before the face of our Lord Jesus.

Your mom and fellow Samaritan,
Bettie P. Mitchell

August 27, 1994
Dear Mama Bettie,
I thank God for the love he first showed us through His only begotten son, Jesus Christ. I am so grateful to have this opportunity just to write to you a word of hello. I thank the Lord because of you, Mama Bettie, and the ministry too. You are a wonderful Mama for having listened to the voice of the Lord and having seen this revelation concerning GSM.
Thank you for taking that necessary action and developing such a wonderful ministry. I am deeply sorry, Mama, for not writing to you. The Lord has protected us all, the children of the late Jenipher Oduor.
We are praying for you and the ministry. We have seen the hand of the Lord since mother left us, and the Lord has done great things to us, the family of Jenipher. I am staying with Rev. Nicholas Okungu and my name is Eunice Otieno Oduor. God bless you so much.

October 10, 1994
Dear and precious Eunice,
If I could have only one letter that came with James or Nicholas, it would have been a letter from you. Anything that comes to remind me of your family, you children, and your wonderful mama makes me feel again in that special family way, that we belong to each other.
I am very proud of you, Eunice. You have done extremely well. I understand that Bettie is quite intelligent and that she is really growing strong. It is a great miracle, you know, to see you children thrive and prosper. I am well aware that you join millions of orphans in Africa and that being an orphan is not unusual. But, I want to say to you, Eunice, and to all of you Oduor children, that you are unusual orphans because you came into the world to bring a special message of hope and healing.
Mama Bettie P. Mitchell

December 14, 1994
Dear and precious Little Bettie,
I wish I could hold you on my lap for Christmas, and sing you a song. I'd sing you the funniest song and you'd like it so much

and we would laugh and clap our hands. Maybe we'd walk to the Center and we'd point up at the place where our name is and we'd laugh some more. Do you know how much I miss you and how happy I am that you live at Uranga? I just ask Jesus to keep you well and to satisfy everything that you ever need. You must become a saint, Bettie, and it's not an easy road, but you will. I trust that with all my heart.
 Happy Christmas and a blessed New Year.
 Mama Bettie P. Mitchell
 P.S. I am still waiting for my letter.

 February 6, 1996
 My dear son George,
 It was such a pleasure to see you. I have one small concern. There is a lot of very loud noise in the Nakuru church. I'm concerned whether the still small voice of the living God is there. It is easy to make a joyful noise unto the Lord, but to hear Him, the whole earth must keep silence before the Lord. When we are quiet, we can hear Him, George. Let Him play His drum for a moment, and record His music on your soul. Then you will write and speak for God. His drum, His music is the "Still Small Voice."
 Your Mama in Oregon, and your fellow Samaritan,
 Bettie P. Mitchell

 April 19, 1996
 My dear little daughter Rose,
 I miss you a lot, my little one, my precious one. I know that you have a sincere and wonderful heart and that you are not satisfied to not give. That is a great and wonderful gift to be able to give. Many don't have it.
 At this time, I am not to send something for you to give to others. I am to tell you that the piece of bread you give, that is yours, is enough to feed the heart and humble the souls of those around you. Don't be afraid to give your little piece of bread. This is the way Jesus was. He taught us to give what we had and the Lord God multiplied it.
 Your mom and fellow Samaritan, Bettie P. Mitchell

September 17, 1996
My dear son, George and your family,
As an orphan, George, I wonder how much time you give to Widows and Orphans. It is very easy to give much time to music. We see it here. All the musicians give time to playing music and singing, but when it is time for them to give from their pockets, many disappear. The music is fun and fills us with joy. The giving seems to hurt us and makes us want to go away. How few people ever gave your mother a single thing that she needed, and yet God blessed her and He gave to her. Always remember, George, you are to give more than the others around you for you felt the suffering of a widow's heart for many years.
Your mom and fellow Samaritan,
Bettie P. Mitchell

October 3, 1996
Dear and beloved Rose,
You are totally aware of it Rose. You are an international family. As I take you with me across the world, the Oduors travel. You are international in that your spirit is something that no one can defeat. Yes, Rose, I want to say this to you very firmly YOUR FAMILY SPIRIT IS SOMETHING THAT NONE CAN DEFEAT! Don't be too concerned with what you don't have. You know that your spirit is undefeatable and incredibly with God. To be with God is to live. I consider your mother as alive today as she was yesterday. Don't make this mistake of not thinking you are too, because your name is Rose and you are not as important to me as Jenipher. This is not the truth. YOU ARE!!
Do you ever get tired of just listening to religion? Sometimes I get very tired of it, Rose. It just seems like words, words, words, words, singing and dancing, but where is the truth? The truth is, we are together, we will be protected and there is something greater than our hardships. That is the friendship that Jesus left behind for us! I love you, Rose, deeply, profoundly. Always remember, you are Rose Oduor, someone extraordinary!
Your Mama and fellow Samaritan,
Bettie P. Mitchell

March 19, 1997
Dear Little Bettie,
I understand that you consecrated and dedicated the Center that has our name on it again on December 15th. I also understand that there is a video. I can hardly wait to see it! Will you tell Papa James to please send it right away? I want to see how big you are.
Do you remember I am coming in July? I am going to stay at your house. That is an important day, when I come. By God's grace, I believe Papa Jerry is coming too. Isn't that a miracle?
I praise God that we are good friends. You are a wonderful sweetheart and very, very smart. Always remember that kindness is the most important thing you can ever do in your whole life.
Your Mama,
Bettie

July 21, 2003
Dear Mama Bettie,
Praise God, Mama, hoping you're doing fine in U.S. We are glad to meet GSM team in Kenya and to have a hello word with them. I myself it has not been easy for me for a couple of months.
But I thank God for healing from malaria. Now I'm fine and energetic. Mama, I would like to thank you for the love you have toward Jenipher's kids. You are the only mother left to take care of Jenipher's kids. I pray that the Lord may give you more strength and bless your ministry, and your husband and your family.
Finally, I really miss you so much. I do hope to hear from you soon.
Your son,
Ben Oduor

Hi Mama Bettie,
I thank God for giving me another opportunity to communicate to you another time. I hope you are doing so well. I'm praying that one day we meet and see one another again because it's long since we met. I'm now busy in school and tackling my final National Examination and it's only remaining

for me one week to complete my secondary education. All this has happened because of God's grace. I thank God for you too, and I take this chance to sincerely appreciate for the work you have done and also to thank you very much for your support on my schooling. Thank you Mama Bettie. After school I will be committed with church choirs for time being before joining university. I would like to be a news reporter. I would also like to tell you that I was very happy to hear that you will include me in your story when you publish books. I would also like to own one of the books please. I don't have much to say but we all keep you in our prayers. I have also grown old, now 21 years. Wow! God bless you too much. I'm missing you and also missing your voice. Goodbye. I have also met another friend, Nubi. Wonderful. God bless you.
From Bettie Mitchell Oduor

December 29, 2008
Dear George,
This is perhaps the last letter I will write to you. I am going to retire and write much fewer letters. This is a letter to remind you of the key role that your family played in the history of the ministry. Needs of Widows and Orphans have been met because of your mother and your family. All the things we could think to do have been helping. You continue to be an honored part of the ministry as a whole. Your children to me are as important as Mother Jenipher or James Opiyo.

I am sure your music continues. You have much laughter and you are very little afraid, George. I honor and bless you! Greet all of your siblings,
Your fellow Samaritan and Mama,
Bettie P. Mitchell

The Story of Bettie the School Teacher, A Tale of Old Bettie and Baby Bettie as told by James Opiyo:
On 15th December 1987, Mama Bettie Mitchell was called upon to officially open the Good Samaritan ministries work in Uranga, Kenya. While cutting the ribbon signifying the official opening, Mama Bettie was carrying the Baby Bettie on her left

hip, and she made it clear that the opening ceremony was being done by both Old Bettie and Baby Bettie.

The Old Bettie is the one who began her career of teaching and later God called her to continue teaching and to teach nothing but the Kingdom of God. Out of that single act, the work is now operational in 19 countries of Africa.

On 5th January 2009, the Baby Bettie, who graduated from high school last year, was enrolled as a volunteer teacher in a primary school, awaiting her results that are still to come. She loves teaching. The head teacher comments that Bettie is a gifted teacher, so efficient and thorough in her class work. God has made both Old Bettie and Baby Bettie to be professional teachers. The Old Bettie is turning 75 this year and she is retiring from her active service. At 22, the Baby Bettie is now BIG 22. She is beginning her teaching career. What do you learn from this story?

Your fellow Samaritan along the way,
Papa James Opiyo

What does it all mean?

In some ways, this story is one of the most significant stories in the history of Good Samaritan Ministries. We are called to take seriously the lives of widows and orphans. We stand firm as a ministry to the individual, a ministry to a person, a relationship with an individual that lasts beyond our lifetimes. It is about an eternal God and the value that we place on one human being. It reveals the value we place on all!

This is a challenge, for the ministries have many. Do they know the few, and are the few the many?

When Jenipher was here, her husband and his entire family were dead. She had an elderly mother, one sister, the nine orphans, and a third grade education. She spoke no English. Jenipher was 39 years old when she died. She died of a blood pressure problem. I know in my spirit the Lord took her to heaven to be a greater intercessor because people here are often too selfish and they don't pray very well. Jenipher loved God and all of us so much

At the time of Jenipher's death, Kenya had 3,000 Samaritan workers, and the families that took Jenipher's children considered it a great privilege to have one of her children because Jenipher was a woman of God.

Among the men, leaders in the ministry in Kenya, many took their problems to Jenipher because she was a person who could be trusted.

The Jenipher Oduor Widows' and Orphans' Fund
Dear friends,

Before her death, Jenipher sent me the list of her children's names and the age of each. What would the list mean to us and what does this list mean in the lives of those children?

In the Scriptures, God frequently recommends to his people to be very careful in affording relief to the widow and the orphan. Exodus 22:21-23 says, "You will not ill-treat widows or orphans; if you ill-treat them in any way and they make an appeal to Me for help, I shall certainly hear their appeal, My anger will be roused and I shall put you to the sword; then your own wives will be widows and your own children orphans.

Deuteronomy 10:16-17 says, "Circumcise your heart then and be obstinate no longer for Yahweh your God is God of Gods and Lord of Lords, the great God, triumphant and terrible, never partial, never to be bribed. It is He who sees justice done for the orphan and the widow, who loves the stranger and gives him food and clothing."

Was Jesus interested in widows? Hear his teaching in Mark 12: 38-44, In His teaching, He said, "Beware of the scribes who like to walk about in long robes, to be greeted respectfully in the market squares, to take the front seats in the synagogues and the places of honor at banquets; these are the men who devour the property of widows and for show offer long prayers. The more severe will be the sentence they receive."

He sat down opposite the treasury and watched the people putting money into the treasury, and many of the rich put in a great deal. A poor widow came and put in two small coins, the equivalent of a penny. Then He called his disciples and said to them, "In truth I tell you, this poor widow has put more in than all who have contributed to the treasury; for they have all put in money they could spare, but she in her poverty has put in everything she possessed, all she had to live on.'"

Finally, in James 1:27, we see the words, "Pure, unspoilt religion, in the eyes of God our Father, is this: coming to the help of orphans and widows in their hardships, and keeping oneself uncontaminated by the world."

Due to the terrible unchecked disease and poverty that has ravished countries in Africa, countries that have been forgotten by the development of Western civilization, the widows and orphans remain a strong Biblical story confronting us face to face. Their faces need to be written on our own lives and memories. We need to willingly bind ourselves to friendships with them so they are the testimony to us of a God who gave us eyes to see, ears to hear and a heart to understand.

Jenipher Oduor spent five years working for Good Samaritan Ministries in Kenya. Although she had only a third grade education and sold a few poor fruits and vegetables in the streets to make a living for her family, she found the time to draw upon her faith and keep her family together and strong. In the family, they prayed and fasted two evenings each week. They prayed for genuine, real Samaritans to be born into this work for the Kingdom. Jenipher begged for ministries of compassion to come upon this earth, and she made herself a living Samaritan forever. Instead of expecting others to take care of her, she expected to take care of many in her lifetime.

On the evenings of fasting and prayer days, Jenipher sat with her nine children on their floor and they often spent three hours in prayer that this organization, Good Samaritan Ministries, would be healthy, a servant to the Lord Jesus, and a true and *worthy purpose for God's wealth on the earth. She sat in dust and poverty and she believed!*

The Sunday before Jenipher Oduor died; she went forward once again and re-dedicated her life to Jesus, believing that church was important, and that she could be a witness to the fact that again and again, we must humble ourselves before the Lord. She was a founding Board Member of Good Samaritan Ministries in Nakuru, the fourth largest city in Kenya.

As Mama Jenipher and I exchanged many letters, it is important to understand that she spoke little or no English, and that those letters were sent by her telling the story in her language, and someone writing the letters for her.

This could be the end of the story and we could walk away and say our work is finished, and Jenipher is a precious memory.

The Lord spoke to me and said that Jenipher's life is only the beginning of the story. The life of Jenipher was a God-given parable in our midst. We are to read it and act upon it. In accordance with the quickening of the Holy Spirit among us, we have been called to establish, in every location of Good Samaritan Ministries in the world, a permanent Widows' and Orphans' Fund named the Jenipher Oduor Widows' and Orphans' Fund. These local monies will then be kept sacred by each little organization in its smallest community form. This will be a place where provision will be shared by all human beings for the care and continuing educational provisions, for needs of those like Jenipher, who struggle along the dusty road praying earnestly for humanity to learn compassion.

Good Samaritan Ministries in the United States helped to begin the Jenipher Oduor Widows' and Orphans' Fund in our international work.

Papa Jerry, Mama Bettie, Joan Baker, and our African team travelled to Kenya, Uganda, and Tanzania in 1992. We dedicated this sacred fund in each local center in those three countries. From that day, each center was to hold this as the most sacred part of the funding of their work. This too would be a fund for African coins, where all the hands of the earth might add to the treasure. **We will say to the widows and orphans, "Indeed, among all of us, you have shown us the light of** *understanding, God's mercy was at your door, and your suffering need has truly made us whole."*

We would ask that every widow bring in the widows' mites, the needed small offerings that your funds might beget all of the funds that are yet to come. Bring them in with prayer on your lips and place them in the giving basket of faith. There is a quickening of the Holy Spirit, and you become a work of our God. We've only seen the beginning of it. Millions of hands will add to it, and the right hands will bring it to the genuine fruit of profound love.

Our prayers: "Father, we entrust Your Word that by the integrity and honesty of Jenipher's life, not one shame will ever come to the work begun this day. We ask You to cover this with Your holiest desire to teach Your children to be a blessing to one another. In the Name of God we pray, Amen."

Jenipher offered friendship, and she kept it. She offered motherhood, and she fulfilled it. She offered integrity, and, indeed, she had it.

Bettie P. Mitchell
International Director
Good Samaritan Ministries

September 30, 1991, Faraday and Angela Iwuchukwu reported from Nigeria:

A girl has been born to them who was named Bettie. Bettie meant to them more than an American lady. Bettie means a wonderful, sweet, wise, caring Godly mother and personal friend to Faraday and Angela. Chiamaka (God is good and Mother is sweet) is her vernacular name. To the Africans, names convey great meanings and influence the future of the child. The little girl is as pretty as Mama Bettie. You will see her when you come in 1992.

CHAPTER 10

SHOCK AND GRIEF, 1992, AFRICA

In 1992, there were 3,500 full-time Samaritans in Kenya, and 12 centers. In late fall, Joan Baker and I were teaching at Uranga. A special tent had been set up for the training. There were 300 people of all ages present. I was teaching about the experience of grief, and the healing of a grieving spirit.

Suddenly, without warning, a man named John, one of the builders of the center, came running in and fell on his knees at my feet. He blurted out: "They have all been killed!" Bishop Tom's van had left Nakuru heading for Uranga. John had missed the van and drove following in a car. The Samaritans were on the way to Kisumu, and about 100 kilometers away from Uranga. There was a terrible accident. When John looked in the van and saw nothing moving, he believed all in the van were dead. To my memory, there were 13 people in the van, and only four survived the crash. As they were on the way to join us at Uranga, their children and family members were sitting with us in the teaching tent. We all received the news at the same time.

I hastily dispatched Joan Baker to go to James Opiyo's house and call the United States. She was to reach Good Samaritan Ministries in any way she could and ask them to call a meeting at the office of every Samaritan. She was to ask them to come in and stand before the Lord in intercession. She was to request that Good Samaritan Ministries immediately send $5,000 to Kenya. Miraculously, her call went through, and 100 people came into the Beaverton office to intercede in prayer.

As I remained behind with people in the tent, you can imagine the chaos, disbelief, powerful levels of grief. People ran out into the road. They ran up and down, tearing at their hair, crying, and screaming. We gathered everybody together and made them sit down. We made them be still. I had to make the announcements and lead the crowd through the most difficult stages of shock and mourning. James Opiyo fell at my feet and begged me to help him forgive. I took him into another area where we could be alone. He explained that he had given his youngest brother, Charles, the money to come to Uranga. Instead, Bishop Tom decided they would all go together to Uranga, and the funds for Charles would help pay for the petrol. Thus, James' brother Charles was in the van and Charles was killed.

James and his family were not only losing young Charles, who at that time was 25 years old, they were losing a dream, a hope for his college education. You see Charles did not go to school at all until he was 13, and now he had been accepted to go to the University of Nairobi. He would have been the only college-educated person in the family. Charles wanted to be a doctor. Out of 144,000 students who took the college entrance exams, only 10,000 students were accepted at University of Nairobi.

Charles was beloved by every person in the family and everyone in Uranga. He had a simple faith, an open and honest faith. He was creative. In 1989, Charles made a work of art, a collage of real Kenyan food, displayed on cardboard. He presented it to us as a gift.

In 1987 and 1990, our time with Charles in Africa had been profound. Joan Baker bonded with Charles as she would with a most beloved son. The death of Charles was the hardest shock of her life. We each groaned and suffered with the whole people. We, with all of the people, went into a state of shock. Charles had been a great servant, caring for his mother, the needs of the family, the elderly. Many considered him the greatest counselor at the center.

We had to sort out who was killed because John had told us everyone in the van was dead. As it turned out, five Samaritans were killed: Charles, Rhoda Abungu, the wife of Bishop Tom, Dan Oloo, our Director of GSM--Nakuru, Pastor Jonam's wife, whose baby survived the crash, and a Samaritan, Jane Onyago, who had led the singles in Nakuru. What of the rest?

About 10:00 p.m. that same night, there was a man who appeared in the dark, Bishop Tom Abungu. Everyone thought Tom was dead and they were seeing an apparition. No, it was Bishop Tom. He had received some injury, but left the hospital to come and be with his children. He explained that Jenipher's Oduor's son, George, was sitting next to him in the front of the van. George had a very injured arm. He and Tom were protected from what happened in the back of the van.

Those sitting in the back of the van had all had their skulls smashed by the impact of the accident. There was no lingering death, only death sudden and absolute. Tom was extremely agitated. It was his van, but that was not the main issue. It was Rhoda, his wife, the most wonderful woman of God, someone that everyone cherished. Her children sitting with us could not believe that mom had left for heaven so quickly. They were bereaved and profoundly confused by such a tragic and unexpected event in their lives. Altogether, the accident left 30 orphans. Eight of those orphans lost both parents. Pastor Jonam's wife was the last surviving parent for her eight children. Only the people sitting at the front of the van, and one baby, survived the accident.

You will remember that Jenipher Oduor died January 8, 1992. Now, we had feared that her oldest son was dead. We praised God that he was not seriously injured, but we learned he had been unconscious for 12 hours.

We were to leave in the next few days to go to Uganda and then on to Tanzania: Joan Baker, Jerry Mitchell, Moushir of Egypt, James Opiyo, and myself.

How did Moushir of Egypt happen to be on this training trip through East Africa? The very day he received my letter asking him to meet us in Kenya in 1990, his father was killed in the streets of Cairo. While stepping down from a bus, he was thrown under the bus.

I had been to Cairo in May of 1992, where 72 counselors were graduated from the Counselor Training Program. I sent Moushir a letter and asked him if he would come with us to Kenya, Uganda, and Tanzania. He agreed.

It was one of those times that was so shocking one cannot speak. Our eyes were haunted with the people of Kenya. Our lives were shaken and yet lifted up. We were receiving the healing to go on. Can you imagine Moushir's time when he realized here too was another shock and another great grief in his life? Besides that, Moushir's luggage did not arrive for twelve days.

At Uranga, as we tried to sleep at night, the mourners wailed. The grave was being dug and the coffin prepared. Charles Anyango, James Opiyo's brother, would be buried at Uranga, the first funeral to be held. Joan Baker and I were asked to preside at his funeral. We were under the trees at the family homestead with most of Uranga present. I knew everyone's faith had to be challenged. I believed the shaking of faith renewed was needed in all of us. Grief paralyzes a living faith. We had to see beyond the moment of death to the miracle of the hospitality of heaven, the welcome of those who had left us.

"I can see heaven thrown open and the Son of Man standing at the right hand of God." (Acts 7:56)

You see, in Africa, there are so many funerals; so many times that children have seen bodies go into the ground! These shocks to their little hearts and their faith have often caused in the people as a whole great grief over the dead. It is this grief of the body being lowered and covered with dirt. Children are concrete and visual. The children don't understand that when the coffin has been lowered and the person has been buried in the ground, that the person is not in the coffin at all, but has long since entered the gates of heaven. Only joy and the realization of the truth of eternal life can defeat the misery and shock of grief!

As Joan and I stood under the trees with 900 people, and led them to the grave to watch the descending of the body into the ground, I asked all the children to look up into heaven, not down into the ground, not down at the casket. We will all say, "Hi Charles!" Many did. We had to draw on our belief, our profound belief that God is good forever! I want to add that always at an African Christian burial, testimonies are given of the person's faith in God. As I was leading Charles' funeral, I chose only one scripture. *"He who is great among you must be the servant of all."* If we are to be an organization truly of His kingdom—then all will be served. That is our great mission.

Before we left Kenya to go on to Uganda, I helped lead a service for Jane Onyango. Before we left Uranga, we were asked to baptize 122 people in the river. James Opiyo was to go with us to Uganda. He remained behind for a few days to be with the family, but joined us later in Uganda, and went on with us to Tanzania.

Our time in Kenya was overshadowed by the accident. The other stops we made, and the other reasons we were there, were fully completed. The teaching was finished. Joan and I worked 17 hours a day, traveling, meeting, and speaking. On this journey, John Oundo agreed to take alcohol training to Africa.

I found it very important to meet with the Oduor children at Jenipher's one-room apartment in Nakuru. They were all able to be there. It was a great victory to come together and to give Jenipher Oduor the International Good Samaritan Award. The award was presented again at Uranga. Jenipher's whole family was present.

I want to describe the last night we spent in Nakuru before we went on to Uranga. We had a large meeting with the Nakuru GSM Center. Our luggage was left at Dan Oloo's house. We were staying at a small hostel. Before we went to sleep, Bishop Tom and Rhoda Abungu came upstairs to pray with us. I will always remember that Rhoda looked deep in my eyes that night and the exchange of the language of our eyes spoke volumes of the Kingdom of God. Ours was a life-changing, penetrating prayer. Later, I understood that Rhoda knew she was leaving. She left 13 children behind, nine of her own, and four adopted.

Rhoda's death hit me very hard because Jenipher and Rhoda were best friends and Jenipher and I were best friends. Therefore, the three of us had an important work to do together.

While our luggage was stored at Dan Oloo's house, some children broke into some of the suitcases and helped themselves. I thanked the Lord that it didn't matter to us, because what mattered were the people in Kenya.

Dan's pregnant widow, Lillian, continued to be a friend. Her loss was profound, the loss of a great and good husband, leaving her alone with her small children. As we corresponded, the months ahead continued to bring closeness.

I want to say, without hesitation, this ministry is a ministry of penetrating intimacy with our God and with one another. There has been no doubt in anyone's mind that The Call at Nineveh was sent from God Himself and that I was only the instrument to deliver The Call and the message. This Call changed many churches as the people became more aware of the greater church, the work that we do each day in the Name of the Lord. Church was no longer only about pastors praying with people, it was about people praying together. Widows' organizations gave birth to intentional development of Samaritan work among the people in each region.

Last letters between Dan Oloo and Bettie Mitchell:

June 23, 1992
Dear Mama Bettie,
Grace be to you and peace from God our Father and the Lord Jesus Christ. It is my great pleasure to write you today and also to report to you our progress in the work of Good Samaritan Ministry in Nakuru.

After the diverse attacks so diabolical that we probably thought we would not be able to get up again here in Nakuru, we have obtained special favour from God our heavenly Father and the Good Samaritan Ministry here has grown wings and is ascending to higher heights.

Since we started Good Samaritan Ministry in Nakuru here, it has been hard to bring heads together and actually make constructive ideas to create for a genuine and effective Good Samaritan Ministry.

Whenever we called on people, both in writing and in person-to-person invitation, we only received a very discouraging turn out. But for the last three weeks to the time when we last had our meeting for Good Samaritan Ministry (21/6/92) and performed an election for the new officials in Nakuru, we've seen God's hand. My house, where Good Samaritan Ministry Nakuru meetings take place, could not contain all the people.

The living room was packed to the capacity; the dining room packed to capacity. We had not enough chairs for the Samaritans. The meeting was held outside in our backyard. Chairs were collected from the neighborhood. The following churches were represented:

1) Kenya City Mission (host)
2) Presbyterian of East Africa
3) Salvation Army
4) Seventh Day Adventist Church
5) Hall Deliverance Foundation Church

6) The Door Christian Fellowship
7) Power of Jesus Around the World
8) Anglican Church (CPK)
9) Catholic
10) Pentecostal Assemblies of God

Yours in Christ, Rev. Dan Oloo Okumu, Director of Good Samaritan Ministry—Nakuru, Rift Valley Province

July 7, 1992
Dear Dan,

I believe that it is important for me to write a letter of encouragement to you, son. I know the great difficulties under which you work and the upward struggle of your soul to meet the Lord with integrity and a clean heart. I deeply understand the churning and the turmoil around you. I know that it is difficult for you to deal with a society of kickbacks, plea-bargaining, and ego building, which is so common in those who try to build with the wrong goal in mind. How often, I am sure, you have seen your work torn down and how much we desire for Christ's work to be built up.

I want to comfort you, Dan, on the loss of Jenipher. Thank you for the ways in which you were a servant through that time of turmoil. I want to thank you for helping to establish a board of the Good Samaritan Ministries in Nakuru, and for choosing the people like Jenipher to work with you. I know that your work can be very great in this ministry. It is a ministry that catches the hearts and the imaginations of the common man, much as the work of Jesus captured the apostles. So too, will this work capture and make us the least in the Kingdom of God for the glory of His Name.

I want you to feel free access to me and be able to write your feelings without fear. I want you to know that I pray for you personally, and for each board member in Nakuru. I pray that you have great faith and that you see great miracles as you give more and more to the people, taking less and less collection and giving more and more until the church itself joins the Kingdom of God.

I am your fellow Samaritan in Christ Jesus our Lord,
Bettie P. Mitchell

September 4, 1992
Dear Dan and all of your family,
I have not written to you for a long time and I am not just writing to you because I am coming to Africa. I am writing to you because I know how much responsibility you have taken for Jenipher and for the work in Nakuru to develop for the Lord through Good Samaritan Ministries. I know, Dan, what a heavy load you carry and that there are burdens on your soul that you can share with no one, except the Lord, Himself. I hear those groanings in your heart as I know the pressure of your soul and this letter is written to comfort you, son, and to kneel down with you and shelter you from the suffering you must go through to receive the people needed to carry on the work of Jesus.

I have recovered from Jenipher's death, but it is something that is strikingly powerful within me and will always be remembered as a central event in my whole life. I wish to go to her little home and to her graveside.

I live under prophetic call and I will deliver the message until my breath fails. When my breath fails, there will be many others to deliver it; and it is those "others" that I am so deeply and humbly proud of, for they have heard and responded to The Call.

Dan, don't be discouraged. Give a fresh message from deep within your spirit. Never let your people go hungry for lack of words of encouragement and living faith.

I am your sister and fellow Samaritan along the road,
Bettie P. Mitchell

[Dan was Rhoda's brother. He too died in the van.]

We were taken to the Kenya/Uganda border. James, Joan Baker, Jerry Mitchell, Moushir, and I bonded in our grief and struggled to live by faith, not only our own, but in faith with a multitude of others.

Osborn Muyanga came to the border, met us, and took us through to Kampala. All of the original Samaritans had stayed with the work.

The water project in Kisengi was finished. At the dedication, the Minister of State, B.K., told the story of us coming and how the work had begun. All of the people were quite astonished that the first thing we did in Uganda, was give a well to the people who were the addicts and prostitutes of Kampala. They considered that the well should go to good people. We considered the wells should go to all people. It is what we are about.

We met with B.K., and we met with the President of Uganda again. This time we met at the State House at Entebbe. We came to a large tent outdoors. All of our team sat together with President Museveni. As I ran ahead of the others, in my spirit, there was a song. It was for this day I was born.

Our conversation began with a discussion between President Museveni and me about education in Uganda. I urged him to make free public education a huge priority. The next generation had to be prepared to live decent lives while rebuilding Uganda. We talked at length about that, and then he asked me for a favor. He said, "Would you be willing to travel a considerable distance to Kanyaryeru School, a school I have built for children who lost their parents in the Civil War? I will send a car for you, a driver, and a guard. Would you do this?" I agreed we would.

As we each significantly chatted with the president, I was led to give him a Good Samaritan pin. Would he wear it? It did not need to be a visible pin. It was an invisible call. Years later, he realized that only as his nation became a nation of Samaritans, helping, building and encouraging one another, could Uganda become, in the Lord's sight, a people of His blessing.

True to President Museveni's word, the next day, a car came to pick up Joan and me. We made the long drive to the Kanyaryeru School. We were in a covered Jeep, and the guard behind us was carrying a weapon. The road seemed long, but the visibility was important to our understanding.

We arrived at the school where over 1,000 children in all grades were being educated. You must remember they had lost their parents and this was a life and death situation for each child. Could they make it to adulthood, and would they be able to support themselves in their future? We spent some time singing with the children and talking with them. I was particularly drawn to the teachers. It was good to see their attitudes of compassion. The children seemed blessed. They did not communicate need; they communicated relationship.

Very late in the day, we returned to Kampala. Our team was very relieved to see us.

By far the most significant visit I remember about the journey into Uganda in 1992 was when we saw the first classroom that had been built to educate 30 small children living in the Kiwangela, Masaka region. The children could meet outside on dry days, and in their little hut on wet days. It was the beginning of the education of the children that Osborn and I had agreed upon that first day we met. It is important to note that the people knew by their intense faith that it would be so. **The children of the Kilwangela, Masaka District would ALL be educated.**

We went to the airport at Entebbe to fly to Dar Es Salaam, Tanzania. We were very weary, anxious to get on the plane and go to a place of rest in Dar Es Salaam. It was not going to be an easy time of flight. We called this plane the "Maybe Airlines." We soon found out the plane had not arrived and, therefore, we could not yet fly. We found that out over many, many hours.

Every time we asked at the ticket counter, they said, "Maybe....Maybe you will fly at such and such a time..."

The Maybe Airplane finally arrived. Wow! It was early morning. We had lived through the night at the airport.

CHAPTER 11

THE SHOCK CONTINUES – TANZANIA AND NIGERIA

Our Director in Tanzania, Samuel Kitwika, met the plane and welcomed us.

Samuel was given the name Gwakisa, which means "the son of mercy," at birth in December of 1961. It seemed that in each generation of the Kitwika family, the first-born child had died. This was also true of Samuel's parents. The first-born child died shortly after birth. Samuel's mother and his father, Ambwene (meaning "God saw me") thought they were cursed since her parents did not like Samuel's father because he was an orphan. All of Ambwene's children from his first wife had died except for Godwin ("God wins").

Samuel became very ill when he was only a few weeks old. The Chief of the village commanded Ambwene to go back home and find out what was wrong. Samuel's parents walked 300 miles on foot to return home that year. Ambwene's in-laws sent someone to kill him. They were ashamed of their daughter because she had married a poor orphan. Samuel's suffering became a big issue with the village elders and they decided to call the in-laws in and command them to forgive their daughter, and to accept her husband. The hour they agreed to forgive, Samuel was healed.

Samuel decided that he had to go to school by any means possible. The family had a small farm in Rudewa Village in the Kilosa District, where they grew corn, rice, and millet for food and for selling. But there were not sufficient funds to pay the $100 school fees required at that time. There were four children, and Samuel was the oldest. When he was 10, he asked his parents if he could go to school. They said that he could not because they did not have the funds to pay the school fees and get the other required necessities. Samuel was determined. He stood up and said, "No! I have to go to school because it is important to my future."

He went out searching for work with other farmers who had money, so as to earn the funds for his school fees, and in 1971,

Samuel managed to save the money needed to attend school. He started first grade at the age of 10.

Samuel worked very hard in school. For the first three years, he would go to school in the morning and work the farms in the afternoon. For the next four years, he would work in the evenings for two hours. He managed to pay his school fees, and to buy his school uniforms and exercise books. On weekends, he went into the forest to cut trees to make charcoal to sell. He also gave money to his parents to help buy food for the family and helped pay his sisters' school fees.

In 1977, Samuel finished class seven but was not chosen to go to the public high school. There were not enough public high schools in Tanzania, so the competition to attend one of them was very great. This was a tremendous disappointment, because Samuel saw this as the end of his dream of succeeding in life. Suicide seemed the only option. His parents, teachers, and friends, all tried to persuade him against it, but it wasn't until the Lord spoke to Samuel in a powerful voice that he found peace. The Lord said, "Where are you coming from? Why are you in the world? Where will you be forever?"

Upon hearing these words from God, Samuel decided to go to church. He gave his life to Jesus at the age of 19. He was baptized and was given the name of Samuel, as the Lord spoke to him again, "You will be called Samuel because you are a chosen one by God for His work. My son, I have chosen you at your young age to serve Me. I have saved you for a long time. I have been following you and serving you so you would come to Me and serve Me for My work in My Kingdom."

In 1986, while in one of the villages of Tabora Region, the Lord had spoken to Samuel: "I have the mission for the widows and orphans. I have anointed you to stand for my people and help them, to give the orphans a future and food to the widows." So in 1991, when Samuel met James Opiyo, who told him about Good Samaritan and its work with orphans and widows, Samuel decided to join the vision. He told us he had been seeing great miracles happening to the people.

Our time in Tanzania was a blur. It was hardly fair to the beginning of the development of the work in Tanzania, but we were all still in a state of shock. To a large extent, it was hard not to remain in grief and shock. We had to press on to meet new people, and come to grips with the assignment that was vital to the training to be delivered from the kingdom of God.

Here we were, James Opiyo, Moushir, Joan, Jerry and me. It was hard for us even to speak to one another, but we had to act upon our faith and set our face to the Lord and His people.

Tanzania is a beautiful country. At the time, it seemed more developed than Uganda and Kenya. The roads were better and there was more electricity. Dar Es Salaam was a modern city on the coast looking out on a vast beach. It was a country that had not been torn apart by civil war and the rights of the people seemed not to be trampled. Their democracy was working well.

As we sat in Dar Es Salaam, in a church, suddenly Jerry felt a small tug on the back of his neck. A hand had reached through the window and this hand tore his gold necklace off his neck. The thief immediately ran away with it. Jerry was pretty shook up. His heart medicine on the chain now was gone. The gold coin attached was a gift from his daughter. For Jerry, it was more than the loss of the coin. It was the absolute loss of a sense of safety.

We found Samuel Kitwika to be a man of structure. He had a business background, as well as ministerial, pastoral training. He was in the process of legalizing Good Samaritan Ministries in Tanzania. He was not a money grabber, and he did not emphasize needs for money.

We went to the Morogoro Region where one of the very significant events of our stay in Tanzania took place. One day, we went out and met with a Masai Tribe. Their leader was Sebastian. The Masai are traditionalists. They live as they did 4,000 years ago. They eat nothing but beef, raw and cooked, and drink the blood and the milk from the animal. They dress in the most primitive ways. Here now, were Samaritans in this tribe.

The Masai are noted as jumpers and they did the jumping dance. They gave us a live goat, which we took with us. Later, I would find out that Sebastian named his tiny daughter, Bettie. Bettie would develop some serious skin problems and it brought deep sorrow to Sebastian's heart.

Sebastian and I remained friends. Several years later I got word that Sebastian had been killed in an uprising between the farmers and the herders. I asked them to look for him to make sure, and lo and behold, he was found alive. This experience badly shook him up. Sebastian's Bettie was the first Bettie in Tanzania.

It was my sense that Samuel Kitwika was not trying to impress us. He had long set his heart on the Samaritan journey among the Masai people. He often showed that heart. He too had interest in education, a common thread throughout Africa.

The education picture was brighter in Tanzania, but because there was a disastrous lack of high schools, Samuel's great dream and hope was to build a high school in the Rudewa Region.

As it was time to leave Tanzania, we took the train north to Kenya. On this overnight train journey, we spent no money for pillows or blankets. We had a bare bones budget that we kept, and our comfort was not a priority. I should add, it never has been!

As the train moved along, Moushir began to pray and write. He sensed the direction of the Lord for the work in Egypt would also include many Arab countries. Before we arrived, he shared this vision with me.

I want to clearly state that the vision did not come to pass quickly. The work in Egypt developed well, but there did not seem to be much outreach. It was only when the digital age came that outreach became enormously possible. Moushir and his team translated many English books and put them on the Internet. The counselor training programs went on the Internet. This led to the development of much of the work in many countries. In addition, the man who had been Assistant Director of our work in Cairo, moved to America and developed an international Christian television station called Al Karma T.V., which broadcasts 24/7 in the Arabic language via satellite to most of the nations of the world.

Moushir's vision on that train ride was from the Lord and the Lord would fulfill His purposes. Many have come to know Christ, not just hear about Him. Not just witnessing reached their ears, but the knowing of Jesus. Their hearts were reached.

We made a major stop in Mombasa, and saw the development of Good Samaritan Ministries there.

As we came to Nairobi, it was time for each of us to depart. Jerry went back to the United States. Moushir went to Cairo. Joan, James Opiyo and I got on a plane and headed for Lagos, Nigeria.

April 3, 1991, I wrote a letter to Faraday Iwuchukwu, our Director of the work in Nigeria. I shared with him that I had a great concern for his work in Nigeria:

I know that you are scrambling to find the core and the key of what to do. Is this a time of testing? Are you passing the tests? Do you know how much I am really interceding for you, that you might be able to find inner strength and walk away from all of the games in Nigeria? We are interceding for you to carry a cross for all of your people. It is not easy to come into the fullness of Jesus. It is so much easier to talk about Him and teach religion around Him, but He wants the fullness, son, of His life, His work, His message, and His purpose. He wants it through your life, and through the Samaritan calling to teach nothing but the Kingdom of God. He wants you to train the people underneath you to be as strong as you are and to walk with an army that is well-trained to deal with the evil, the cunning, and the disparity of your culture.

I'm sure, Faraday that many nights you wonder why He would pick a person like you, and that since the very beginning of The Call on your life, it has been a struggle for you not to hide from Him.

Our trip to Nigeria was the hardest of all. I knew in my heart that would be so. There were two reasons. 1) The humidity is terrible and the living conditions exhausting; and 2) Faraday is a man with much head knowledge, and therefore, great need for practical development training. He had a doctorate degree and was studying to be a lawyer. You can imagine how it was to get through all of that and find heart and the simple development stages of this work. As a man of prominence, he had now been reduced to live the life of a digger, cultivating the soil with the Samaritan laborers of his country. This was a real revolution in Faraday's life. In 1992, as we met and spent our time together, we were able to make much progress. We visited several centers outside of Port Harcourt and the trip to Nigeria was successful, but painful and growth producing for us all.

The final shock and grief of the 1992 journey to Africa took place on the road in Nigeria. We were going to another state. James Opiyo and Joan were in the back seat. Faraday and I were in the front seat. As we were driving down a sort of freeway, we saw in the middle of the road, lying in the form of a cross, a man, seemingly dead! Although we were Samaritans, we didn't stop. Although this bothered us all, we kept it in and said nothing to each other.

We went to lunch at a restaurant. We tried to go to a museum, which was closed, and then we drove an hour to the home of the parents of Faraday's wife. They lived in a village and her father was the chief.

Suddenly, Joan realized she had left her camera in the restaurant where we had lunch. Six hours had now passed since morning when we were on the freeway. Now, as Joan and Faraday were driving a second time down the same freeway to find the camera, they saw the man, lying in the form of a cross, still there on the road. Again, they passed him coming back. It was almost dark when they returned. Joan did find her camera sitting on the back of the chair at the restaurant. Although there were only five tables, none of the people had noticed it.

By this time, the fan belt and alternator were broken and our car would not hold water. It was 20 miles to a gas station or anyplace where we might get a fan belt. Having no choice, we set off down the freeway, in the darkness, to find a schoolteacher who might know where to find a fan belt. We made it the 20 miles, we found the teacher, we found the part, and we went on down the road.

Coming toward Port Harcourt, all of a sudden, with no sign or warning, the freeway disappeared and we hit huge ruts. We hit the ruts at about 60 miles per hour. Our heads hit the top, but the car miraculously did not turn over. It did come to a complete halt like a pile of junk. By God's grace and much prayer, we took a very broken car more slowly down the road and we made it one hour later to Port Harcourt. It was 10:00 p.m. We had been invited to a dinner at 7:30. We went to the house. No dinner was made. The man wasn't there. We eventually located the man. I told him the story. He took pity on us and took us out to dinner, but he didn't have enough money to pay the bill. This is one day in Nigeria. It was the sixth African death. The man on the road was by far the hardest because we were Samaritans and we didn't stop.

The Good Samaritan
By Beatrice Akinyi, West Kenya Region

Down from Jerusalem to Jericho
A man went, When Robbers
Attacked, stripped and beat him up
Love and Compassion are very important Factors.
A priest going down the road
Saw him and walked on the other side
Leaving him half dead, he had no
Love and compassion which are very important
A Levite also came, looked at him
And went away, also leaving him
Half dead by the road.
Love and Compassion are very important factors.
The two are rushing for the
Kingdom of God and not caring
For the welfare of their fellow man
They had no love and compassion
A Samaritan came up, his heart full of pity
Poured oil and wine on the wounds
Bandaged them and carried him on his own animal
Took him to the Inn, he had Love and Compassion
Now brethren, let us do as the Samaritan did
For one cannot prove of loving God if he doesn't
But love his fellow human being.
Let us be compassionate and we shall be Good Samaritans.

It was while we were on the journey in Africa, the Lord gave me revelation: The Africans are diggers. They dig in the soil with their hoes. The Lord showed me that a Samaritan is a digger, and if there is no money for a hoe, we can still dig with our hands. If we don't dig, and we don't do the work of the Kingdom of God, the Kingdom of God will never come on earth as it is in heaven. Jesus asked us to pray for that, but He also showed us the harvest was ready, but the laborers to prepare the soil were few. Evangelists will plant the seed, but the soil must be continually cultivated. The problem of harvest is the work of the laborer. The preparation of the soil often has not been properly done. Thus, many seeds are not going in the way they need to go in. During the following year, I thought much about the digger and I kept an African digging tool on my wall at Good Samaritan from then on.

A Good Samaritan is a digger, building the Kingdom of God.

In 1992, one word that the Lord impressed on my soul from this journey: "Many are looking for position and money. Few are interested that I bring The Call of God directly to them. It is The Call that I am to deliver, not the position or the money. Position and money have nothing to do with this work. I can only bring the gift of the Holy Spirit's teaching and The Call."

I encouraged James to always look for the true givers, and when you find them, encourage them to go on the giving road. This is the key for all of our work. It is the transition for every nation that we raise up, in that nation, a central core of people, the whole part of a nation that understands the pure and sacred value of living the life of a true giver in Christ Jesus our Lord.

CHAPTER 12

I MUST BE ABOUT THE FATHER'S BUSINESS

In the first six months of 1993, I had incredible pain. Many bones were out of place as a result of the whiplash in Nigeria. During those six months, Joan and I worked steadily, pushing down the road with the things that needed to be done in order to stay faithful to our commitments. We were often exhausted beyond words. The ministry grew here. So many needy people came. They never ceased coming through the door and asking for help.

James Kabvalo, the National Director of Good Samaritan Ministries, Malawi, Central Africa, tells the incredible story of how he was called to become a Samaritan:

"It was on May 5, 1992, in the late afternoon, of which I received a stranger in my house from Tanzania. I never met this man before, just as it was the same with him. He was led to my house by a certain woman after he struggled to find where my house is. This woman just left the stranger in my hands and off she went. The stranger introduced himself as Emanuel Moses Kashakwali, from Dar Es Salaam, Tanzania. He was an evangelist. He came to Malawi to conduct crusades in Blantyre, Lilongwe, and Mzimba. The man who invited Brother Emanuel to come to Malawi was a Ugandan by the name of Stephen Kato. Unfortunately, Stephen abandoned Brother Emanuel while they were in Lilongwe. He did not take care of Brother Emanuel. The proposed crusades died prematurely. Not even a single crusade took place. Then, brother David Kazisonga of Lilongwe, Malawi, gave my address to Brother Emanuel, who was staying in his house by then. He boarded a bus from Lilongwe to Mzimba where he got me. I kept him in my house. My wife Nancy and I provided food, accommodation, and transport money to Brother Emanuel, who was in desperate need. We are poor, but we gave what we had. Then, this Tanzanian was very touched with the way we treated him. He called me and Nancy after we kept and provided for him for many days. He opened his mouth and expressed his gratitude for all that we had done for a man we had never met before. He said that we are surely, 'Good

Samaritans.' Then, he opened his notebook and gave me your address. He said, 'Please write to your fellow Samaritans as soon as possible as they plan to come to Tanzania this year.' Then he left for Tanzania. My wife, Nancy, and I, took aside two days to pray for your ministry to be established in Malawi. Then, I wrote you my first letter on May 21, 1992. This is the way I got the information of your ministry."

In 1974, James Kabvalo married Nancy Konyani, and they were blessed with seven children. In 1978, the Lord called James and Nancy to full-time work. They both went to Assemblies of God Bible School in Dedza and completed a three-year diploma course, passing with distinction in 1980. Between 1981 and 1994, they pastored four Assemblies of God churches.

In his biography, James states, "In 1988, the Lord laid a burden on my heart to serve the needy, the sick, the lame, the broken-hearted, the lonely, the disturbed, the aged, the orphans, the widows and the like. I prayed in tears to the Lord that He will open the way for me to fulfill the vision. The vision came true in 1992, when I came in contact with G.S.M."

In 1993, at Uranga, Kenya, a rural area, the work in Africa began. They have been able to develop a program that is suitable for cities and rural areas throughout Africa. I told him Pastor James had been our full-time director of Kenya since 1987, and the Continental Director of Africa for approximately one year. I shared how James Opiyo had trained with me extensively in Egypt, Israel, Pakistan, and America, and that he was a man who could be deeply trusted.

I gave James Kabvalo some key teaching about being a Samaritan in a letter I wrote to him in June of 1992. I said, "Your job, as a Samaritan laborer and as a Samaritan developer in Malawi, will be to train hard yourself and be a genuine Samaritan visible among the people. You are to see and do what Pastors generally do not do. Pastors don't serve as a Samaritan laborer in their ministry because they're serving as a leader. Your job is to centrally be a Samaritan, to give up only teaching by words and to begin to teach by actions and by deliberate acts of kindness. People need to see the work of the Gospel. The second job you are called to do is to call and train others. You are to begin to train and develop real Samaritan workers, specifically developing a labor, a mission of mercy, acts of mercy, things needed in the community that have been neglected, never thought of, never dreamed of. You will train with Kenya GSM. You will go on down the road and do the things you finally see are so necessary. Eventually, you will develop a National Board and a national organization that will carry the message throughout Malawi. In the process, you are to develop the support of pastors and leaders, sharing with them that every Christian must be an effective Christian for Christianity to mature in them. We must each do the work we are called to do. This is not a work just of leaders it is the work of all the people. All the people can be turned around by this work.

While James Kabvalo was in Oregon at the International Conference in 1994, his house was broken into and all of his furnishings were stolen, though his family was saved. Even the bars on the windows were taken. James' son woke to see the thieves, but was threatened at knifepoint to keep quiet. This set back did not deter James or Nancy from the Samaritan vision.

The battle between Satan and Christ raged over the head of James Kabvalo. Before Good Samaritan Ministries came, he was pastor of the largest Assemblies of God church in the capital of Malawi.

One Sunday, a foreign man showed up at the service and left a large financial gift. When the elders found out about this, they dismissed James Kabvalo, for they thought they had a new source of significant income. The man never came back. The elders did not pass the test. By losing his position, James Kabvalo would lose his life in order to find it. He was shamed for many years by his denomination, but he endured to keep The Call.

The African Continental Training Center

It was a dream to build the Continental Training Center for Africa, to build it in Uranga. By May 1993, 500 people each day worked on the building. During the school holidays, all of the school children we sponsored came to help build the building. Everyone was very excited about this project. It had gone rapidly because we extended as much as we possibly could to complete this important project so the training would be available to Africa. The cost of the building was $40,000. 1000 people attended the dedication.

When the Kenyans asked me, "What will we teach? What will be the curriculum?" My reply was, "You will develop the curriculum. God will help you."

The first Continental Training School was held at Uranga in 1993. Samuel Kitwika of Tanzania and James Kabvalo of Malawi were among the trainees. From that year on, the training school lasted three months each year. It was funded by a lot of sacrifice from Oregon and from other centers in the United States. I went to the Lord and I said, "Lord, what can we do? This seems an impossible task." He spoke to me simply, "Sell your treasures."

Thus began in Oregon, "The Annual Treasure Sale." This is how it was. Every person connected with the ministry was to pick out their greatest treasure and decide to give it. They were to write a story about the treasure and tell why it was a treasure.

It was challenging. People like to give up some things, but seldom was it their greatest treasure. It took a lot of consideration, and a deep amount of prayer, for only the Lord could point out what the treasure was. People purchased the treasures, LOVED the stories, and continued to look forward to this as an annual event. After several years passed, it was discontinued. It had taken its toll in effort, and, perhaps, on our willingness to dig deeper into the life's treasures of the heart.

During those years of the "Treasure Sales," we entirely funded the Continental Training School. This funding required us, not only to pay for the food and meet the needs of the students who came to Uranga, but also to help the people coming with transportation, passports, and whatever was needed for them to get there. No one coming paid anything for the training. Almost all of our directors in Africa took the training, and each marveled at the changes they experienced within themselves.

I want to report that it was generally agreed upon the food was terrible, the accommodations were not good and that the experience was shattering to what they expected the school to be. Instead of opening books, studying, and taking tests, they did field work most of the time. The fieldwork might be bathing an old woman who could not bathe herself, feed a person who could not feed himself, working in the gardens for the women who were too exhausted, cleaning the town. Yes, this was a different kind of school, a school that brought pride down, down, and brought humility, up, up.

Although many complained, all agreed upon leaving, they had been completely changed from the inside out. They had received a new spirit. Here was a pastor, perhaps even a Bishop, being reduced, in order to be a teacher of nothing but the Kingdom of God.

At one time, the Continental Training School had 22 volunteers. The new building had 17 rooms, a very large teaching room, many offices, storage areas, and places for small meetings. It was a great challenge for us to help furnish the center, and to provide the chairs or benches needed. By God's grace, this was blessed. We lived the core value of the words, "Teach nothing but the Kingdom of God." We taught by what we gave. They would teach by what they gave, and those who learned, would later teach by their experience in His Kingdom.

I shake my head over the faith needed to believe we could make it. We could not only make it in the lives of many, but we could make it in the outpouring. You see, we gave everything we had in the Name of Jesus, and we gave everything as a gift. What we gave was God's unexpected grace, freely poured out upon the lives of many.

It was my decision to keep in faithful touch with the directors as they were developed. That often required lots of phone calls, many letters. This was before e-mail and cell phones, but the communication was essential among us, for we were working through the Kingdom of God to touch the lives of many. Our lives had to be touched daily. We helped one another.

There is a scripture that says, "Love covers a multitude of sins." It was my decision not to cover up the sins of the weaker, but to cover them until they had learned and were strengthened. I never gossiped about any of the people, neither the workers in the Samaritan centers here, nor the people directing the programs overseas. It was enough for each of us to bear the cross of The Call. To find fault or weakness would be beyond bearing.

There was great trust from the beginning, and that trust deepened as the years went by. We knew we had to trust the Lord absolutely.

I cannot begin to tell you the struggles to make it financially. They were not struggles of raising money; they were struggles of intercession, crying out, calling out, and seeking where the spirit had fallen and the true giver would come forth.

In January 1993, I wrote a letter to Faraday Iwuchukwu in Nigeria:

I had a dream and I was standing in front of you with a sealed envelope. It was a message in the envelope. As I send this training and instruction to you, this is key, not my presence in front of you, but the instructions that come through the Holy Spirit. Sometimes, you look at me. The Lord would have you look at the instructions. I am small, but the instructions of the Holy Spirit are the key issue in the development of your life's work. He does not want you to focus on me. He wants you to focus on the work and on the instructions that will come on the days that you need them. It is hard for you to not focus on a person because you love greatly, but it is a special instruction for you to understand that it is the message that I bring that is the key to your calling. Listen closely to the message and follow it.

I want you to begin to develop people who will have major responsibility working with you. Begin to locate your most gifted teachers and counselors. You need to develop a team that is highly functional to relieve you from some of the administrative duties. These need to be people you can place high trust in and that you can assign to the most delicate jobs. I believe the secret of the work in Uganda and Kenya has not just been James or Osborn, but the teams they developed around themselves where they could place high trust. Osborn has two very key men and then Flora Mutaka as well. They could be assigned anything and do the work with the highest integrity. James in Kenya has developed 15 or 16 people around his leadership that will do anything at any time and function as Samaritans. I realize that in Nigeria, people are hung up with many other things and that they are weak in what they do for the mercy of the Lord. I will pray that you use a team approach, and that you feel great spiritual freedom to select a team that will be Samaritans for life.

I know there are many Christians in Nigeria, but I want you to know, quite frankly, there are few Samaritan laborers. There is that resistance to labor, for words are so much quicker. Do you understand my meaning?

Peace Talks Israel/Palestine

In September, I wrote to Moushir in Egypt:
We were most happy over the Peace Meeting in Washington D.C. Did you know that President Clinton read the book of Joshua the night before the signing? The Lord awakened him at 3:00 a.m., and he spent the rest of the night reading the Bible.

January 27, 1993, I received a fax from B.K. of Uganda:
My dear daughter, Bettie:
Your fax has given me happiness for you to have thought the way you have thought. God willing, I will meet your humble request, that is to say that on the 7th of February, I will be with you, so you can do whatever you wanted me to do for you.
Your loving father and friend,
B.K.

B.K. did arrive. He intended to stay three days. I told him he had to stay eight days. He stayed eight days.

Upon B.K.'s visit to Oregon, he brought the news that in the Fall of 1994, the President of Uganda was committing to free public education for children through the 8th grade. The school fees will be removed. I know this doesn't solve all of the problems, but at least it is a start.

On February 10, 1993, B.K. preached at Christ Episcopal Church in Lake Oswego. 700 people attended.

In the Episcopal Church, sermons are only to last about ten minutes. B.K. spoke for an hour. They had to cancel communion. He kept them in that church service longer than expected. When he asked them to take out their Bibles, there was a stirring in the crowd, as none of them had Bibles.

Because of B.K.'s talk from the heart to these people, Christ Episcopal Church began to support the work of education in Uganda, which they have done up to this day.

B.K. was wondering why so many women came up and hugged him after the church service at Christ Episcopal. I replied to him, "I think I know why. The women immediately sensed you as 'father'. You are one who can be trusted, one with whom they are safe. There are few fathers in the United States who provide this type of covering for their daughters. But the women recognized the needs in their souls when they heard you. Their hugs were out of gladness that for a moment a need in their soul had been met. It is quite possible that one moment of physical contact is enough. It clears the path for them to be able to connect with their Heavenly Father, for they have experienced the need being met with a physical presence, which moves them to the spiritual."

Jackie Wilhelm wrote a letter to B.K.:

Your humility, B.K., is a standard for my soul to measure against. Truly, you have kept your word to God to be His person at all times, and in all places, doing whatever He asks. When I think of the word "servant," I will always think of you, even if we never meet again. The image is alive, fresh, and one I draw on for guidance and as a standard.

Osborn Muyanga was nearly killed in Uganda. He was robbed, beaten and taken out into the bush to be killed. Osborn wrote about it:

It was one week after I had got a dream in which I saw that I was shot by unknown men. It happened when I was trying to help someone who was shot before. I thought in my spirit that though he was shot, he could be helped. When I was shot, I knew I was dead because it seemed the bullets came up to my heart. After some time, I realized that, although I was shot in the arm, I could still stand up. So, I went ahead and told the other brother who was shot that he was not dead, and I tried to take him by the hand and he stood up in great fear. Then, I woke up from the dream. I failed to understand what it all meant. I prayed about it, but I still didn't understand. Instead, it stuck on my heart with a great fear inside me. I decided to share it with Richard, who was sick in bed at the time. The next day, I was supposed to travel to Masaka, but I could not get peace. I felt like praying. The day the incident occurred, I was in prayer and fasting, bound inside by my spirit, asking God to set me free.

It was on August 12, 1993, I went to the bank to collect money for our Camp arrangement. It amounted to six hundred thousand shillings, Uganda money equivalent to $500 U.S. dollars. I had left Dithan and Richard at the office doing other work. I came back at 3:00 p.m. to meet a client for an appointment. The counseling was long. It ended at 8:00 p.m. and I left for home.

But, I had to pass by another home, which was on the other side, a distance of five kilometers to our home. When we were about to reach the home, in a corner, men stopped us. I was in a pick-up truck of a friend who got saved in Karamoja Mission in January, Mr. Lawrence Sentongo. This driver is a Samaritan who has helped us so much with his vehicle. Though the vehicle is very old, and it keeps breaking down, he always sacrifices it to do Samaritan work. At many occasions, we use it. During the camp, it helped to carry food from Masaka, carrying firewood and many other things.

When we stopped, at first we thought they were security guards of the area. Surprisingly, they harassed us to provide everything we had. Immediately, the man saw my bag, he took it away from me. We were harassed back into the vehicle not to make any alarm, but to squat down and be quiet. One of the robbers sat on the steering. This made the driver to be beaten seriously on the spot because he did not want to move from the steering position. Then, we were squeezed down in on our backs. The place was too small for two people. We were suffocating and as the other robber was driving off, this one was stepping on our back and he went on beating us with his gun, knocking our backs terribly. We could not see where we were going. Instead, we heard the robbers insisting that they were going to kill us by all means. Other men were at the back of the pick-up. I didn't know the number and they could not allow us to look in their faces. After a one-and-a-half hour drive, they stopped near a bush and they said they were going to kill us. All the time they were driving us, I was praying, crying to God in my spirit that He may spare our lives for His work and for His Glory. I was disturbed inside my spirit. Why had it happened to us brought a great shock inside our hearts. When they stopped, they pulled us out of the car with the intention of shooting us. We begged them, in tears, to take everything and spare our lives. By the time we were doing this, another vehicle came towards the road where we were. When it reached where we were, it stopped. The man in this car wanted to see what was happening. Instead, he was harassed to produce everything he had. He jumped out of the vehicle and he tried to run away. They ran after him and brought him back. They started beating him terribly and asking for money. They got a hold of him; put him down in his vehicle and they drove off with him. This was the time that we narrowly escaped death by God's Grace. They went with the vehicle together with the owner. We ran to the police and reported everything. We reached home past midnight.

Not only was the $500 camp money taken, but much of everything else of importance.

After two days, the other man they took was found dead beside the road and his car was nowhere to be seen. The police investigated very seriously, and, after five days, the car was found at night, and it was stopped. One robber was caught on the spot, but the others ran away.

Up to this time, I have not recovered anything. What brought a great shock in my life was to hear that the other innocent man was killed. I knew we were to die, but this man died in our place. It was very tragic. We remember his family in our prayers. Otherwise, the driver, Mr. Sentongo, is recovering. Only he is disturbed by chest pain and a rib problem. We are praying and we believe he will be alright.

GSM--Uganda had developed a camp for all sponsored children. Despite the difficulties, we kept our word and a camp was held. The first camp had 126 students, 35 adults and 91 children. It was held in Kampala.

The children's camp was wonderful. They planned activities and experiences to help the children bond, broaden their world through a visit to the zoo at Entebbe, the museum, and the burial place of the kings. Through stories, games, and songs, they grew connected as children of Uganda and Good Samaritan in a new way. God truly blessed it and we are proud of the staff in Uganda who worked more than 20 hours a day for the five days of the camp.

Osborn wrote:

I felt so good during the Camp because the children gave me a very good company. They made me laugh at all times and this brought healing in my spirit. I remember in the letter that was also taken in the bag, you had advised me, Mama Bettie, that I should get about 10 people to be my intercessors to pray for my life and for my strength. I can see the importance of it. This is the time that I feel most in my life that I need a lot of prayers so that God may heal my spirit and restore my joy. During these months, I have seen great miracles of God and at the same time, many attacks from the devil. I know the devil hates me, but God loves me so much so that I will live to see the goodness of the Lord in the land of the living. The work will grow and we shall continue to serve in the Kingdom of our Father through Christ who strengthens us.

Morris Cerillo came to Kampala immediately thereafter and our people went to his crusade. It so happened that he taught on the Parable of the Good Samaritan. It also just happened that President Museveni gave a speech on the Parable of the Good Samaritan and our organization at the crusade, and B.K. did also. So, it was with thousands of people hearing the story, that these events were used by God to turn the ears towards the action that God would have us all to take in the significant history that we are allowed to live through Christ Jesus.

It is not easy to be a Samaritan. Osborn Muyanga found many challenges to his life, not the least of which was four children who were willed to him by a mother who died of AIDS. When Osborn went for her burial, he was handed the Will. Pauline, the mother, was 26. Suddenly, Osborn had four children, although he was not married. He kept them all and educated them. After his marriage to Louise, they agreed to keep the children, minister to them, and develop their characters. **The story has turned out well, as integrity became the parenting of these children.**

These are the stories of the four orphans Osborn received to raise:

THE LIFE HISTORY OF JOSEPH MULONDO

He is the firstborn. He was born in 1982, a healthy and good-looking boy. When he was two years old, he had an attack of the stomach. The medication results provided that he had a hernia. It has been his problem up to this time. It has been off and on and he is very much disturbed when he a carries a heavy thing. He started nursery in 1985, and by the time his father fell sick in 1987, he was in Primary I. He was not able to go further because no one could pay his school fees. It was not until 1993 when he resumed his studies in Primary Two at the age of 11. His performance is good and he likes school very much.

THE LIFE STORY OF ALLEN NABISALU

She is the second born, born in 1984. In 1988, she left nursery school due to the father's sickness. Her life has not been so good because when she was two years old, she got a terrible cerebral fever, which later developed into epilepsy. Her life is always on drugs. She is taken once in a while for medical check-up, and this has helped her to go from continuous attacks to a mere fever attack. At school, Allen is doing excellently. After passing the interview very well, she was promoted to Primary Three. She is very active and quick in doing the work at home. She likes singing very much.

THE LIFE STORY OF GEOFFREY KIKONYOGO

He is the third born and was born in 1987. He did not get a chance of going to school. At the age of starting school, the father passed away and the mother could not afford. Geoffrey has been suffering from syphilis since his childhood. It has affected his life so much that he looks thin and his skin is rough. But, now, he is physically fit and has started schooling in the Nursery's top class. He likes sleeping and eating so much. His health is improving greatly.

THE LIFE STORY OF BETTY NAKAWESI

Betty was born in November 1979. She is the lastborn in a family of 11 children. Her late father, Simon died of AIDS in 1989 when Betty was 10 years old and in Primary Four. Her mother died in September 1990 when Betty was in Primary Five. At that time, Betty left her home and came to stay with Pauline, who then adopted her into her family. Since Pauline was very weak, Betty started to take care of her and the younger ones. Pauline counted Betty as one of her children. She is now in Primary Six, and is a healthy and good-looking girl. She behaves as a true Samaritan.

Two others were also adopted by Osborn, street children who followed him wherever he went.

July 22, 1992, I wrote to Osborn:

Ours is not the only important work in the Christian world, but it is that little bit of work that is often neglected by the others, so press into your little bit of work, Son, and train all of your people to be extraordinary laborers.

Early in 1993, I received a letter from Lillian Okumu, widow of Dan Oloo:

Dearest Bettie Mitchell and Ministry,

I greet you tonight in Jesus' Name. We are doing fine in the Lord. He has remained my refuge and comforter. I am writing this letter to thank you for the $450 American dollars you gave so as to help in Dan's funeral, and some to help us later on. I was so grateful. God bless you abundantly.

The Lord has continued to be my comforter, even during this time of loneliness. The young ones are doing fine. He blessed me with a baby boy on August 12, 1992. We named him after his father, Dan. We keep on missing Dan since he was so lovely to us, but what I know is that the Lord is merciful. He keeps on giving me comfort. Dan preached in most of his sermons in the church that when we miss him here, he will be present in Heaven. Therefore, today, when I miss him here, he is present with the Lord in Heaven. I continue to remember you in my prayers. God bless you as you serve him fully.

It is because of Calvary, Lillian

You see Lillian was pregnant when her husband, Dan, was killed in the van accident.

In 1993, Joan Baker and I spent three and a half weeks in Pakistan and Egypt with Judith Sellangah, a Board Member from Kenya. We travelled all over the country. Almost always we slept in one bed, and we called ourselves The Three Mamas. How Judith happened to be able to come is an interesting story. She was with us from October 25th until December 9th. You would laugh because I told her she could not come unless her husband gave her written permission. Well, Josiah got up at 4:30 a.m. the day she was going to leave, and without her knowing it, he sat down and wrote me a letter. In that letter, he specifically said, "I give Judith Sellangah written permission to spend (such and such dates) with Mama Bettie and her team, traveling to Egypt and Pakistan." That wasn't all he said in the letter. It was a friendly letter and had many important things in it. I knew this was a gift from God, and it was an especially unusual gift due to the fact that Josiah was an alcoholic.

Judith's children were alright while she was gone, although the whole family had bad Malaria, and even Josiah was laid up and had to stay home to recover. The absence of a woman leaves great appreciation in the heart of a man when the woman returns.

November 1, 1993, I wrote to James Opiyo from Egypt:

I'm sitting next to Judith Sellangah. We are returning on a train from Alexandria to Cairo. We are looking out the window at the people working in the fields in the most ancient ways, and yet driving automobiles and growing in their use of modern conveniences. Judith is holding up well. Her milk has dried up and she is now resting well and feeling more relaxed and confident in this journey. (Judith had recently had a baby when she met us in Pakistan). I am so pleased to have Judith sit with me and lay in the room with us as a support. It is the greatest gift Kenya could give us to give such support to the work, for Judith brings strength and such great humility to serve, to learn, and to grow. I also feel the presence of your prayers and Mama Jenipher.

On June 7, 1993, I wrote a letter to John Oundo:

I look forward, greatly, to the International Day of Prayer next week. I am going to spend a special time just laughing, thinking about all of us praying together. What funny little characters we all have! How strange it is for God to gather us all up for such a day of prayer. Surely, there were better people, more important ones in the world, to do His work, but He chose us, His very own, to do this for Him.

In a letter received from John Oundo:
*Surely speaking, on that day you came to the family homestead at Uranga, I judged wisdom from cleverness, and today, **I believe that wisdom is a divine gift from above. I met Mama Bettie Mitchell, who used wisdom to conquer the devil's cleverness in me, and on that day, all devils of alcoholism left me. And I am saved in the Name of Jesus Christ!***

In July 1993, I received a letter from Obuda Sylvestre from Uranga, Kenya. He gives his testimony of the tremendous help the Addictions Recovery Program played in his life, and that he was moving through the program to be moved to help others. **This letter reminded me never forget the one for the many.**

May 1993, James Kabvalo wrote from Kenya, while he was taking the Continental GSM Training:

I have learned many things that I did not know before. To be a Samaritan is not just something we speak through our mouth only, but it is through action. When I go back to Malawi, after my training the end of July, I will teach and train my fellow Samaritans to be practical people. In Malawi, we have taken this ministry so seriously.

The Lord is speaking to my heart that from now onwards, I work full-time in Good Samaritan Ministries. I am willing to work full-time as per the direction of the Lord. I give myself fully into this work in ministry no matter what it will cost. This is a voluntary work in the working field of the Lord. The Lord is working for men and women who are willing to serve Him without looking back.

In May 1993, I wrote B.K.:

I'm greatly blessed by the fact that Osborn has recently been in Kenya with all of the leaders of East Africa. Our men are growing and it is good. They are not foolish with their time. They are not wasting coins on superficial religion. They are friends of God, called to the highest level of friendship with their fellow man. They lead, and there is wisdom in their words. This is a blessing, which happens too seldom in this world.

In July 1993, B.K. wrote:
My dear daughter Bettie:
I praise the Lord very much for many things, especially for facilitating for you to communicate with us. I find it difficult to get suitable and adequate words to express my gratitude to you personally for the wonderful letters you usually write to us.

May I assure you, my dear daughter, that I do sincerely love, pray, think, and remember you. Our relationship has been very much cemented by the Holy Spirit, and it will not be broken at all until we meet in heaven, and I do still think, that when we meet in Heaven, it will be more strengthened and confirmed.

How is Jerry? Please give him a big hug for me, and tell him I still remember the time and energy he used to keep us.

Also, in July 1993, I wrote to B.K. and Grace:
I agree with you about the Holy Spirit leading President Museveni along into the next stage of his political life. It is our job to pray so intimately for his relationship with Christ, and the sensitivity of his soul to the Lord's work and to the Holy Spirit, that the final stages of security for Uganda are achieved. The angels' wings are heard over your land, and peace is nearby. You stay well, B.K. Tell President Museveni that I miss him a lot, and that I believe mightily for the things he will accomplish, not only in Uganda, but among the other leaders in Africa. Let him speak out with a strong voice for real human justice. Surely, that was the lesson of the years of suffering among your people.

In 1993 Papa Jerry received the International Samaritan Award.

In 1993, five members of G.S.M., Kenya received awards: Pastor Dixon, Samaritan of the Year, for his work in Mombasa; John Oundo, Best Program Report for the Year; Old Lucy, the

Mama Samaritan Award; Elder Henry, Father of the Year, Domatila received the Widow of the Year, for her work on the construction of the center. She brought stones and water all day long. Domatila was 50 years old.

January 13, 1993:
Dear President Museveni,

This letter is written to tell you that the visit we had with you at Entebbe was very important to us; and to say that I believe, my brother, it was important to you, also. I pray that the little Samaritan pin, which you may not wear on the outside, may stay on your heart, deep inside, where no one can take it away from you.

As you know, we did get out to your school in the Western part of Uganda. I want you to know that it was an important trip and I am deeply glad that we went. We liked the teachers. We loved the children. We are proud of the spirit of that school. We did meet the man that you wanted us to meet. He came just as we were leaving. We laughed at how God had provided for that.

Although we are called to help in many school situations, we feel that it is important to help with your school, as well. We will be sending along some boxes to help the teachers who have a huge job in keeping their morale up in a really difficult living situation.

Continue to take a personal interest in Good Samaritan Ministries in Uganda, Mr. President, and don't be afraid to contact, at any time, our Director, Osborn Muyanja, P.O. Box, 4428, Kampala. Minister B.K. knows the location of our office and his house. Osborn is a man you can trust with a small task or a larger one. He has been sorely tested and he has passed that great test of compassion from the heart. So many men would seek a position. He sought the lost, the brokenhearted. He sat with them and made it his life.

I consider us very close personal friends. I also look deep into your soul, my brother, and see that you made your people your life, as well. I am very proud that we know each other and I believe that in the years to come, it will become an increasing blessing for both of us. Please greet your wife and Minister B.K. with a word of encouragement. My husband, Joan Baker, and

myself and all of the team pray for you daily, but more than that—we pray for the people that you serve; the people that you so much believe in. May your Nation become a blessing to all of Africa and, indeed, to the whole world.
I am your sister and your fellow Samaritan,
Bettie P. Mitchell

April 25, 1994
Dear Mr. President,
As your beloved friend and brother, B.K. is aging and perhaps preparing in the months ahead to leave political life and retire, I know that you press into the desire for men you can trust around you. I want you to know, my beloved brother, that I cover you deeply and personally in prayer and that I am very proud of you. You have, in your country, a Christian movement that is different than all of the countries in the world. Christ is from the heart of your people and the souls of your people are being touched. In the years ahead, you will receive your reward for being a faithful leader and for suffering with them as you struggle to do what is right.

This fall we will be bringing Osborn Muyanja to the United States for six weeks with the National Directors of all 12 Good Samaritan countries.

I will be coming to Uganda again in 1995. I beseech God to give you the money to open free public primary education for your children and to really improve the life of those who are in the wilderness areas with little help of medical care and nutrition.

I love you dearly, as a real brother, for you indeed love your country and you are a man of all of your people.
Your sister and fellow Samaritan,
Bettie P. Mitchell

August 23, 1993
Dear President Museveni,
I appeal to you that you might know that Osborn Muyanja nearly lost his life. He is our National Director, the one you met. He was robbed, beaten, and taken out to be killed. A car came, stopped and intervened. They narrowly escaped, he and the

driver. Please make it your business to ask B.K. about him and to check up on his needs. He is a man of profound calling.

The money taken was $500. It was money for a camp for all of the Samaritan children that we sponsor in school. There were over 120 coming to Kampala. The camp began on August 20, and lasted until August 24th. It was not just the loss of the money, but the loss of the documents and the difficulties of the road. Many hands came to help with the camp. I want you to reach down as a President and know that we called all of our children from many regions of Uganda to come and be at a camp. We are taking care of them. How much we believe that God is with you in this work.

Your sister and fellow Samaritan,
Bettie P. Mitchell

Reply from President Museveni:
March 9, 1994

Mama Bettie P. Mitchell,

Please refer to your letter dated August 23, 1993, to H.E. the President. We are taking both investigative measures as well as to see what help can be given. We shall keep you informed of steps taken in this direction. We are sorry that Osborn Muyanja nearly lost his life.

April 18, 1996
My dear brother, Dithan (Uganda),

Recently, it was pointed out to me by the Lord, Himself that no one in the first century asked Jesus for money or things. When they met with Him, they were overcome with their own shallowness, their own inadequacies, and their own sin. I was reading Chapter 5 of the Gospel of Luke, verses 4-11. Read it and see how Peter is overcome with his own sinfulness when something is given to him that he neither worked for nor expected. I have been moved by this scripture. I believe that it will move you and it will move your people. It is time to teach it in a new way. Ponder it and use it.

You are deeply in our prayers, great and wonderful friends in Christ Jesus,
Bettie P. Mitchell

CHAPTER 13

PRAYER SUPPORT TEAM/SATELLITES

All that developed at Good Samaritan Ministries was led by the Holy Spirit. There came answers from Heaven to develop the ministry at its highest level.

We had a prayer support team of 25 to 30 people for many years, and they provided many hours of volunteer work. We also had the fun, community, and fellowship of Samaritans working and playing together. We all knew each other, and we laughed a lot.

As the name "Prayer/Support/Team" had been given, it came to my realization, prayer was the first for which we were always to be accountable.

PRAYER: On-going intercession without ceasing.

SUPPORT: Every person connected with Good Samaritan would have to give strong financial support for the ministry to make it. Often the giving was deeply sacrificial, shocking, and surprising to them what they could do. We had many fundraisers. Personal funds were given for this ministry to prosper, not just to survive, but to prosper for the needs of many.

TEAM: We were to work together as a single team. When divisiveness tried to come into the ministry here, it was difficult to move the people into teamwork. At times, the most difficulty was with the staff in Beaverton. Over-worked, not paid or underpaid, it was hard for them to come into the fullness of the agreements, but we managed year after year to together surmount our differences and find the team approach.

Team meant all action was of one accord, and above all things, in one spirit, the spirit of Our Lord.

It was hard to know how the ministry would grow. **Would we allow the ministry to come to many countries? Would we slow or stop it, hemmed in by our own limitations? Could we make it? Did we make it?**

We made it! We opened the possibility of this ministry in many nations, and at the time of my retirement, that included 38 countries. Each country deserved a fair opportunity to develop the work, and each national director needed enough income in order to give their lives and their families to the movement of the work and the training of the people. The people learned the difference between the believer and the person of action through the Holy Spirit.

I prayed for months one steady question before God. How can we do this? Finally, the Lord gave me the word, **SATELLITES.**

The ministry would function in one spirit, but each nation needed a satellite group from our region to help believe in the work, to travel to the country, to help with their funding, and to be consciously and deliberately involved in the development of the work and in the maintaining of new relationships.

I begged the people to come into agreement for satellites to be formed. This came to pass. As each nation came into the work, it required a new satellite for that nation. We were often desperate for people to step forward for this assignment. I would beg the people to develop a satellite for a designated country, not to be a temporary work, but a lifetime work. I would beg the commitment. I would plead for more laborers. Very gradually more came, but I must say, honestly, there were never quite enough. Was it our lack? Only God knows what was needed.

The satellites went to work helping to organize the coming of the Internationals in 1994. They became excited and passionate. We believed much in the miracle of visas to be granted, and the arrival of many airplanes bringing people from across the world. It was the biggest undertaking by any of us in our lifetimes.

What did the word satellite mean? It meant we lifted up our prayers to God, our intercession, our many works that had to be done in the Spirit of the Lord, as a satellite, up into heaven, and then the light would beam down on the country that was being served. Twice a year, from that time on, all of the Satellite Leaders met together. When our local satellite leader for a country came into the room, instead of taking role, I wrote on the grease board, Uganda, Kenya, Malawi, Egypt, I wrote each country by name. It was not our names at issue, but the country named. Only by coming into the fullness of The Call by our shared faith and by the movement of our lips to definitive action, could we change lives across the world. Education, widows and orphans, recovery programs, training of leaders, counselor training, getting people to continental training, the list was endless. The need nearly sucked my breath away, but I continued to correspond, and I continued to believe that with the Prayer Support Team we would stand firm in our commitment.

Finally, it was decided, in early 1994, to remodel and expand the size of the office in Beaverton. By God's grace, we nearly doubled our size. We used a warehouse and did the work ourselves. I will always remember the time and effort given by three people in particular. Jim Dreiling (plans and construction), Carrie Ward (mudding the walls), and Joan Baker (on duty with the workers). This project involved every weekend throughout the summer of 1994.

Finally, we had a large group room, a wonderful kitchen, a wheel chair access bathroom, and an increased number of offices.

The Parkside Business Center, who collected our rent, agreed that we would only have to pay for warehouse space, for we had used a warehouse and done all of the remodeling ourselves as fellow Samaritans.

CHAPTER 14

WE MUST SEE BOTH SIDES

January 8, 1994, I wrote a letter to B.K. and Grace Kirya in Uganda:

This last week, I was teaching the first three chapters of Genesis. I was thinking about the word "woman" a great deal. We are working on self-esteem issues in group. B.K., I asked the women and the men, "What do you call yourself, and what do you call God?" I call myself, "holy" and I call God, "My Father." But, I thought about it a lot, and I have to add the word "woman." You see, you are right. It is what we are to be called. It is the call of God upon the women to be "woman." Most people take little or no responsibility in the value they place on themselves. They just let any old incident change their value. However, very clearly, in Genesis, God placed the value, and He said, "It is very, very good!" The creation, finished, was very, very good.

The more I think about your teaching about the word "woman," B.K., the better I like it. I am woman.

God bless you both

I was unrelenting in the pursuit of writing significant letters to develop the ministry. My core value for others: your life will bear fruit, and you will see the Glory of God.

January 26, 1994, I wrote to Faraday and Angela Iwuchukwu in Nigeria:

I was at Mt. Sinai with my mother, an elderly friend, and another woman friend. I had run short of money—in fact I was out of money. I wanted to ask my mother for money, but I had too much pride. I asked the elderly friend. She looked at me and said, "You need to ask your mother."

Sometimes the reverse is true. It is easier to ask our mother than it is to ask someone else. But, I want to truly say to all of us, to myself, to you, to everyone in the ministry, we need to ask our God and our God will show us the way and open the door for us to receive what we need. He will show us whom we are to ask.

Lift up your countenance, and try to think less about money, Faraday. The Kingdom is paved with giving. Whatever we are to receive, it will be according to what God feels is just in our case. There is something beyond our culture and our pride. That something is the Lord's will. Few ministries ever discover the Lord's will, for they stay in the world of money with God, instead of beyond money in His Kingdom.

May God bless you and keep you. I challenge you in your faith and in the priorities that you will set in 1994. I am your fellow Samaritan and dear friend along that hard road.

March 31, 1994
My dear Father, B.K. and Sister Grace,

I was so happy to receive your letter, Grace, and to know that my father is safe and being strengthened by God. I can imagine the cares that you carry, and I am deeply humbled, Grace, that you would write me a page. Don't feel guilty when you can't write. Always feel that you can call collect, for sometimes a call is easier than a letter. We are part of the innermost family in the spiritual realm, and whatever is needed among us, must always be shared.

This fall, September 1st, the International Directors will be gathering here at our headquarters in Oregon. The Director of each country will be here for six weeks.

B.K., you are well aware that six weeks can bring us together. I am sure that you are pleased that I have chosen to strengthen communications between peoples and nations. I am like you, B.K. That is why you are my father. We believe in strengthening by the meeting of people.

Living at our house right now, we have Doctor Emil Zaky, a psychiatrist from Cairo. He is offering some supervision for our counseling programs in Egypt, and he is here for two months of training.

David Bhatti is here. He will be full-time in Good Samaritan in Pakistan. He is assigned to develop our local organizations in Pakistan. He flew in this week from Pakistan for seven months of training. You can laugh, as you know we have an International House again, "just like you."

God bless the President and let him know that I sit in Entebbe often, and pray for him and with him.

I also want to comment that the massacre in Hebron touched me deeply. Our son Mohammad's first cousin, 18, was killed in the mosque. It was over the tombs of Isaac and Rebecca that the killings took place. Surely, the desecration of tombs, and the aborting of the peace agreement is a victory that this world must never allow. I stand firm that we will see the Day of the Lord.

Your daughter and fellow Samaritan,
Bettie

June 14, 1994, I again wrote to President Museveni:

Mr. President and my dear Brother,

This letter is written to inform you that I miss you. It is also written to encourage you and your nation, that is still so needy and crying out. I want to encourage you to press in for the funds needed to do what other African nations are refusing to do for their people. Often this is due to greed and the funds going into the wrong hands. I want to say to you that I believe, with all of my heart, you are a trustworthy man. I want to encourage you and the people working for the government. The funds must go to the real needs of every person in Uganda.

We grieve with you over the tragedy in Rwanda. It is a tragedy that you know well—death camps, killings, orphans—it is the hell of this century. I join you in prayer for your brothers and sisters found floating in Lake Victoria, and I bow down and bend over and grieve with your God and mine to say, "Enough!"

This letter is written to request a special exemption. In speaking to Osborn Muyanja, the Executive Director of Good Samaritan--Uganda, yesterday, he told me that the only way we could receive an exemption on the packages and parcels that we mailed from Good Samaritan Ministries in Oregon to Uganda, would be if that tax exemption were authorized by the President. I request for you to give an order for tax exemption on packages from Good Samaritan Ministries, USA, to Good Samaritan Ministries, Uganda. You know we are a non-profit organization, registered with your government in Uganda.

June 6th was my 60th birthday. On my birthday, I received $6,000 to go for needs of widows and orphans in Africa. We used part of that money to mail 111 boxes of much needed materials to African countries: books, clothing, medicine, eyeglasses, and school supplies. Last week we mailed 27 boxes to Uganda, to Osborn Muyanja, and the Good Samaritan Ministries in Uganda, for widows and orphans. This is the reason we need this exemption with the postal authorities.

Mr. President, we are small and weak, and we are called to do a mighty work. You know me. You know me well, and you know my heart. Please respond to this letter and meet this need. The burden on our small organization is too great if the parcels are taxed.

BALAKI KIRYA IS DEAD.

August 9th, I wrote to Osborn and all Good Samaritans in Uganda.

Today, our father, who helped us on earth, went to be with Jesus. It is a day for us to pause and consider what God did to give this man the strength to meet with everyone day after day until the very last day of his life. The courage of this man has been a testimony and a witness to the greatness of our God. I meet with all of you today, the mighty, the great, the lowly and meek, the unlovely. I meet with you as a Ugandan, a mother, and as a personal friend to every one of you. We here meet with you to make intercession for your nation, for Grace, for B.K.'s children, for the schools of Uganda, and for the leaders. We meet with you to make intercession together, for we know your needs have often seemed beyond bearing. We know this because we bear it with you. Heavy burdens hurt. Sometimes they are frightening.

I want to say to Moses Ssemanda, who is Osborn's brother and chairman of their GSM Board in Uganda, "I am so proud of you for the way you have handled things. I know you are a real brother to all of the Muyanga children. I am sorry about your accident. We will take care of needs in your work, as we must help you. I pray that everyone who was in the car will not be injured in the spiritual realm, but will receive special kindness from God to heal the fear that wounds such as these leave behind."

As we draw Osborn out of the nation and bring him here, we are drawing all of you unto all of us. Never think that we are bringing one man—because, when we bring him, we are bringing all of you. You are so "one," so inseparable from each other in Christ Jesus, that whenever one of you goes, you all go.

To my sister Flora, "Do not be afraid, for heaven is close at hand, and B.K., Grace, Bettie, Osborn, all of us are there with you. You have done well, and each day from this point forward, you will bear greater fruit, through His Name."

I ask for peace, grace, and kindness to unite the whole ministry, today.

August 9th, I faxed President Museveni:
One of the great men of God of our times has died today. He was my father and the father of Africa for Good Samaritan Ministries. His loss in Uganda, as a statesman, is incalculable, but the gain in heaven of his prayers for your nation will bear fruit beyond your eyes, beyond anything that has been seen. The Glory of the Lord is coming upon your nation to keep you, to bless you, and to heal the wounds that are too deep for words.

I know that you will be at B.K.'s funeral. Somewhere in the crowd will be Osborn Muyanga, our young director, who is now raising six orphans, as well as handling this ministry in Uganda. You probably will never see each other, but I want you to know we are all best friends, and that you can talk to us, and you can trust us like you did B.K. We are with you, and we will take up the cross and bear it for your life and for the work.

My dear brother, Mr. President, I will need to call upon you when I must, and I know from this day forward, we will always hear each other. I respect your grief, for to find a man who can be deeply trusted, as B.K., is the greatest gift a leader can have.

As B.K. died August 9, 1994, that very day I wrote to his wife, Grace:

I was at the office today, when Osborn called me from Kampala. He called me immediately when he heard of B.K.'s death on the radio. The crowds have been pushing into my office, and there has been so much work to do here today, but now I have come outside the office. I am standing on a little wooden bridge overlooking a stream, and it looks like Uganda to me. In my hand is a dictaphone, and now I can weep. I am alone. That doesn't happen very often. How well you know that!

Some scripture words came to me a few moments ago. They were strange words. "The Glory went out of Israel." It is the desolation of a nation. The loss to Uganda is great, but the gain is greater, for a great intercessor has gone to heaven. B.K.'s beloved children will be saved. His grandchildren will know Jesus, and his nation will be changed again and again for the better. The prayers that he has prayed for other nations, presidents, and governments will be answered, and the victory of Christ will come sooner. But, today, the Glory went out of Israel. It will return!

I'm sure that many of your family members will come, and thousands of people will stand with you, Grace. I was his daughter and you know that, don't you? I will stand there too, and the Glory of God will come from heaven and it will consume us all where we are, one in His spirit.

You're such a great woman—hospitable in heart, gracious of spirit. Go on with his work, Grace. Continue to speak to your nation, continue to teach the president, continue to reach out and minister far beyond your strength or your time.

When you are lonely at night and you have those quiet moments, I will sit beside you and say nothing that you will know that I am there. We've known the loneliness and grief all of our lives, Grace. We were born to carry the message we carry. I am so proud of you.

As I was writing this letter, a staff member came and got me. You, Grace, were on the phone. You hung up, but it is alright, Grace. We were talking. We've been talking a lot today, and we will talk a lot in the days to come. No one will hear our words, for our language is the language of heaven.

In the midst of the grief and all of the decisions, I ask you to be a mother to Good Samaritan in Africa, and to take up where the father left off. This is something that you understand. Hardly anyone understands as well as you do, for you were always a Samaritan.

Osborn Muyanga has been sick and terribly burdened. 180 children, and the people who take care of them came to the

Children's Camp near Wobulenzi. There was an accident with our GSM truck just before the camp, and there were many trials for the staff. Flora Mutaka, a woman of great leadership, has AIDS. In the midst of all of that, Osborn called today to say one thing. He called, immediately, Grace. He told me about the last day he had with B.K.

Osborn said, "We spent a long time talking, and B.K. wanted to go to the camp so badly to be with the children, but he was too weak." B.K. sent a message for the children's camp instead. Osborn told me B.K. asked about James Opiyo. Osborn told me that he and B.K. prayed a long time together.

Now B.K. is resting a little while before his greater work begins, and we must go on. I will call you "Mother Grace" from this day forward, Mother of Africa.

By the end of August, preparations had been made for the International Conference. We knew that 15 were going to be here for sure: Majed Alloush, Jerusalem West Bank; Nicholas Okungu, James Opiyo and John Oundo, Kenya; James Kabvalo, Malawi; Samuel Kitwika, Tanzania; Maqbool Kamal and David Bhatti, Pakistan; Alick Malama, Zambia; Osborn Muyanja, Uganda; Moushir,Egypt; Fager Batarsa, Jordan; Galina Bidenko, Ukraine.

There was a surprise: our leader from GSM--Kingston Ontario, Canada, met Yesu from India. They decided to send him. Therefore, India not only was represented, but the work of Good Samaritan Ministries, India, began at the International Conference. There was one other: Mervat Isaac. She was here for some training. Her country of origin: Egypt.

One country was going to miss the conference, Nigeria.

August 31, 1994,

My dear son, Faraday,

There are no words to describe exactly how I feel. I have been upset for several weeks about what is going on in Nigeria. We are somewhat aware of the political upheaval, the oil strike, and some of the instability in the government. I have no idea whether you will get this letter. We have tried for days and days to reach Doctor Omotoso, in Port Harcourt. We sent a telegram to your office.

We did get word about one week ago that you had picked up your ticket in Port Harcourt. We did receive word yesterday that you had cancelled your reservation from Lagos, and that the plane left without you. What these things mean, I do not know! I can only imagine that there have been problems, and that you are hard-pressed what to do.

There has been one other tragedy. John Oundo of Kenya had his passport, his visa, and his ticket stolen twelve hours before he was to fly out from Nairobi. We are trying to make arrangements for him to get another passport and visa. The ticket can be replaced. Other than that, all are arriving and everything is as it was planned.

We are concerned for your conditions, for what your family may be going through, and for the particular hardships in Port Harcourt. I am astute enough on African tension to know that there is always danger of sudden eruption of violence.

Yesterday, when I got word from MTS that you did not take the ticket and go to the airport, I was quite depressed and full of sorrow. I want this to be a time of joy, and of course Satan tries to rob the joy by crushing the heart of a mother for her children. However, as I was in the car driving with Papa Jerry, your face appeared before my inner-eyes, and you spoke to me. You told me not to worry, and you reassured me. That was a miracle!! Therefore, by God's grace, you did get a message to me, and I did receive it. I want you to know that I've been in intercession for weeks for you, and I have agonized week after week to the point of total exhaustion for you to get out, knowing that Satan was going to attack there, and yet feeling helpless to prevent this.

They all arrived on time. This meant meeting several airplanes, taking very weary travelers to destinations of rest, and the final preparations to house, feed, clothe, and protect them in the training that would occur for six weeks. I met each of the airplanes.

In a day or so, John Oundo called me from Nairobi. John was really grieving at not being able to come. I said firmly to John, "You are to get a new passport, a visa, and come within the next 10 days!" John arrived 12 days late, but John arrived. This was a miracle! You see, in Kenya, if a passport is stolen, it takes weeks to arrange for a replacement, let alone, a second U.S. visa. This was a miracle!

On the first day of the conference, we started with play therapy. The men and women sat on the floor. Denny Nkemontoh brought toys for them to play with and helped them reflect upon the needs of children. They were our first children to have a need for play therapy.

The six weeks of time were full of tremendous amounts of communication among us all. Each of the directors came to know each other intimately. They shared so many stories. The grief was poured out of hearts. We paused. We rested, and we went ahead.

We all had to learn. We taught the Internationals the importance of their communication to us on a regular basis; how and why to do annual reports; budgeting, and prioritizing money; development of teaching and counseling skills; personal self-care; leadership; and management of teams. We pressed in again and again to the Parable of the Good Samaritan. We all needed to address victim mentality, abuse, enabling, and how not to be emotionally used up by peoples' neediness. We had to learn to be born again daily of water and the spirit.

We also travelled to the other GSM centers in the Northwest. Each Center had a tremendous celebration and a great plan for community on both sides of the world among us all.

In Pendleton, all of us went to the Pendleton Round Up, and the men received cowboy hats. Each local center in the U.S. was beginning to understand commitment was among us all and unless we worked together, in an absolute spirit of caring for one another, them for us, and us for them, we could not do the work of the Kingdom, and, ultimately, we would not make it. There were huge miracles, and such great daily joy.

We chose several drivers to transport all of us. You can imagine the huge job of each local center housing all of these people. In this experience, we would all know one another face to face.

We gave the internationals several experiences that were unusual. For example, I took them all to the American grocery store to see what our food was like. As we looked around the

Albertson's store, I almost got sick to my stomach, for I saw how much we had, and I knew how little they ate. It made my eyes hurt.

We took them to several stores for them to learn what it was like to shop and buy things in the United States. Believe it or not, we took them to Nordstrom's to show them the price of shoes. Then, we went to Fred Meyers, and finally, we took them to the Goodwill to price shoes. They could see the differences, and they could see that all Americans don't have money. We had a variety of experiences and opportunities. Most of us in this ministry had little money and great heart.

We had a retreat near Sisters, Oregon, at a conference center. All regional center directors came.

It was particularly moving to see the children participate in this retreat, for a large number of children were present. They washed the feet of the ones who had come to be with us, the internationals. Each country had a special table of gifts to represent their country. We shared by shopping and studying, to learn ourselves. We were children, learning things we knew little about. Willing to learn much, our love was genuine.

One of the hard adjustments during the six weeks, was Majed Alloush was a Muslim. They came from countries where that was just not acceptable in a Christian organization, and it was shocking to them. It was hard for them to believe that God had called and chosen Majed Alloush to do what he was doing in the West Bank by developing and hugely impacting the community of addicts and their families. After a settling in period, which was particularly hard on Majed, they all finally broke the barriers and became one team. It was a great breakthrough.

Another test, another day, I asked them to take a piece of paper, and write down things they would like to take home, things they felt were important to their work. Then, I asked them to turn in their lists. In some ways, their lists terrified me, for they had so little reality in their list, and so much materialism. It was significant to me, personally, that Majed Alloush had only one thing on his list, a used suitcase.

Getting each of them to be on time to meetings was a very big problem because Africans don't keep time; they keep what we call African time, which means "sometime in that day...."

Gradually, slowly, and with much intentionality, we trained them hard to understand that we needed to be together during those times that were given for all of us to meet.

One of the biggest problems we had was the use of the telephone. In 1994, there was not much access to telephones in some of the countries, and there were situations going on in some of their countries that were really difficult for them. Although we set phone limits, and I worked really hard to get them to understand that we had given everything we had and we couldn't give more, they had some failure. The biggest offender was Osborn Muyanja. When he left, the phone bill for Uganda was $700. These were hard lessons for us, but ultimately they did take the lessons to heart. We were changed by the Spirit that lived among us, a Spirit which joined us together. **He kept us all as one Samaritan working together.**

One day, I took the men out to the park to play basketball. There was a very small basketball court in the park, but we had no basketball. I had to trust we would find one. It was a hot day, and when we got there, sure enough, there were men playing with a ball, and they let us use it. When we came back, I handed them some deodorant in my naivety. In their naivety, they put it on under their arms, over their clothes. There was often cultural humor. This brought us again to what was real; we were together.

Yesu was not able to stay the whole time, but his time at Good Samaritan in Beaverton, became crucial in the next stages of his life. He went home to develop a significant work in South Eastern India. We stayed strong with him as a team.

There were times of confession. There were times for prayers that were too deep for words.

I asked them what their priorities were for the work in their countries. They spent a long time working on those priorities. They were learning how to manage and prioritize. I remember that James Opiyo said his number one priority was a house for Nicholas, because Nicholas did not have one. Each of them was honest. Each of them had integrity, and each of them spoke candidly the way they were and how they were able to be.

During the International Conference, we received a letter from South Africa. They had heard of us, and wanted to become part of the ministry. We all prayed and believed this was a miracle.

We sang, we danced, and we studied hard. Vonda Winkle taught a full first aid training course. That training went on to create first aid programs in some of their countries. The training was so effective because they could see the point. We sent them home with the right information.

One of the problems we had with our people here was they all wanted to bring something for the Internationals to take home with them. None of them from this end had any realization that there were two suitcases allowed, weighing only so many pounds each. They came in with generosity, but this created for us frustration and some hard decisions of how to handle the stuff that was brought. We were learning what was effective, and we were learning when we were not effective.

The International Conference was a huge effort from all of our people here. The staff worked day and night. They taught by what they did. Our people grew up to the realization of the great call upon their lives to be fellow Samaritans. When they all left, we were exhausted, but satisfied. Financial recovery was slow, but we had no regrets.

The International Conference was the toughest teaching job of my life, but the results were good. I blew my foot out, and two months later, I was still limping. It was the day of the big stress, when everybody was going down the tube, and something dramatic had to happen. It's like when evil hits a certain point, the victory comes when someone is wounded. I'm glad the wounding was in my body, for my heart was truly with them all.

James Opiyo was the toughest of all. He felt lonely and frightened and needed much encouragement. The years had wracked his soul, for he was the one who went out and faced the enemy, single-handedly, until he formed a strong team. The evil one had crucified him many times.

One of the reasons Osborn called Uganda so often was because Flora Mutaka was dying. September 29th, the word came she had died.

In a letter written to Faraday on September 30th, I shared:

I want to tell you that Mama Flora Mutaka died yesterday in Uganda of AIDS and tuberculosis. She had one surviving relative, besides her five children. Her daughter, Pauline, was five years old in July. Osborn, Dithan and Richard took her to Osborn's mother's house to stay until she died. They kept her in Osborn's room, and took care of her until the end.

We had been expecting to hear of her passing. Three days before she died, she sobbed all day. She was irrational. She was broken from the terrible tragedies in her life. Her daughter died of seizures at age nine. Her husband was murdered in front of her, and she was raped and robbed by three men. She went on to be a great Samaritan and a hero of the faith, and I'm sure we are going to do something special in memorial of her life. We sent $500 to take her through her last medical care because there was no funding for her, and now, we sent more to bury her.

In addition, James Kabvalo's son became very seriously ill with a blood crisis, and we had to send funds for him. It has been a hard time for us financially. We've really been stretched. Right now, we are $13,000 in the red in our general fund, and the rent is due tomorrow. Please keep us in prayer. People love us, but they don't realize how much we really give. They have no comprehension of that. We had a special memorial service for B.K., and a special memorial service for Flora Mutaka.

One thing I will always remember about Flora Mutaka was the day we had lunch at the simple place where she lived. She had no table, so she set a box out as a table. She had cloth napkins for each of us. I have never seen this since in all of our visits to Africa. Flora stood out as a real lady. She did great work in establishing Good Samaritan Ministries in Wobulenski. Even today, the work is still strong.

After the conference, on October 19th, I wrote a letter to Osborn Muyanja in Uganda:

There has been a great miracle here. You would not believe it. Last night, Cindy Womack called on the telephone from Pendleton. She said Stephen, the oldest son of Flora Mutaka, was at her house spending the night. He is traveling with the African Children's Choir throughout America, and here, suddenly, is Flora's son at Good Samaritan Ministries! Can you believe that? Is that possible? Surely this is God!

Stephen will be coming to Portland Saturday and I hope to have him spend Saturday night with us. He knew of his mother's death, but he knew nothing of the details, and he had not seen her since last January or February, just before she went to Uranga for training. He was deeply moved that God had moved in such a way. He said he knew who I was. He had read many of my letters, and he was well aware of our work in Uganda through his mother's life. It is a great miracle, Osborn! I'm sure that Flora's prayers will be answered. It is the first of her great prayers to be answered we can see. Expect more miracles, for Flora was an intercessor, and when she agonized, God heard every word. Perhaps it was her intercession that brought the great service when you preached at Christ Episcopal Church in Lake Oswego. How happy I am about this. It made Flora's death come home to me, and now I will have time to grieve.

November 1st, I wrote to Osborn:

We are continuing to make plans to try to get a synthesizer musical system for Stephen. I don't know how we will do that, but I feel it would be a crime not to, and enough crimes have been committed against his life. I did interview Stephen about the death of his father, and what really happened. He told me some of the stories that are important for us to know. We will be able to help the whole family.

Stephen was six years old when President Idi Amin's forces broke into his father's church. His father was the co-pastor and singing in the choir. Stephen hid under the bench. The Army arrested his father and tortured him for a year that he might deny Christ, even throwing him off a second story building onto a cement floor. Stephen was ten years old when his father was shot in the heart and a spear put in his side by President Obote's men. I'm going to probe this young man as much as possible. It seems the African Children's Choir program and the school education programs are good works programs, but they seem to be pushing the children to get over the sorrows, instead of developing the children spiritually to integrate their past with their present. They are trying to separate them from their past. Only as we integrate into a whole can we truly be born again of water and the spirit. I think that you as a therapist know what I mean. Each trauma has its teaching event, and each part of the life is valued. Don't throw away the past, but recognize the value in teaching the meaning of the present.

When Stephen was in Beaverton, I had a terrible time getting the African Children's Choir to release him to spend some time at our house. I explained to them that we've had much word about his mother's death, and we were very close to the family. I told the people the whole story, but they were still very unhappy that Stephen departed and came with me for a time. I persisted, for I had things to tell Stephen, and things to show him.

I had all of the letters I had written to Flora Nyakayilu and all the letters she had written to me. I gave Stephen those letters. I had the video made at the Uganda Children's Camp. It was made just a few days before she died. In the video, his mother was lying on the floor, with her head propped up, singing beautifully and praising God.

The Mutaka children have continued to be part of Good Samaritan Ministries, and Stephen's sister, Hannah, has had a great deal of influence developing professionalism in the work at the office. Flora is still very much present in the history of this ministry and deeply remembered also for the three months of training she took in Kenya.

November 9, 1994, Osborn Muyanja wrote the following letter:

It is true Mama Flora went to be with the Lord. I no longer see her. She no longer answers like she used to when I call her. When I walked into the office, I can see the gap. As I hold the burden on my soul, I am looking for one to intercede earnestly. I have come to understand it so well that Flora left. Sometimes I dream to wait for her until she comes, and I come to realize that she left forever. On November 3rd, the center's leaders and board members visited Wobulenzi. As I moved out from the car, I could not hear Flora's surprising, shouting, joyful welcoming voice. It was sad again. Deep down in my spirit, I grieved again and again for Flora. I have missed her deeply.

I have heard all the stories of how Flora suffered and died. It is healing for me to hear how my mother, the children, the Samaritans, did a lot for Flora during her days of agony. She rested loved and in peace for eternity.

The day we were at Wobulenzi, we mourned together with all the Samaritans. It was a special day to remember Flora and the wonderful work she accomplished for the Kingdom of God. She was an intercessor, a Samaritan with a servant's spirit that will never be forgotten in the memories of many.

I found all of the people fine and well here when I returned. The work never ceased. The Samaritans worked so hard, more than the days that I had lived with them. I want to commend Richard and Dithan, who were left in charge, for having done such a wonderful work. They cooperated so well with all the Samaritans at every center.

My family, the Samaritans, especially my family, was overjoyed to see me back happy, well-looking, and healthier than when I left. As I give them the stories, one by one, since there are many, it is wonderful to hear the testimonies of what the Lord did among us all.

Since I came back, I am out and in, visiting centers, calling Samaritans, and teaching the concepts this time deeply more than ever before. There is revival in the work, a great change, which is done by God. I hope to have one week off to rest in December. If you pray, pray for me so that God relieves me a little bit. I travelled safely unto home with all my luggage. It was good for me that I came to USA meeting with my fellow directors from other countries, together with the many Samaritans I happened to meet there. It was great and life changing. It gave me a broad understanding in the work, and a wide heart of the Samaritan. All the people I met were different and important to my life. I can see and understand very well where the work was born and how it is being done. Faith in God, depending on the Holy Spirit, love, relationship and endurance, are some of the many things I learned at the International Conference. Most of the people I met had a lesson to teach my life.

Thank you, Mama, for loving us. You took care of us. You protected us in many dangerous things. You gave us so much. Only our hearts can tell these. During my stay, the greatest work was done in my spirit, which is important. I came back strong, encouraged and excited. I will never forget the great love and comfort the Samaritans gave us in the USA. It was healing to our souls and bandaging to our wounds.

In our many weaknesses, fear and ignorance, you dared to hold us. You remained loving and a true mother, an unusual teacher to all of us. We over-worked your life, overwhelmed you with our needs, but you could still smile to us the last hour we left. I will always call you mother, and call you whenever you need it because I have come to know what you bear. You are there always for us. I have missed you deeply. I miss being with you in your house, together with Papa Jerry. I love the way he can detect your weariness when you are back, and prepares food and everything ready for us to eat and rest. We need him in Uganda to teach the men to help their wives. It will be wonderful for the families.

Finally, as Alick Malama from Zambia was at the conference, I must write a little about him.

Zambia is a big country, a little larger than the state of Texas. It was formerly the territory of Northern Rhodesia, administered by the South Africa Company and the U.K. The name was changed to Zambia upon independence in 1964. There are nine provinces.

Alick Malama and his wife, Sellina, were pastoring a church in Luanshya in the Copperbelt Province in 1993. They were also counseling abandoned pastors, and taking care and teaching four orphans. Alick states, "It so happened that one of the abandoned pastors I was counseling brought me a yellow-paged paper from a Yellow Pages phone book. It was not the full page; it was torn. He handed it over to me and asked me if I needed to contact Good Samaritan Ministries in Beaverton, whose address was on that small page. He said the name of the ministry sounds like what you are doing." Alick wrote to Bettie Mitchell, who promptly responded and invited him to be part of GSM. During the conference, he was appointed National Director of Zambia.

At times, God leads his servants in seemingly very strange ways. Imagine finding a fragment of a page out of a Portland, Oregon Yellow Pages directory in the middle of an African country with just the right name on it. This could only be God, who had been preparing this Samaritan long before that date.

Alick was born in Luanshya in 1955. His father worked in the mines, and his mother was a nurse and a housewife. Alick was the second child in a family of eight girls and three boys. Life was difficult as both the father and mother were alcoholics.

Consequently, Alick did not start grade one until he was 10 years old. By the time Alick was in the 7th grade, he was also working part-time to help buy his school uniform, shoes and books.

Throughout his life, Alick felt drawn to help the helpless, and that is what he did. He helped the downtrodden. A man he did not know, with a prophetic anointing, pointed at him and said, "You are Barnabas. Many who are wounded will come to you and will find the heart of a father. I will establish you that no man will move you." Alick and Sellina have five children.

They have the Lord's love for the brokenhearted, the lame, the poor. Their home and hearts are open to anyone in need. They have been instrumental in opening a school in the slums of Lusaka, where more than 400 students who would not have had an opportunity to go to the school are being taught.

Satan attacked often, but The Call has prevailed in Zambia.

CHAPTER 15

DEVELOPMENT! DEVELOPMENT! DEVELOPMENT!

In 1995, I led a tour of 47 to Egypt, Israel, Palestine, and Jordan. I traveled for three months to ten countries.

In the fall, I left Portland with a team of ten to visit and help with the development of the work in Kenya, Uganda, Tanzania, Malawi, Zambia, and South Africa.

I could see the forest and I could see the trees. What I saw and discerned was that most people had little or no development. They took the days as they came, but they seldom sought personal or spiritual growth. I saw this in clients at the office and I saw this in people who were interested in going on tours or visits to Africa, I saw this sometimes in myself. It is easy to be busy. It is hard to stay effective.

It is so difficult for a human to cut a piece of rice in half. We want to keep it all for ourselves for we have so little. It is hard to give half of all we have to our neighbor. It is truly, truly hard to love our neighbor as ourselves. I think we are all struggling, and it is very painful to learn this lesson, but when we've all learned it, and it lives deep inside of us we manifest action. No one will be hungry.

I traveled because I saw the necessity, as the person receiving The Call at Nineveh to teach nothing but the Kingdom of God. My presence and the repeated pronouncement of The Call was my witness of God's priority to teach nothing but the Kingdom. The shaking up of ingrained cultural habits and the development of those who would see, those who would hear, those who would come to know vital actions must be taken in the Name of Jesus on behalf of His Kingdom.

In order for development to occur, it is important to recognize that we are under-developed. We have often called countries in the third world, "developing countries." This included most of Africa.

My personal definition of a "developing country" is their strong urgency to receive instruction, and to learn new ideas and ways to implement them. Highly developed, effective individuals will change the priorities of countries from sickness to health.

Often, in Africa, the church developed pastors better than they developed the people. This ministry was to bring a balance in the development of the people and their leaders. It was to bring forth the work of Christ among us all. I had to become a passionate developer, not only fighting for development in many, but training developers as well.

Since 1976, I had a high priority to take as many as possible to the Holy Land, and other middle-eastern countries. Getting them away from their environment gave each person a chance to move into new places of internal growth. They had to learn to get along with others in close quarters, often frustrating, but very developmental. The harder the tour, the greater the change that would take place.

GSM countries in Africa were still at tender places of development. They needed a ton of encouragement, intercession that would move heaven and earth on their behalf, people who knew them and cared about them and would remain faithful.

My life was never just about going to Africa; it was always about the development of the people going, as well as the people receiving us. It was about the challenge for growth. Would we be changed? What would move each of us to a lifetime of effective action?

Often ministry people traveling to other countries see themselves as the teachers. They see themselves as essential in the ministry. From my viewpoint, what was essential in the ministry was experiencing the hardship of the life on African soil. The cultures seldom met our desires or expectations. Could we relate to a person who had few teeth and would never in their lifetime see a dentist? Could we relate to on-going genuine hunger? Could we relate to never going to school? I saw the needs as our teacher. What was I looking for? I was looking for the Holy Genius, the Holy Spirit moving. I was looking for people who would pay a long and hard price to stay on the road. I was looking for people who would not manipulate, use, or look for advantage for themselves. I was looking for people who could be crushed by the cross, and raised by the resurrection.

In May, 1995, I wrote to Samuel Kitwika in Tanzania:
I know you're struggling as a man, Samuel, but I want you to know that we're struggling for Christ, and our struggle is to learn how to carry a cross without looking like a baby and acting like a jerk. I struggle. You struggle. I pray we both pass.

Osborn Muyanja suffered from Cerebral Malaria in January. He was under tremendous pressure. His soul was broken. By a shocking miracle, he got to Washington, D.C. in the spring. There was only one problem with this. No one in Uganda, including the woman he was engaged to, knew where he was. He had been missing for several weeks. The Samaritans in Uganda were frantic with worry and thought he might be in Rwanda. No one dreamed he was in the United States, except his pastor, Robert Kayanja, of Miracle Church, Kampala. He had taken Osborn to Washington D.C., but Osborn was fearful to let any of us know. Robert Kayanja stayed with Osborn for a short time, took off for other states, and told him to raise money. Osborn became desperate and fearful.

Finally, the week before Easter, while I was quite ill with a bad flu, I had signed up to go to the altar at our church every morning to pray. This was a 24-hour-a-day Prayer Vigil for Holy Week. I was to be alone at the church between 5:00 and 6:00 a.m. each day during Holy Week. This required me to leave home at 4:30 a.m. On Tuesday that week, I went into very profound levels of intercession and deep begging of God for Him to answer the prayer, locate Osborn, and relieve me from the pressure and worry about his life. I begged so much and was so broken on that altar, not only for him, but also for many. The ministry had come to a point where it was far beyond my bearing. Only Christ could bear such a cross.

Well, the Lord gave me a Scripture, found in Mark 4:35-41. As He gave me this scripture, He came to me, stood up in my face, and said, "This thing will be finished!" He even told me my own faith was weak, and asked me where it was. As He stood, He said, "I will answer this, and I will answer it now." Thus, I have no doubt, that this was the will of God. The next day Osborn called from D.C. I arranged for him to come to Oregon. I picked Osborn up at 3:50 a.m. at the airport on Good Friday. At

5:00 a.m. on Good Friday, we were praying at the same altar of my church where I had prayed for Osborn to be found.

Osborn spent ten days at our house. Ten days of counseling, challenging and listening. Ten days of the final breaking of his soul to be delivered into this work permanently. Papa Jerry and I played a key role in Osborn's life. We worked together for his healing. The healing occurred.

At the end of a few days, I said to Osborn, "I'm going to send you to North Carolina to Lisa Earnhardt's house. She is a widow with two children, and as you must stay for several weeks until Robert re-appears with your ticket, it would be good for you to be there. She will be gone during the day. You can rest, you can be alone, and you can read. This private time will be unique in your whole lifetime. It will be your time before the Lord, and His time in your face. God with you."

After much agonizing, seeking, asking for help, I recognized the deepest need of the ministry was for 12 men to be intercessors for myself and for the ministry as a whole. After much prayer, the 12 men were chosen.

The 12 intercessors were not going to be given prayer requests. They were to intercede for the whole, and not be distracted with the part. They were to keep this intercession in the spiritual realm, knowing it was the will of God that it takes place.

The Spirit chose three Internationals: David Bhatti of Pakistan, Faraday Iwuchukwu of Nigeria, and Osborn Muyanja of Uganda. Another man chosen was Pastor Ron Mehl of Beaverton Foursquare Church. He was the pastor of a church of nearly 8,000 people. He was struggling with leukemia and heart problems. He agreed to take the assignment. He understood the cost. These 12 men needed to seek righteousness with all their hearts. They needed to be willing to profoundly train deep, deep in the spirit to be intercessors, men who would know and understand the burdens that were being carried by the few, and men who would be faithful in prayer regardless of their circumstances.

It is an enormous task to be an intercessor for this ministry for the enemy would like to eat us up as fast as possible. We destroy the power of evil and we declare the Kingdom profoundly.

From a letter I wrote to John Oundo, February 1, 1995:
I miss you around the house, John. I miss your steadiness and that little twinkle in your life that I love so dearly. I want to tell you that Papa Jerry was pretty seriously ill, but he has received much healing and the Lord is doing mighty things inside his body. He had blood clots in the leg and they were very infected. He is taking a blood thinner, and will be taking it for several months. He spent six days in the hospital.

This is a ministry to those who are so failing on the road that nobody wants to stop for them. It is a ministry done in spite of the church. Because it is the ministry that Christ Jesus Himself performed when He created the church, we are all recovering sinners training hard. You and I well know that.

I found, John, over the years, that we will be broken many times. Do not be dismayed if breaking comes again. It is a way in which Christ prevails, and we have to give Him the glory, the credit, and the work.

From a letter I wrote to Faraday in April:
The longer I go on, the more I realize we are the two, strongest, toughest and most broken intercessors in the whole ministry. I count on you and Angela to suffer with me our prayers for the saints and the sinners.

From a letter to Samuel Kitwika, June, 1995:
I have spoken to James Opiyo on the telephone upon his return from Tanzania. He is so supportive of you and helpful in solving the problems. I urgently sat James down to straighten things out, and to get things into correct spiritual order. For, it is he and I who have headship over you, not the people in Tanzania, who would hurt you in the spirit, instead of helping you. The beginning of any ministry is like this. It is Satan to discourage the soul and tear it apart. Do not submit to Satan, but continue to call upon the Name of the Lord Jesus. As you do that, and put your head in the King's corner, He will sustain you, Samuel, until the crowd lets up and stops stoning you. I have felt

the stones myself. They have bitten into my flesh daily, often for years at a time, so I know what you are going through.

James told me they have chased away the woman, the mother of your last child, to Dar Es Salaam. How foolish it all is that they would throw a Muslim woman out, but if she were a Christian woman, they would probably stone her even worse. God help us all as we learn to be compassionate. Where is mercy? Where is forgiveness? It is so difficult to find, isn't it Samuel? Remember the mercy you found while praying in my room up at the retreat. Remember the mercy of my hands of prayer and God's heart for you, Samuel. Be sustained, for that is the mercy of Christ. Those who are humbled and thrown to the ground will be lifted up. In the last day, they will be kept.

I know you are learning many things the hard way, and sometimes you have been foolish, Samuel. I want you to know that I know all about the foolishness, for the Lord speaks to me from the deep. But in the foolishness will come the breakthrough gift of wisdom. I say to you, son, it will come. Be encouraged today and be lifted up. Know your God is very near you. Your God is very good to you, Samuel.

Written to Bettie from James Opiyo, August 1995:

John Oundo is doing very well, as well as the other workers. We are all in agreement and we pray for the work to grow. I have trained people to work together without competition, personal greed or ambition. I have trained everyone to work with Nicholas, and they have collective responsibilities. I am very happy that our people respect each other and they tackle matters wisely.

Mama, I must also thank you for the encouragement I have received from you. It has not been easy bringing the heads of people together, especially Africans. It is a long road for people to learn to be humble and submit to each other. I am totally convinced that when we continue holding our heads together, nothing will be impossible because our God and the power of the Holy Spirit is in charge.

We are training people on the line that they have never been trained. We are dealing with pride, selfishness, greediness, which are all properties of the devil. We need people to come out of these spirits unharmed. It is very hard, and we have a long way to go.

The man from Burundi came and we had a very nice weekend with him. He decided to take the GSM concept back to Burundi. We came to an agreement with him that he will come back to Kenya when you will also be in Kenya.

Letter to James Opiyo, August 1995:

Dear and precious James, I wonder what we will do when we go to heaven. I hope the rest is long and the laughter is a lot. I personally want to see your face with the smile I saw in the very beginning days of our relationship. The Lord took us to the door of tragedy. You and I walked in. This is a heart ministry. Many don't want it. They want everything superficial, with professional distance for personal privacy. Bury them, marry them, but don't know them. My Lord and my God, James, we knew them all. It must have been the way Jesus felt, for He knew us.

We are sending Faraday a ticket to come to Kenya and Uganda when we are there this fall. I want you to really think about what you are going to do to train him, and have him train you. There needs to be much interchange between the two of you and very deep time of prayer and spiritual bonding between you, Faraday, Nicholas, and John. As you well know, we are action people, but the spirit must be touched deep inside by that bonding prayer. Faraday needs your arms around him. He needs to weep. He will pretend he doesn't. You will need to hold him and make him cry. He is tired. He has burned in hell by the Nigeria soils. You will minister to him. Wash his face. Wash his feet. Hold him like a boy. Ponder my words, James, for there is a great truth in them.

To Faraday and Angela, Nigeria, written during the International Day of Prayer:

I have a very important word of the Lord for you. The word, specifically, is to you, Faraday, and then through you, to many, "Do not strut as the ministries of others, or as others have strutted before Me," sayeth the Lord, "But put your feet on a new soil. You must walk each and every step that you take in My Name. I will look after you, and I will look after the ministry in

Nigeria. You will see Me as never before. You will see Me as if you have never laid eyes on Me. All pride will become dust under your feet. Your submission must be final in the days to come." Thus, sayeth the Lord.

Another letter to Faraday in 1995:

According to your wife, and according to what I see in your letter, I believe that your list of things to do in this world is too long, Faraday. I have learned never to operate off lists, but to operate in the small things I can do one day at a time. When you exhaust yourself with endless work, you have missed the point of the simple tasks of loving your neighbor as yourself. Never make your list more important than the person you are working with at the moment. A busy mind brings disaster to this work. It is a peaceful heart and a quiet mind that brings the greater healings. When people meet with a saint, Faraday, they must give up positional Christianity.

Always remember that the Lord spent His nights alone in prayer. He did not entertain others, He did not do ministry. He spent the nights alone in prayer. He was not dependent; but He was with His Father. I don't believe Jesus made intercession the way we do. I believe He was just glad to be with His Father, and in that time alone, He was strengthened for the next day. Never, under any circumstances, can you do this work without that time.

In the midst of all of the travel, counseling, training, teaching, and daily decisions to be made, I had to gather a team of people who would go to Africa, a balanced team of men, women and children.

Xavier Rueda was Chairman of the GSM International Board when James Opiyo signed the first agreement with Good Samaritan Ministries to take this work to Africa.

First of all, I found that no one from the board wanted to go, but I am a persistent person when I feel it is the Lord who is leading us. Xavier was thinking, as he sat at our board meeting, "I do not want to go to Africa!!"

No other board members volunteered, and the Board went into prayer as to who should go. After a time of prayer, both

Bettie and Jackie Wilhelm indicated that Xavier was called to go, representing the board.

He quickly responded, "I can't go to Africa." He gave three reasons why he could not make the trip. I asked if God removes the three reasons you gave, will you go to Africa? He responded, "Yes, I will go." Within one week, two of his reasons were removed, and the third was removed during our stay in Africa.

Xavier shares, "I was called to go to Africa. On the day we departed Nairobi to come back to Oregon, James Opiyo indicated that the high point of this trip for him was my coming to Africa because I represented the board, and it was important for the board to know the work that the Samaritans of Africa were doing, and the commitments they continued to make to keep the work alive."

Development is an inner choice. It is the responsibility of each person to have a teachable spirit, to remember we know little, and there is much we can learn. Development does not necessarily depend upon talents; it depends on the use of them. It depends on the relationship gifts that we will have if we stay on the hard road that leads to life. Would you be willing to give up all you know in order to learn what you do not know? Would you be willing to walk away from the clutter of your mind and your life's experiences, and into a road of faithfulness and love that will lead you to where you must go? Development! Development! Development! This will never be a "feel good" ministry!

CHAPTER 16

MISS APRIL

Miss April -- Seven Years Old
~by Grandma Bettie

When I have laid my head to rest,
One child will lie upon my breast.
Funny little freckled face, crinkle,
Laughter, pout, or frown –
Nothing can make April's spirit stay down.
Tragedy struck from the very start,
To cut down her soul and her heart.
When she saw the shadows of sorrow's doom,
Her precocious look lit up the room.
Mother of nations and child who is ageless
Lead forth with honor to develop the pace
That one day may benefit the whole human race.
Someday, my darling, I'll lay down my life
And send you to conquer and win, o'er the strife.
Jesus, feed this Lamb.

Written July 11, 1991
April, Grandpa Jerry and Grandma Bettie
Traveling in South Dakota on the way to Wounded Knee

I was in the room when April was born. April's neck was caught in the birth canal. She had to be yanked out hard. Her mom, Laura, was courageous. Her dad, Mark, was excited. When April was born they wrapped her in a blanket and handed her to Mark. He proceeded to carry her around the sleeping hospital. It was 3:00 a.m. My neck had a crook in it for two years.

April saw her dad until she was 4 years of age. During those beginning years of her life, he was a severe drug addict and alcoholic. He had to watch her a lot because Laura worked to make the living. She invested in property so Mark could not put his hands on money to use for drugs. It was a rough beginning.

When Mark was into drugs, guns and dealers, Laura divorced him. She was so thin and worn; I took her to the Holy Land and baptized her in the Jordan River. Grandpa Jerry babysat April and her little sister, Melissa, while we were gone.

When April was 11 years old, she and her family lived near Lincoln City, Oregon, in a fifth-wheeler (camper). There were four children. They each had a box for their clothes.

In school that year, April did well. She received an award from President Clinton for scholarship, and several athletic awards. She took and finished Level I Counselor Training in Beaverton. She also took Intensive Training, learning to be a Samaritan, a person of action, who could profoundly touch the world with God's love.

When my aunt died and left me $17,000, I earmarked that for traveling opportunities for our grandchildren. They did their part to raise funds as well.

I decided to take April to Kenya and Uganda in 1995. I was leading a team of nine from the U.S. She would be gone three weeks and she would miss school. I did not even fly home with April, as I was in Africa for two months, from October 17th until December 17th.

She was the youngest to travel with us, in fact, the youngest I ever took to Africa. She got on the plane like a champion and held up well. When we got to Kenya, landing in Nairobi, we spent a couple of days seeing the work there, particularly in the slums, and a nursery school. She held her hand a little bit out of the car window; then, suddenly, someone grabbed and stole her wristwatch. She was really shaken up.

Nicholas Okungu, the National Director of GSM-Kenya, took a special interest in watching over and protecting April during the rest of the journey. In fact, as he and his wife were childless, she became as a spiritual child to him, and he became as a spiritual father. He has covered her in prayer through all of her trials up to this day.

We made many stops along the road to Uranga. April would be the first in her family, and indeed, the only one of her family, who went to Uranga, the birthplace of Good Samaritan Ministries in Africa.

April was profoundly gifted with children. When they saw April, I don't think the children saw the rest of the adults. They saw in April a friend. She was a moving force to inspire children, and trust me, the children inspired her.

The night before we left Oregon for Africa, I took April to the jail where her father was being held. He had been arrested for six robberies, two of them, bank robberies. She saw him commit a bank robbery on her television at home.

Because of this trauma, it was my desire for her to work through and find some peace. When we got to the jail, they said Mark was in "the hole," and they would not allow visitors. We sat there rather stunned and then went home, preparing to leave for Uganda and Kenya the next morning. Jerry and I had gone to see Mark several times, praying with him and ministering to him, knowing his life had tragically been destroyed by profound addiction.

In Africa, April did not hang out with the adults; she hung out with the children. She focused on her work. She was a listener, someone who played with the children and talked with them heart-to-heart. She shared experiences with them. Towards the end of the journey, April styled her hair like an African, in many braids. Africa had taken hold of Miss April and made her see the bigger picture of permanent relationship through God's inclusive love for all.

While we were in Kenya, we visited several schools and we visited the Lake Region, where there were more than 1,000 Samaritans. It was an exciting area to visit. James Osewe, the center director, was thrilled with April's visit. James had a special love of children, just like April, and he had himself come through a horrific, long period of addiction. They clicked.

I particularly remember one of the events of that visit: James presented to us the teachers and students of each grade in the school. Good Samaritan Ministries was helping to sponsor school children. James had appointed a spiritual covering for each teacher and class at the school. I was particularly impressed by two things that happened. The spiritual covering for the first grade teacher was a man who could only walk on his knees. God had provided a man who would be the same size as the children.

Secondly, James Osewe had a profound understanding of the importance of play therapy. He demonstrated all sorts of play therapy he did with the kids, so many of them traumatized by tragedies, lack, and loss. I will always remember the cardboard airplane he had made. He flew around the field wearing it. The children laughed. In the airplane, he had hidden cookies and suddenly they were shared.

After April went home, James Osewe wrote a letter entitled: "Why We Named Our School April Sweitz School" Uyoma people have welcomed many missionaries from overseas, but they never welcomed an 11 year-old. What surprised them, again, is how April Sweitz spoke to 1,200 people without fear. They wondered whether God could use an 11-year-old to be a missionary, and that is why they named the school April Sweitz Primary School. It is a historical name for Uyoma Good Samaritan Ministries' School.

James wrote, *"Due to the government of Kenya Policy of Cost Sharing, the school building, books, and other educational materials are provided by the community, and our school is for community. Our community has done a lot. They have built 12 permanent rooms, eight classrooms, headmaster office, deputy headmaster office, staff room and storeroom. They have already bought desks for 350 pupils.*

We have eight teachers and they are paid by our Kenya government so we have no problem with teacher salary.

Now what we request is a prayer for the Widows' Mite Project for April Sweitz Primary School. Most people think Widows' Mite is a small contribution, but before God, Widows' Mite is a big money and a gifted contribution."

When we returned to Uranga, April and I both planted a tree at the school. The tree she planted survived the drought. Mine didn't. The Principal was very pleased her tree survived.

We crossed over into Uganda. As I watched April from the corner of my eye, this Scripture came to me, "Never tire of doing good." Miss April did not have high energy. She had consistency and willingness to see and learn.

When we visited the school up in Masaka, it was a sight to behold. April and about 40 children were running across the fields. Running, playing, being! Is this not the Kingdom of God?

We were so excited to be at Masaka to visit the teachers, to go into the classrooms. We needed to understand most of the children had no parents, as their parents had died from AIDS.

In November of 1995, while I was still in Africa, I wrote this letter to April:

I'm so proud of you. You really held up well. You were very relational. You were a help to many people, and you were an inspiration to a lot of kids who don't have very much to inspire them. I want to thank you for making the trip. It was a dangerous thing to do. It meant risking your life; however, I believe that in the years ahead, this decision will bring healing and help to thousands of children.

I wrote to Nicholas Okungu:

You did a wonderful job with April. She had a good journey. I believe she has grown much and benefited from it. I spoke with her mother who said she is getting straight A's in school this term. That is a considerable feat considering she was gone for almost three weeks. It shows her commitment.

I saw her on Christmas day. She said, 'I'm never going back to Africa.' Then she paused a little while and said, 'At least not until later.' The videos and slides are good. She did much better in Uganda, as she strengthened and lost some of her fear. Your ministry to her was so good. Nicholas, you strengthened her faith.

I wrote to Osborn in Uganda January, 1996:

April is, I think, a changed person by the journey. It will be slow, and it will take time. She got straight A's in school despite missing three weeks.

That day at Masaka school when she played and ran with the kids, that was a beauty that none of us will ever forget; one white girl and many black children, in permanent relationship with each other.

I went down to the coast in the summer of 1996. I saw that April had grown much from the journey. She and her class collected many things for the Uganda school. I brought one box back to mail. I will put the return address: April Sweitz and her school.

I wrote to Dithan in Uganda, March of 1996:
April Sweitz is doing pretty well. She is beginning to talk more about the trip, and she is learning more. There was growth. I have seen her two or three times. We taught all the kids at her school about Africa. Papa Jerry, Judith Sellangah (Kenya) spoke at the school. April and I don't say much, but there is that deep-down understanding. I know that what occurred in Africa will affect her for the rest of her life. She is on her mission, with us, in her own way, chosen.

Her father is going to be in prison for 12 ½ years. She is ashamed of him, and it is hard, but she is a brave soul. She has already been through more than most of us would go through in two lifetimes.

In June 1996, Obuda Sylvestre, an addict in recovery, wrote:
Mama, I was really blessed during that trip with the words of encouragement you gave us at the GSM Continental Headquarters here in Kenya.

Thank God for April Sweitz. Because of her boldness, she was not afraid of the African children. Most of the children are still remembering her.

In remembrance of April Sweitz' trip to Africa, especially at Uranga, Kenya, there is a nursery school named after her, known as April Sweitz' Nursery School. This nursery was started this year. There are 70 children and two trained teachers.

Mama, pray for this, our nursery school, so it should improve in its standard of education.

While in Uganda, April and Osborn really clicked. He, as Nicholas, took a spiritual role in her life, and in that role, he has sustained her life up to this day. Later, in April's life, she became a severe drug addict. She used drugs for seven years. During that time, she also went to college and graduated. She was fighting to do well, but darkness hovered over her soul. I wrote to Nicholas and Osborn of the vast need to cover her in prayer and absolutely not to give up.

Finally, April went to a drug and alcohol treatment center. While there, Osborn Muyanja made a visit and spent half a day with her, encouraged her, and built her up. After two months of treatment, April made her way out of addiction and into recovery.

As Miss April climbed out of addictions, once again her spunk and her spirit grew. She and a friend from high school, Mike Ashmon, fell in love, and decided to get married in 2008. It was a beautiful church wedding, a traditional bride, and a lovely family event. Osborn Muyanja came from Uganda and performed the wedding ceremony with me.

Very soon April became pregnant. It was a hard pregnancy, as the doctor said there were complications in the size of the baby. They took seven ultrasounds. She and Mike had no health insurance, but they fought their way to pay their bills. Gabriella Grace was born quite healthy, quite beautiful, and truly full of God's grace.

In February 1997, I wrote to Nicholas:

Today is Sunday and April Sweitz called me early this morning. She made $45 yesterday babysitting. She has considerable babysitting employment ahead. She told me she had decided to help sponsor a student. That student would be one of John's children. It was a wonderful way to start out Sunday morning. It made grandma feel really good. April's grandfather, Bruce, her father's father (that is to say her father, Mark, who was in prison), died last week. He died in his sleep. He had been a horrendous addict, and although he was in recovery, he was not a well man for many years. Mark called me from prison immediately when he got the word. The chaplain allowed him to call again the next day. God is really working in our family and He is not finished.

In 1999, April wrote the following letter:

Hi, my name is April Sweitz. In 1995, when I was 11 years old, I got to go to Africa. I went to Africa, representing the children of the U.S., and now I would like to go again. My trip is scheduled for July of this year, but I don't have all the funding I need. The reason why I would like to go again is because I feel I am needed there. It is my responsibility to go there and help anyone in need of my help. As I said, I represented the children, and now I represent the teenagers. I go there to show people there is hope that someone like me cares for all of the people. People like me can make a difference. I had a fundraiser and gathered hundreds of clothes to bring with me. When I do go, I will give the children all of my clothes, notebooks and other school supplies. I would like to go back now, and maybe again someday so I can teach the children of our culture. The best reason to go is to be their friend and have fun with them. Thank you.

March 2002, April wrote:
Uganda and Kenya Schools
~by April Sweitz

Through a personal experience, I have developed a concern for the importance of education in other countries, particularly Kenya and Uganda, Africa. Though Africa is just another continent, and a problem to deal with, it has many issues involving education.

I believe that it is very important for every child to receive some type of education and, more importantly, a good one. It is very hard, though, to receive any type of education in Africa when there is no money, but intense interest in pursuing education. In the United States the schools are paid for by the government and are maintained through U.S. taxpayers. Most of the books, desks, teachers, and other supplies and costs are taken care of through different types of funds.

Spending several weeks visiting existing schools in Africa, I personally began to witness a lack of education there. Each day, as I passed through another city or village in Kenya or Uganda, I saw hundreds of children just roaming around the streets with no type of education being offered.

As my group and I visited some of the schools, we saw many of them were only halfway completed. Some had only partial walls, dirt floors, and even no roofs. With these conditions, it seems hard for any child to successfully receive a good education.

Without schooling there will be no future for Africa and its people. Education is very important to any country in that it leads to that country's future. Education is key to the country's success.

One of the reasons why I went to Kenya and Uganda was to go to the smaller schools and give as much aid to them as possible. As I went to each of these schools, I saw that there was one writing utensil for every five children. Paper was scarce, as well as any type of coloring utensil.

I brought with me three suitcases full of crayons, pens, pencils, markers, staples, paper. This was not nearly enough, but it helped. Any school that received any of these items was very grateful. In order to distribute these items to the students, the teachers held them and checked them out, just like a library would with books here in the United States.

For as many children as there are in Africa, there aren't nearly enough teachers to teach them. Under my grandmother's program, Good Samaritan Ministries, we sponsor many of the teachers by sending them food and rent money. We have also bought the ground and helped build schools. A lot of the children are full orphans. Unfortunately, there is not enough money to send to all of them, and so many teachers donate their time.

After I left Africa at 11 years old, I received word that two schools were named after me to show their appreciation for everything I did for them. I went to visit these schools again, along with several other schools, in 1999, at age 15. Since then, I have helped raise money for many of these schools to be completed and maintained. I currently send as much money as I can put away each month to my schools to help finance them. As well as sending money, I help fundraise for postage, books, clothes, and other supplies and send them over as much as possible.

Even though Africa is so far away, their education is just as important as ours. Just like any parent from the United States would like to see their child grow up and get an education and succeed in life, so would the parents of the African children.

With more people showing interest in the education of Africa, they too can have a successful future ahead of them.

Though Africa's lack of education is just another problem to add to everything else, it is an important issue to deal with sometime in the near future. **How long can children wait?**

When April sold her house to pay for her drug treatment programs, she gave a large donation to Good Samaritan Ministries for African education.

Today, Miss April owns a resale shop in Lincoln City, Oregon. This resale shop is for children from 0 to 5 years of age. The shop provides all necessities for those children. It is in a rather impoverished area of the state of Oregon. People can come in and trade the clothes they have for other clothes, as the children grow. There may not be much gain at the store, and some people would consider it a loss, but I would say that is the great fruit of educating a child in the way they must go.

I will never forget the last night we were in Uganda in 1995. The ten team members gathered and were asked to each give a speech. Eleven year-old April gave the last speech. It was the shortest and the most said.

"I came to Africa representing the children of the United States. I go home from Africa representing the children of Africa to the United States."

Everyone was astonished.

I end the story of Miss April with this poem I wrote in 1991:

Purpose

~by Bettie Mitchell

*The wind blew heavy on
My soul.
Threatening dire destruction
To my goal.*

*Quiet Moment. Faith renewed.
Another day as seen and viewed.
Word my song, dream, and
teach.*

*Coming close to end of time –
Chose to laugh and die to whine.
Delight my soul how many
grew.
I only thought there'd be a few.*

Thank God, Me Too!

I can only say to those who went to Africa: "Why did you go? Did you know your purpose and your bigger assignment?" Many went, there were few Miss Aprils.

CHAPTER 17

BUILDING THE CHARACTER OF TEAMS

A letter I received from John Oundo of Uranga, Kenya, December 22, 1995:

My people say, and I also agree, that you are peculiar wasungu (white man) for many come in our midst and they do not dare eating with us together. It is my strong belief that this ministry was inspired of God to reach His people who are down in the dust. It is from this dust that the Lord lifted me, and it is from this dust I want to lift people. For David said in Psalms 30, verse 3, 'O Lord Thou hast brought up my soul from the grave: Thou hast kept me alive, that I should not go down to the pit."

I compare Vonda with Issachar, a strong ass crouching down between two burdens, and he saw that rest was good and the land that it was pleasant, and bowed his shoulder to bear and became a servant unto tribute. Through dust, bumps, as a result of bad roads and bushes, I tell you, Vonda managed it.

Nancy Paul mourned our countries and I could see the burden she had with the work and the people who were doing the work. People could think that Nancy was attacked by flu, but the Lord told me when we were at Ragengi that she was being loaded with the work of GSM in Kenya. I joined her in prayers and before we left each other the next morning, I saw the hand of the Lord. Nancy called me back and gave me $50 to buy a cloth with this money. I bought a very nice long black trouser and a brown jacket. Nancy has a merciful heart.

Jane, as a priest, will always be remembered with the remarks she made at Ragengi. I could see Jane in spiritual angle how much she was touched when a young boy sang and led everybody in shedding tears. Lisa is another different widow. Our country's widows wait to be helped with food and materials. Unlike what we know here, Lisa has given to help our widows. May our Lord uplift her and add her more for His own glory.

I cannot forget the star of the trip. This was granddaughter to Mama Bettie, April. April, I tell you until now; our people never believed that April is 11. A person of 11 years of age is a very small person with April comparatively. I have appointed April to be International Director of Children.

John Nichols was very busy with sponsorship part. John was really touched when we visited Ndiwo Primary School. It was a need experienced for John, and really, God is going to use John to do many things.

I lastly want to share a little about Eric. I first met this man in Beaverton when all the directors were there for training. Eric is someone who knew how to build relationship. He was very cooperative, and could sometimes drive both Alick Malama and me back home. I drove in his van to the falls and lastly, to the family camp.

When Eric was here in Kenya, God forced me to say something before him and Mama Vonda. I said, "When God shall bless me with a baby boy, I shall name him after Eric, and when God shall bless me with a baby girl, I shall name her after Vonda."

God did a miracle, and on the 17th of December, 1995, the promise was fulfilled because a baby boy was born and his name is Eric.

Xavier's Journal – 1995 Journey to Africa

Xavier Ruweda, who was the GSM International Board Chairperson at the time, shared his journal of his first journey to Kenya and Uganda. Nine of us from the United States traveled with him. I use parts of his journal because it is fresh, written on the spot. In addition to those coming from the United States, three Internationals joined us: Faraday Iwuchukwu and Linda Tokuta from Nigeria, and Jeremie Ndayishimiye from Burundi.

4:14 p.m. – Nakuru Bettie dedicated the new office and presented a plaque made in Palestine "The Only Way to be Right is to Give Up Being Right."

We met in a classroom with about 40 present. Bettie gave a lesson on the need to forget how important we the leaders are. We need to make those we serve more important than ourselves.

10/23/95 We visited the site of the accident that had occurred near Kisumu in 1992. A bush of the crown of the thorns has been growing at the site.

10/24/95—Uranga Richard Omollo was one of the first intercessors for Bettie in Africa when the ministry first came.

Bettie presented a gift of $150 to Richard and he "jumped" for joy. His gratefulness was genuine. Bettie praised Richard for his work with the children, and then said, "Richard, I could look at your face for five years because I love you." Heartfelt laughter and joy brought smiles to all.

Parents presented a skit of Bettie Mitchell healing a troubled person. After healing, as portrayed by a parent, Bettie rejoiced and danced. The Parable of the Good Samaritan was done next with the Prayer of St. Francis being sung between scenes. "Whatsoever you do to the least of my brothers, so you do it unto me." Each scene was chorused by the song, The Prayer of St. Francis.

A GSM meeting was held outside. The International GSM Award was given to Pastor Dixon Oloo for Courage. In the beginning, he was the only pastor to acknowledge GSM and the importance to the church. Pastor Dixon never went to school, but his children will be sent to college. Dixon did not realize he was to receive the award. Tears welled in his eyes.

Today was a great day. Tears of joy welled in everyone's eyes by all the gratefulness shown for the teaching. Love had opened the door of self-respect and purpose that Bettie brought to the Luo Tribe. This changed their lives forever.

10/25/95   What GSM has done for Kenya is to change the way people live. Relational living, purpose, and meaning are now a part of life. Control was released (empowered) to these people to learn themselves, and that is the difference. After Eric told us of his pet python Joshua renamed Eric the Snake Man. A water storage tank is Joshua's dream (top priority). Water quality is bad. It is brownish in color. Cost for the tank is estimated to be $1,500.

10/27/95   Pastor Jeremie Ndayishimiye arrived today. He just completed Bible school, is married, and has one child. He and his wife had to sell all of their household possessions to raise $600 for travel expenses to come to Kenya for several months of training.

10/28/95   Question: Why do we visit these centers?

Answer: EACH CENTER IS ANXIOUS TO HONOR BETTIE MITCHELL AND SHOWS HER THE PROGRESS THEY HAVE MADE. IT IS IMPORTANT TO ENCOURAGE

THEM FOR THEY SACRIFICE A LOT TO DO THE WORK OF A SAMARITAN. THERE ARE MANY PROGRAMS BEING UNDERTAKEN AND STARTED ON FAITH, AND WITHOUT FUNDS, BECAUSE THEY ARE NEEDED TO HELP OTHERS. ***NOW WE HAVE COME TO LEARN FROM THE AFRICANS WHAT IT MEANS TO BE A SAMARITAN!***

The people want more than material things. They need to have fed their three areas of humanity: soul, spirit, and body. Bettie and her team came in 1987 and taught. She comes again to learn from those she taught. The Bondo Center office was dedicated. The office was one room, 12 by 12, with signs on each wall, reading, "Client," "Secretary," "Library," and "Director." Nicholas Okungu, National Director of Kenya spoke. There are 36 centers in Kenya. Nicholas called the nine Coordinators up to meet the team. Without Coordinators, this Center could not have grown. Peace, love, unity is the GSM objective. The main work is counseling for healing of soul and spirit. Owimbe Center changed to Jerry Mitchell Center. James Osewe has little education, but is powerfully gifted by God. Also present at the reception was the doctor who provides medical services at Uyoma Center.

Reflection: *I truly believe that GSM was not begun by God for work in Oregon, but was begun for the people of Africa. Someday, it will be Africa who will lead the world to the Kingdom of God.*

10/29/95 James Osewe was not a Christian when Nicholas first met him. Nicholas told James that if a person is walking in darkness and the sun is shining behind him, he doesn't continue walking in the dark, but makes a U-turn, changes direction, and walks towards the light. Nicholas did not say anything more to James Osewe, but turned and walked away. James thought about it all night, and because Nicholas did not preach at him, like most pastors, he decided to become a Christian and a Good Samaritan.

Uyoma District has over 1,000 GSM members. There are three Directors. Since the District is so large in area, Membership Coordinators have been assigned to help the three Directors. The Coordinators are highly educated. Most are retired teachers, government workers, trained in humility to serve the ministry. They were trained to be humble and to work in humility. The work they do is tremendous. 300 to 500 members for each Coordinator. This concept of Coordinators was James Osewe's.

10/30/95   Bettie began to give a teaching after Nicholas spoke. Nicholas was standing at her side translating and mimicking Bettie's gestures. Bettie said she felt sick and laid on the floor. Nicholas translated and also laid on the floor. We all thought it was part of the teaching Bettie was giving. As it turned out, Bettie had actually passed out, and Nicholas, not wanting to panic the people, just reached out for Bettie's hand and prayed for her. About three minutes passed without a word spoken, and then Bettie came out of her faint and continued the teaching.

10/31/95, Day 15   Today we leave Kenya for Uganda. The town of Jinja is on Lake Victoria. The area is more tropical and more developed than cities in Kenya. It is cleaner and there is landscaping and island turn-arounds. There are 50 members in this Center, and there were 200+ people to meet us. **Osborn told the story of how the Center was started. A body of a boy was found in the Nile River after it had been there for three days. Jeremiah Okwaare, who later began the center, called all of the churches in his area to help transport the body to the boy's home, which was 300 miles away. No one would help. He finally called Osborn, who quickly came to his aid. A coffin was brought, and Osborn helped to take the body back to the boy's home. Jeremiah was so touched by Osborn's actions that he asked why. "This is the Samaritan way," replied Osborn. Jeremiah began a GSM center on the actions of this incident. It is what we do, the way we live that influences people.**

11/1/95 Wobulenzi Center. The sponsored Children's Choir sang a version of the Parable of the Good Samaritan. They also sang about their feelings of Bettie Mitchell for bringing work to the area, "Samaritan, you mean so much to me. Samaritan is where I find my joy. Samaritan is my home. "There were over 200 people attending. **Osborn addressed the group, "We learn from one another. We have come to learn from you."**

11/2/95 Kiwangala, Masaka. We met in a church building with no roof. A sense of humor was quickly displayed by the Master of Ceremony's comment about awnings and sunshine.

Muslims, Catholics, government officials, all were present at this meeting because they are Samaritans. In 1990, there were four Samaritans. In 1995, there are 200, plus an addition of 126 children. The number one Samaritan is the Muslim man who allowed Osborn and the sick people with AIDS to stay on the floor in his store building at night.

The people of Kiwangala, Masaka, do not have the sparkle in their eyes, as did the people in Kenya. The suffering experienced in this area is great. Over half of the adults are dead, leaving many orphans. Also, many of the children are infected with HIV AIDS virus. The spirit and effort they put out, however, is unsurpassed. They are rebuilding their community of Samaritans. Even the local Catholic community has embraced the work GSM is doing. Neighbor works with neighbor without regard to denomination. Not even in America do we have pastors working with pastors to make relationships better.

10/5/95 Kampala. We held a seminar at church for all. The problems Jesus had training the 12 Apostles: They wanted to know the source of Jesus' power, "Lord, who are you?" Jesus does not answer directly. "Who do people say that I am?" Jesus is trying to get them to think. Bettie Mitchell is trying to get Africans, Ugandans to think. The apostles learned by Rote, the same as Africans, and Jesus was trying to get them to think. What are you learning? "If you are in school with Jesus, He is going to test you to see who you are following."

"If you want to be a follower of mine, you must be like a little child." Bettie asked twelve men to sit on the altar facing the congregants. Bettie went to the back and picked up a little boy. She put the little child in front of the men. "Big men wanting big results using powerful persuasion? No! Humble yourself!" The little boy, whom Bettie put facing the men was standing alone. He didn't move. "Why do you think this little boy is still here? Remember this child whenever you start to think you are above others. To be a Samaritan, you must be as little as this little child." Five minutes went by, and the child was still standing where Bettie put him. "Isn't it amazing this child is still standing there? This child was teaching all of us what it means to stand in the Kingdom of God. When we teach, we must be as this little

child. Make ourselves plain and simple." Bettie picked up the child and took him back to his mother.

Jeremie Ndayishimiye of Burundi, Africa

It is important to tell the story of Jeremie.

Burundi was the scene of horrendous genocide in 1993, when the first democratically elected president was assassinated and more than 200,000 were massacred out of a population of about five million. Few families of this small country, about the size of Maryland in the U.S., were spared from having some family member killed. Jeremie lost four sisters and many other relatives.

Jeremie accepted the Lord as his personal savior in 1980, at the age of 14. Jeremie said, "I still remember that day. The Lord forgave my sins and Jesus Christ came into my life."

By 1984, Jeremie was preaching the gospel all over Burundi, and in 1987, with another Christian brother; he trained 25 young people to work as evangelists. Jeremie had just completed his secondary technical school of business and administration.

In the year 1994, Jeremie founded the Christian Deliverance Ministry, and obtained registration with the government. He also married Jeanne.

After being thwarted from using several scholarships due to lack of recommendations, the Lord finally opened the door for more training. Jeremie received two scholarships in 1994; one from the U.S., and the other from Victory Bible in Kisumu, Kenya. Jeremie and Jeanne went to Kenya.

It was in Kisumu that Jeremie and Jeanne talked to George Kadega, one of the teachers at the school who was familiar with Good Samaritan Ministries, as he had been one of the first trainees at Uganda. George introduced Jeremie to GSM, and Jeremie and Jeanne, along with their first baby, Carlene, went to Uranga for the Continental Training and to stay for a period of time to gain more training and understanding of this ministry.

"We had very hard training, but it was the plan of God, and we obeyed him. We went back home to start the work of GSM in Burundi in March of 1996. Many people told us at the time, don't go back to Burundi because it was very hard to stay in our nation. If you have somewhere you can stay wait for a good time. We have seen God protect us for His purpose. Through hard times, God has trained our hearts to love other people, to love even our enemies, even if that is very hard."

In the beginning, Jeremie worked together with brother Gordien. He sent Gordien to Uranga for training. Gordien then became one of the key leaders in Burundi. Since then, Burundi has sent many to Kenya for the three months of training. The ministry of GSM has expanded dramatically. Now, most of the country is covered.

God helped them to train pastors, evangelists, leaders of churches and different tribes. **"Our vision and call was to train and teach people that they may work for God in every situation."**

Jeremie says, "God has helped me forgive the hindrances to my training, and to ask forgiveness for every mistake I have made for lack of teaching. I remember, after my Bible studies in Kenya, I went back and I asked for forgiveness for the situation we had passed in Emanuel Church. That was very good for the leaders of the church."

Jeremie has become known for his work of reconciliation in Burundi. His example of forgiveness and his ability to teach others the benefits of forgiveness and humility were, and will continue to be, an avenue through which God works to bring healing to Burundi. So devastated by war and destruction, he speaks boldly for healing as a nation and as a people.

Jeremie was invited to attend a Conference of Reconciliation in Nairobi, and also in the United Kingdom. He said of these experiences, "When I can give my contribution to restore peace in our country, and also in our region, it is a good time."

May all of us be able to say with Jeremie, "In all situations, I have seen God." Things can be hard, but God is able and He is over all situations, even genocide and war.

While in Uranga, Jeanne delivered a new baby. By God's grace, we collected enough money after their training, to fly them back to French-speaking Burundi.

Since the time of meeting Jeremie, he has embraced his whole country. He is recognized as a leader by the government of Burundi and the President. He has gone on to spend much time in the United States and other areas, ministering to and bringing Burundian people through a reconciliation process. He feels he is called to all Burundians, and that GSM bring the truth that will reconcile all the people.

As I went to Africa for two months, and as the journey involved not only many people going with the team, but also the foreigners and Internationals meeting with us, it stretched me greatly to be able to give the quality of training time for the development of the key leaders who would go on to influence the ministry in Africa.

I asked Nancy Paul to be in charge of the U.S. team, and continued to meet, day after day, the challenges of developing the Spirit of Samaritans, the Spirit of Christ among all the people.

It was hard for me to recognize and eventually accept the fact that many would go to Africa, but few would receive The Call to keep the burning fire of passion alive. My hope was all would become fellow Samaritans, together, followers of Jesus the Christ.

CHAPTER 18

WE WENT ON

As the rest of the team left for the United States, James Opiyo, Vonda Winkle, and I flew to Dar Es Salaam, Tanzania. We were beginning the second part of our longer journey to Tanzania, Malawi, Zambia, and South Africa.

Our plane was four hours late. When we arrived at the airport in Dar Es Salaam, Samuel Kitwika was not there. We looked and inquired, and we hung around the airport for three more hours. We decided to take a cab and find a place close by to spend what was left of the night. In the morning, we went back to the airport, continuing to inquire.

We did not find Samuel Kitwika for two and a half days because he had an old schedule, and did not read the last letter I sent carefully enough.

After two days, we decided to make our way to Morogoro, and see if we could locate Samuel. To refresh the team, Bob McGill and Gary Metternich were joining us in Tanzania as part of the team. They were already in Morogoro waiting for us.

There is a funny story about our time at Dar Es Salaam. By this time, I was just about at the end of my rope and I said to James and Vonda, we're going to go out to eat and I'm going to have a drink. James had a fit. He was sitting in the front seat with the cab driver. I also said we were going to a nice restaurant along the beach. James had a bigger fit, and the cab driver said, "You'd better give her what she wants!" Thus, the one great time of breathing a sigh of relief and just resting and enjoying ourselves healed the tension and made things a lot better. I still tease James about that day. He understands me and we are in total agreement that we did the right thing.

As we developed the ministry in new countries, I understood that the development process could take up to seven years. We had to, first of all, develop the people who would be in charge of the work. We had to develop our understanding of the country, the culture, and the teams. Both sides, theirs and ours, had to become relationally aware

of one another, and at all times and in all seasons, uphold both sides in prayer.

Each country had a national director and each of those directors had different talents, experiences and unique visions. We weighed this together and found a place where things could come together well for each country.

One of the hard questions always for me has been, are we equitable in our funding? Are we equitable in our encouragement to each country and the Samaritan servants?

After finding Bob and Gary, we visited various projects. One that was interesting to me was in a clinic immediately after the birth of a baby. I found out that African babies are born white and turn black within an hour or two after their birth.

Bob and Gary had to make a lot of adjustments. They had never been to Africa, and they didn't know a great deal about Tanzania. You can imagine that African culture can be very confusing and often disturbing to our expectations. **Are we supposed to be like one another, or are we to like one another?**

The Lord arranged bonding among us to occur. We took a long road trip across Tanzania together. We stopped at certain destinations along the way, including a game park where we spent the night.

Our goal was to go to Mbeya. We loved the region. We saw fabulous education, places where young people could really truly develop. We saw the work that was possible when Tanzanians believed in it, organized it and paid the price of making it happen. I personally developed a lifetime relationship with two brothers, Adam and Benjamin in that area.

We left for Malawi by car. When our team arrived at the border of Malawi, it was late at night and the border was closed. Bob was able to rouse someone and they opened the border so we could go through. There were two very serious problems. The first problem was that they wanted to know how much money I had. I was not willing to reveal that information, but a guy with a machine gun looked at me. In a very quiet voice, a whisper almost, I told the man the amount. Then they announced this aloud.

The second problem was even more serious. We were supposed to be met by James Kabvalo, our Director of Malawi, and he was not there.

James Opiyo arranged a bus for us and we headed out on the road. Finally, in the dead of night, two cars were approaching us. James Kabvalo was rushing to meet us. He had been greatly delayed by vehicle problems and was desperate to find us.

Malawi is a long, thin country. It has one major paved road that goes from the very north to the very south. It has one major body of water, Lake Malawi, and a population estimated to be six million.

Our road was long and tough. It was extremely hot and Malawi had suffered drought for three years. The riverbeds were dry. People were trying to dig for water near the riverbeds. One morning, just outside a place where we were going to teach, a water truck came. A child ran with a cup in his hands and got some water. The truck driver did not see the child and ran over the little boy who was about six. Bob McGill and Vonda were called immediately to administer first aid to him. His pulse left and he died. That was the beginning of our day. We encouraged our workers. We knew we must help them make it into an active Samaritan life. Immediately after the little boy's death, we were in a room with 13 widows and all of their orphans. We all gave a special collection, the Samaritans and us, to help some of them. We saw so much heartache everywhere. (See Vonda's poem, page 374.)

The Kabvalo's lived in Mzuzu. It is fairly centrally located and a region of much beauty. We spent four days in Malawi before heading to the capital, Lilongwe, to fly to Lusaka, Zambia. During those four days, we met many interesting people. We met with children, and saw Kabvalo's passion for small children's education and for the widows and orphans. We enjoyed the hospitality of their home and we continued to develop our understanding that each country in Africa is unique. Malawians have a sense of spiritual freedom. Sometimes religion tried to destroy that freedom. The Malawians do best in their long, narrow country, meeting with one another along the road, and recognizing their dependency on one another as a people, as a nation. We were very satisfied by our time in Malawi. James

Kabvalo was the right man in this season for the development of the ministry.

We flew into Zambia and were met by Alick Malama and his family. We stayed with the Malama's while in Lusaka. We traveled considerable distances to different parts of Zambia, and met in different regions with people who were Samaritans developing unique work that spoke highly of what could be done.

I personally found Zambia more developed. A sense of unity in the country was there. Neither Malawi nor Zambia had been involved in wars in their modern history, and both countries have a strong, free government.

Alick Malama is known and valued by the government leaders of Zambia. He has a wide outreach of influence on others. He and his wife were passionate for Christian education for poor children. They have developed some significant schools.

We met with Andrew and Patricia Kayeski in the Copper Belt. They were an extraordinary couple, trained in the medical field, and absolutely committed to the AIDS victims and to their survivors. They were highly capable of making significant action happen.

We went on and met Maggie and Joseph Chikumbi in Kasembe. Both Joseph and Maggie had been afflicted with Polio. Joseph had one shortened leg. He had problems walking, but he was mobile. Maggie had to walk with a brace, crutches, and great effort. They had five children.

The Chikumbi's were people who did not give into self-pity. They did not get aid from anyone, and they found ways to support and develop their family. Alick and the team encouraged Maggie in her development of a school, which provides education in the region for children through sixth grade. Maggie was the principal of the school.

One of the things I will never forget about Zambia was Maggie Chikumbi lying on the floor, scrubbing her floors. Joseph, in order to better himself, went on to Bible College. I found in Zambia, a spirit that is needed. It reflects the Lord the healer, and the Lord the friend.

We were pretty exhausted by the time we got to South Africa. We stayed in South Africa five days.

David Wango, who had written to us in 1994, met us at the airport in Johannesburg. When we left the airport, we traveled on a very fast freeway to Pretoria. In a van full of people we didn't know, we had a severe blowout. I immediately got out of the vehicle and flagged down a car so we could go into Pretoria and wait for the vehicle to be fixed. It was important for us to rest.

The driver had no spare tire and no jack. It took four hours to locate a spare tire and a jack, then the spare tire didn't fit and the jack broke.

Near Pretoria, we visited the black township of Mamelodi, a township of cardboard and shacks, a township where Good Samaritan Ministries had developed a nursery school for a large number of children.

James, Vonda and I were deeply impressed with South Africa. It was not a backward country; it was a forward country.

David Wango had formed a Board of Directors, headed by Pastor Willie Booysen of the Pretoria Elim Christian Church. Pastor Willie, a Dutch Afrikaner, was committed to aiding each ethnic group in the community. **He saw, in the passion and the possibility of The Call, exactly what was needed to change the direction of the needy to the servant-hood of many.**

David Wango, from Kenya, had developed a team: two Mormon Ugandans, and Moses from Zimbabwe.

I must say that David was the founder, but I must also say that he was weakening from terrific emotional problems and, in many ways, he became like a lost child. We went on to send him to Kenya for training and to Uganda to meet with Osborn.

We had become tired, bedraggled children. As we were in South Africa, there was a strong birth of relationships. Some heard The Call, many knew the ministry. The Call still goes forth. Willie Booysen is still with Good Samaritan Ministries even unto this day and the saints proved faithful to learn the power of love and genuine sharing.

Back we flew to Kenya, first landing in Mombasa, where again, we spent four days training educators from many regions of Kenya. Vonda and I took our place with the educators. James Opiyo and I reached deeper levels of conflict and resolution as we continued to learn to work together, two stubborn, hard rocks rubbing against each other. Much growth. Tremendous breakthrough, great blessing!

On February 8, 1996, I wrote to Alick Malama in Zambia:

Since I have returned home, I have written 650 letters, each one of them personal letters. You can imagine that the work has really piled up. It has been a great problem. I am still working my way through the letters to your country.

I wrote a letter to Alick and Selena Malama May 21, 1996:

One of the policies of Good Samaritan Ministries needs to be, "Never do anything for someone that they can do for themselves." Don't believe people every time they cry, for they cry often for money; and seldom are they really truly absolutely grateful for what God gave them, which is true forgiveness and the acceptance they need to survive. If we love our life and if we love our circumstances, then God can be the Master, and He will lead us with leading strings of love.

Again, on June 14, 1996, I wrote to Alick and Selena Malama:

Today, the Lord gave me a teaching that is KEY. After Jesus was baptized and received His relationship with the Father, the second personal relationship He recognized was with Satan. He went out into the wilderness and developed His strength against Satan. This was His KEY to where weakness could be in the ministries among us. Do WE develop our strength against the Tempter?

June 14, 1996, I wrote to Joseph Chikumbi in Zambia:

Good Samaritan Ministries are the field workers. We are out in the field digging and working alongside the people. We all go to our respective churches, but the work of our lives for Jesus is out where the needs really are. We are hard workers. We don't cave in, but ask for the hardest tasks. Believe me, the Father will give them! Always remember, it is no longer your life to be lived, but you are doing His work and using His name, and you are doing the things He will have you to do. Also, remember that Jesus has never changed since He was here on earth. His work is the same as the work He did then.

CHAPTER 19

PAPA JERRY AND MAMA BETTIE

October 12, 1995, I wrote a letter to Arthur Davies in Sierra Leone:
I'm highly pleased, Arthur, with your integrity, with your small beginning, and your willingness to dig deeper and find out what it means. There are many who read Scripture; there are very few who stop to implement it. The Lord Jesus cries out, "Every African, a fellow Samaritan!"

August 22, 1996, I wrote to Grace Kirya in Uganda:
James Opiyo was in a very bad road accident in Kenya, he and five other Samaritans, including his brother. The car was demolished. James was in the hospital for one week with four broken bones in his arm and hand, and three broken ribs. He was knocked unconscious for 36 hours, and they thought he was dead. By God's grace, he is healing and the others were only wounded enough to keep them inside and resting for several weeks. There was a drunken Mutato driver who crossed the lane and hit his vehicle head on. He was able to swerve slightly, or they all would have definitely been killed. Even the wheels came off the car. The station wagon now looks like a coupe. Dear God in Heaven, things are scary.

Old Lucy died. She literally cried herself to death over the accident. It completely broke her that "her James" was hurt. However, the Lord comforted her, and she had a vision before she died. She reported to everyone that Grandfather William and James had come to her bedside and prayed with her. She died very peacefully and the funeral was July 31st at Uranga.

In 1996, my husband Jerry and I went alone to Sierra Leone, Nigeria, Egypt, Jordan, India, and Pakistan.

February 26, 1996, I wrote to William Mbina of Uganda:
In your letter, you talked about the need for a place to teach. I want you to know that the Lord did not have a place to teach. He used the places that were available. I have found so often that people are looking for financial answers to spiritual questions. I want you to ponder my answer very deeply. Are we willing to teach anywhere that we are: under a tree, in a borrowed home, on a front porch, even in our own bedroom? I want you to know that I began Good Samaritan Ministries in one room in our house. I worked in that one room for five years. It was agonizing work, as often 10 to 12 people came to be taught, to be counseled, and to be encouraged. My husband and I gave our whole house unto the Lord's word.

June 3, 1996, I wrote to John Kajjabwangu of Kampala, Uganda who served as a board member there. (He really connected to Papa Jerry.)
I will always see you bending over and washing the front porch at Osborn's mom's house. God bless you. Continue to serve. Share your meals and live as a great friend of Christ Jesus and a wonderful fellow Samaritan. Be a deep encouragement to your wife. Don't just pray a little for her; pray deeply and from the heart. Let her weep sometimes, because sometimes she needs it, John. Be compassionate and understanding of her fears.

From the Journal of Papa Jerry Mitchell
(Written to his students at a Beaverton public school.)

Sierra Leone

As soon as you landed, you knew this time was different. People were getting off at the back of the plane also; either way, you were faced with 20 steps down to the runway and an overwhelming blanket of heat and mugginess envelopes you. Beads of perspiration came from every pore you possess. I was dressed way too warmly with a sweatshirt and a jacket. It took $150 to get our party and our luggage on the airline bus to the ferry.

We arrived at the ferryboat landing to find that they had landed it wrong, and people hurrying to get off had put the ferry into the mud. It took over an hour to get turned, and landed so people and cars could get off and on properly. This is the only ferryboat running right now. Two are in for repairs. We boarded, climbed to the passenger deck, and sat and watched teeming society mill around, eat and drink from the snack bar, including the consumption of a large amount of beer by a lot of people. We finally landed and claimed our five pieces of luggage, squeezed them into a car that was on its last legs, and moved to where we would be staying.

All the time, drops of perspiration are playing chase down all parts of your anatomy, especially your neck, forehead, and face. We fell into bed around 1:00 a.m., and slept very fitfully because of new environment and new sounds. The bed had only a bottom sheet, as one needs no covers at night.

We are staying in a home belonging to a female doctor and a television filmmaker at the one and only government-controlled T.V. station in the country. It has a dining room, living room, kitchen and bathroom, with running water, and a flush toilet with a toilet seat that works.

Sunday was church at 10:00 a.m., and along with more perspiration, we were bombarded with a two-hour procession of screaming and ranting evangelists. The music was loud and accompanied by two large African drums and with very noisy, always-on-beat clapping. The African gets a louder clap than I ever dreamed it. It must be because their hands are large and can form a larger echo chamber.

We spent the afternoon touring Freetown. We went to the large cottonwood tree where all the freed slaves rested on their way uptown from the wharf. We saw the original steps they climbed in the center of town. We then went up Parliament Hill. From Parliament Hill, there is a beautiful view of Freetown and the harbor. It has ruins of fortifications. The elected Parliament is 80 members of women and men. The guards, (I didn't see any weapons) took us all through the building. We even stood where the President stands when he visits.

The electricity continues to go out in more sections of the city. It is a common occurrence, as everyone has lanterns, candles and matches handy.

The city is a street city. Everybody is on the street all day, if they aren't in school or have an indoor job. Cars are taken apart and repaired. Everyone else wheels and deals by selling any and everything from a store with barred windows and only an order area for purchases. There are other, non-secure cubicles, where people sell one or two products and then take everything home at night. Other people sell one thing from a blanket placed any and everywhere on the sidewalks along the streets.

Electricity is back on again. It was only out about three hours this time.

Today we are heading for a refugee camp housing 800 men, women, and children from their recent civil war. We are taking a lot of things to give away, including 600 individual small gift soaps.

The streets and sidewalks are bursting with activity. I forgot to include the children who walk around selling their wares. Color is everywhere. Each of the 43 tribes must have a female or male native outfit.

We went to the children's hospital, and were escorted through; a very unique hospital when compared to the ones in the U.S. There is no running water or electricity in the whole building. The second level floor has so many ankle-breaking pits in it that I negotiated my way very slowly and carefully.

"Why not put each crib over the deeper holes so nobody could fall in them?"

"We never thought of that."

The mothers sleep right next to their child's crib and do most of the needed non-medical caring.

We then visited the office of the new Government Cabinet Department. We talked extensively with the head of the Women's and Childrens' Department, or better known as Gender Affairs. A wonderful, intelligent woman, with an eye for the future, was in charge. She explained about money contracted out for the water and electricity at the hospital. The money was gone, but the job wasn't done.

Our time at the Displaced Camp was gut wrenching; children were everywhere with absolutely nothing. If I had given a toy, we'd have been mobbed. We both talked at a gathering and my hand puppets were a pleasing sight and something for them to try their skills.

Rules at the camp included no begging on the street, and respect for each person and their belongings. As we had brought bars of soap to give them, several of the children started eating the bars because they smelled so sweet.

We then visited a radio station where Bettie was interviewed about Good Samaritan Ministries.

Next, we went to the office of the Mayor, a robust, grey-haired woman, of Freetown. I could have stayed in the woman's office several more hours. They were air- conditioned. Just to sit and have droplets not play tag down your face is a wonderful sensation. Bettie and this woman talked with a few side comments from me, and our Sierra Leone Director, Arthur Davies.

We then visited a courtyard of the city's government building. This had been given over to the street kids of Freetown. They have teachers and athletic instructors. We talked again. I talked about Isaiah Ryder and his street-gang habits that prevail, even if he is a millionaire several times over. I admired the instructors greatly. It reminded me of working for Tualatin Hills Park and Recreation District, where the kids only stayed because you made their time worthwhile and they wanted to stay. This was an all-boy group with different levels of gang leaders.

Incidentally, Freetown is built on red rock. It goes down quite a ways from the views of the street repairs underneath. Everything is dead red dust everywhere.

Today we visited two refugee camps. I wish every one of you could have accompanied me today. You kind of play games with the little ones with a tear in your eye. Incidentally, the street gang members unanimously agreed to trade places with any students in Beaverton. You could live in their shacks or sleep on the street.

Everybody and their second cousins wanted a tip. One nearby black lady stated to a group of them, "Just because they're white, doesn't mean you have to over-charge them." The whole society is based on what you can scrounge from any and everybody. I guess it's African revenge for the pillaging by Europeans of African colonies.

Let's think a few minutes about conclusions traveling in the tropics. 1) Thirst becomes all-important to overcome. Perspiration occurs constantly, and the rest of your plumbing goes on nearly 100% strike. 2) It has been raining heavily at Freetown, and you are still sweating. Afterward, even more as there is no humidity relief. 3) African culture is built on getting anything you can, any time, and under no obvious rules. 4) Unemployment is rampant, with dozens of men sitting near lumberyards or grocery stores waiting to see if they could load or unload for a small fee. 5) The tropics are an outdoor society. Anything and everything is done in the street or on the sidewalk, selling anything, repairing cars, or just socializing with everyone.

We only went to one instead of two Displaced Camps yesterday. It was one with 800 people in an old England brickyard. In fact, it is called the Brick Yard Displaced Peoples' Camp. We met with the leaders of the camp and didn't get among the people. It was kind of a Board of Directors, including four Muslim Mosque leaders. It was all business.

Later in the day, we visited a fishing village; everyone on the beach pulling in the ships as they returned and unloaded the catch. It was noisy, colorful and exciting.

It is Thursday morning and we are finally at the airport. Through all that high confusion, it would have made a great movie plot. To start with, no one woke us up. Luckily, I was sleeping lightly and waiting for the sun. Up 30 minutes and the electricity is off again! Next, the taxi driver is 30 minutes late and shows up with a girlfriend. Then, we got stopped by the police for having luggage sticking out of the trunk. Arguments ensued, bribes offered, rejected, and time marches on. We had to catch the only ferryboat at 9:00 a.m. to reach the airport, a piece of land in the Atlantic Ocean. We now find out that we need papers from the police station and hurry there. Meanwhile, Arthur wants us to pray for his mother and pick up his wife. It is now 20 minutes to 9:00, and we are still tied up in downtown Freetown traffic. The ferry landing is a long way out, and we get *there at 8:55. We need a stevedore to wheelbarrow over 200 pounds of luggage aboard and buy tickets. Luckily, the President's lady and all of her supports are going also, so we make room for many: for Army, Security, Police, and everything in between. Off the ferry, we get another cab to the airport. Then, it's time for Customs, metal detectors, interviews, $80 for overweight luggage, and $40 each for airport tax.*

Arthur Davies, Sierra Leone, West Africa

Through an unusual set of circumstances, Arthur Davies of Sierra Leone, West Africa, made the journey to Uranga, Kenya, for African Continental Training in August 1995. This was a life-changing experience of The Call and the priorities of ministry. We funded his ticket and expenses.

Bettie had asked Arthur if he was interested in accepting The Call to start Good Samaritan Ministries in Sierra Leone.

In a letter dated February 1995, Arthur said, *"I accept The Call wholeheartedly, and I promise to work with the Spirit of the Samaritan. May God be my helper."*

Arthur Davies was born in Ghana, in the City of Accra, in April of 1957. His mother and father were both Sierra Leoneans. His mother was from a middle-class Creole family. The Creole's are people from different parts of West Africa who were taken to America to work as slaves. When they were freed in the 19th Century, they were brought back to Freetown, which is how Freetown got its name.

Arthur's father was a rich man doing business in Nigeria. He came home to Sierra Leone, married Arthur's mother, and took her with him back to Nigeria.

Arthur's mother had difficulty carrying a pregnancy to term and when she did, it seemed the child would die within a few months or years. When she became pregnant with Arthur, she traveled to Ghana to live with her older sister, and she gave birth to Arthur Joko Davies. Joko is a "Yoroba" word meaning "sit down." The "Yoroba's" are from Nigeria. The mother wanted Arthur to "sit down" and not follow the other babies that had died. After eight months, Arthur's mother took him back to Nigeria

Arthur's mother believed that "Ju-Ju" would not allow her to carry a pregnancy, so when she returned to Nigeria, she went to see a witch doctor so she could keep the next child. After two years, she gave birth to another boy, and kept him until he was five years old, but fear caused her to send him to her sister in Sierra Leone. She had already sent Arthur at three years of age to live with his aunt at Freetown.

Arthur's father would not transfer his business to Sierra Leone, so in 1964, when civil war broke out in Nigeria, Arthur's mother went back to Sierra Leone alone. Arthur never saw his father again. He died in Nigeria when Arthur was 21 years old. Arthur's father had been a rich man with many trucks and buses, and he ran a hotel, but he died a poor man. Even though he had been rich, he never sent any financial support to his family because he wanted his wife to move back to Nigeria. Arthur said his father always attended Methodist church services.

Arthur's mother worked hard to support the boys and educate them. She was a very strong and highly respected member of the community in Freetown. To finish high school, Arthur had to sit for his exams twice. He failed the first time.

July of 1986, a relative invited Arthur to church. It was a new church; different than the one he had been attending. This church prayed and sang differently. He was impressed with the smiles on the faces of the people, which showed they had joy in their hearts. It seemed to Arthur that they were alive, more alive than he had ever felt. The preacher even preached differently. Arthur was so moved, that he gave his life to Jesus. Arthur now pastors a church in Freetown called The Upper Room.

Sierra Leone is an extremely poor African nation. The economic and social infrastructure is not well developed, and the serious social disorders continue to hamper economic development. Since 1991, civil war between the government and the Revolutionary United Fronts resulted in tens of thousands of deaths and the displacement of more than two million people, well over one-third of the population. Many stayed as refugees in neighboring countries that were also struggling. The conflict continued until May of 2002. Sierra Leone is slightly smaller than the state of South Carolina.

There were many continuing problems with a great number of dependent widows and orphans left from the war, as well as uncountable disabled persons, whose hands, legs and/or feet were chopped off by the rebels. Another problem facing the society is the thousands of young children who were conscripted by the Rebels and forced to kill or maim others. This has left all with psychological scars upon their young lives. This is certainly a country where the people need the comfort and counseling of Samaritans, and the healing power of the Holy Spirit.

Arthur Davies is a strong man who cares deeply about people. He has deep compassion, but he has to be very tough because of the many games played by the people in Sierra Leone. He has weathered his own tragedies. His family had to flee their house, as the rebels were coming to enter the house. They were beating and torturing as they went. He witnessed the death of his aunt, who largely raised him from the age of three on. She had run back to get something she had left and was shot by the rebels. The family house was completely destroyed by fire. His mother lost her sanity from the war. He and his wife, Elizabeth, cared for her daily until her death in 2000.

Arthur has had to endure false accusations, yet he continues to care for the people. He is a wonderful and creative teacher, often using his own brand of drama to communicate a truth. He and his family are up every day promptly at 6:00 a.m. for devotions. He is a man of prayer, and a man of the Word.

Arthur is a tough individual. He believes others must be responsible for their actions and words. He is a true Samaritan, one that has a keen sense of humor, and one that often laughs at the absurdities of life.

Arthur is an intercessor for the world. Even in the midst of one of the most savage civil wars ever, he would pray for the larger GSM family. He particularly prayed for Palestine and the work of ASTA. Arthur's heart is broken by the suffering of people.

December 4, 1996, I wrote a letter to James Opiyo in Kenya:

We did some very good things while we were in Freetown. The best was visiting the Displaced Persons' Camps where we set up a Counselor Training program for leaders, who will be going back to the villages. There were over 8,000 people in the camps. All of the religious leaders, Muslim and Christian, met together with us to set up the training programs. Arthur will be working with them weekly. It was quite a remarkable meeting because we were all in agreement. We are talking about the religious leaders from the Mosque, as well as the Christians. At the end of the meeting, we all held hands and prayed together. I believe it is probably a first for such a significant event as this. I want to say to you, James, that I believe there was a good job done in training Arthur, and that he has a feel for the spirit of the work. He seems to be a man who is well known and highly respected.

December 26, 1996, I wrote a letter to Arthur:

One thing I would warn you about, don't get too wound up in projects. Give people simple things to do and make sure they do them. Don't promise more than you are able to accomplish. **Most important in the beginning development is to do inner healing with people, and to really bring the Spirit to the worker. Many people run out to work and believe they operate in the Spirit, but there are many spirits. Always remember, above all things, we are living through the Spirit of Jesus. The Holy Spirit is not only "a" spirit, it is the Spirit of Jesus Himself. From the Spirit of Jesus, you will see great and profound fruit for which the world has awaited all these millenniums.**

From the Journal of Papa Jerry Mitchell

Nigeria

One of the customs here in Nigeria, and I'm sure most of us wouldn't like it, is bowing. It's kind of like the bowing when introduced in Japan. One bows further according to the importance of the person you are meeting. Nigeria custom is like that. Only one drops a knee to bring your head below the level of the head of the more important person. When women are introduced to me, they go completely to one knee. I'm embarrassed. The male, to me, bows about six inches to two feet. It is still embarrassing to me, but I'll get used to it.

Nigeria is a militarily controlled country, with the highest population, and population-increase percentage of all of Africa. Oil is Nigeria's main product and its claim of importance to the world. There is an ex-Nigerian playing basketball for Houston. He is now a citizen of the United States, and he represented us in the Olympics.

Faraday, our National Director in Nigeria, narrowly missed being killed in a plane crash. He was on his way from Port Harcourt to Lagos to meet us. He had a ticket and he was in a line ready to board the plane, but at the last minute, the Spirit led him to change lines and get a new ticket from another airlines. They said there was no room on that plane. He said, "Check again." They checked several times and said yes, he could have the last seat available. He met us is Lagos.

While in Lagos, we learned all 143 people on the first plane that he was originally scheduled to fly, were killed in a plane crash on the way to Lagos. This shook us all up very much as two Samaritans were killed on that plane. Faraday created a stir when we arrived at Port Harcourt. His family came to the airport to meet us, but believed Faraday was dead. His name was on the passenger manifest of the ill-fated flight. Reporters surrounded him at the airport seeking reasons or feelings he had that made him avoid the flight. In the meantime, Bettie took a picture of her namesake, Bettie Iwuchukwu. This brought down the thunder of security. The camera was taken and hustled into a private room, as we all milled around outside. Finally, the camera was brought out with an apology from the airport director as we were not in a non-photography area.

This is probably one of the greatest mornings of the trip. I got rid of 45 pounds of books, printed material, and a portable amplifier from my suitcase. We are finally getting smart with our carry-ons, as they insist on checking them, so we struggle across the runway towards the plane and the 30 steps upward. No overweight charge today. They unloaded five bags from the cargo hold and four of them were ours.

What does the tropical climate do to you, physically, mentally and emotionally?

Your body is covered with droplets of perspiration so that no clothes, tight ones, underwear or socks, will slide up without almost two people pulling them, tugging and coaxing. Your fingers, hands and wrists swell. Rings are un-moveable, and watch gets put on a looser notch. You are inclined to be a little more short-tempered, and long cuddling takes a vacation and is replaced by a pat here and there.

We awoke with no fans and lights, but to music. The people are used to entertaining themselves, so there was singing coming from every nearby home. It was like hearing four for five radio stations at a time. Nigeria is very crowded with people. The northern half is almost 100% Muslim, and the southern, almost 100% Christian.

Moving around seems to be more effort than usual. Sometimes, when I go quickly from upright to prone, I get what I call the "whirlees." The room seems to pivot counter-clockwise several times. One looks forward to his next prone time and to close his eyes. This is day nine and I'm figuring this is 2% of our 47 days, so we are 18% done with this journey right now.

We always are the first to eat and I find myself mathematically dividing with my eyes every dish by how many eaters there are, and then taking a little less than that. I'm sitting in a meeting room, looking at an audience, listening to Bettie talk. Our Director has a set of twins. They are sitting in the first row, and in the second row is a kind of Lloyd Free, who was on the 76'ers NBA team during Walton's time. All Africans look completely different from each other. They dress nicely with ties on the men. I'm not sure how this started, as I am hot in a red t-shirt.

As we head to climb a narrow stairway up to the Good Samaritan Ministries office in Port Harcourt, the electricity is out and the single banister is not fastened to the wall in half the places it should be. You start down carefully with a bad right leg. Then you discover, as you feel your way down, that the stairs are not the same width, and shock of all shocks, they are not the same height, varying from three inches to ten inches.

At Faraday's home, they have enough rooms, but the electricity is lost many times during the 24 hours. There is no running water in the house and no toilet seat. Every time the toilet is used, one pours in a bucket of water to flush it, then that bucket has to be filled from outside the home. When we arrived at Faraday's house in Port Harcourt, his twelve year-old son, Chinomnso, who was a Board Member of GSM--Nigeria, gave a welcome to Port Harcourt speech. It was a speech he wrote himself:

"Permit us to say, in the words of the Scripture, that the ministry has built many old waste places, raised up the foundation of many generations, even as it has tilled the desolate lands and they have become like the Garden of Eden, fenced and inhabited."

Then, the night was spent in prayer, praising God for deliverance and upholding the families of those who died in the plane crash. We visited one of the families that night.

Hands and fingers are really swollen. I almost had to tear my wedding ring off, or otherwise I would have had to cut it off today. I guess, with my plumbing only working once a day, no matter how much liquid goes in me, some of the liquid not flushed goes through the body's extremities. I have heat rash on the inside of both arms, but otherwise, I keep going. Today, we looked at a water hole for 5,000 people. It was mud, muddy, and muddier. It was about 15 feet long, five feet across, and probably two feet deep at its deepest. I'm using hand puppets with most of my lessons.

We were on a freeway yesterday, even part toll road off and on. The only trouble is that huge potholes, thousands of access *roads, and trailers and salespeople were everywhere on both sides of the road.*

The cars here are in advanced stages of death. They rattle, wheeze, exhale huge clouds of noxious gas, and threaten to shake themselves apart. Peugeot appears to be the main make. They all are rusting through.

Yesterday was a good day and a bad day. Which do you want to know about first? The bad—okay! I had picked up a bad eye infection in my right eye, and slightly in my left. We started antibiotic drops, but it had had an all-day head start. The good, I was named a tribe elder of the local tribe at Mbano. I was given a knit stocking hat, a shield with the word, "avoner" on it, and a walking cane of the elders with a bird handgrip. It just barely went into the suitcase.

By the time we were ready to leave Nigeria, both Bettie and I had severe eye infections. They were not responding to the medication. Since one of my eyes has a bad cataract, I'm having trouble seeing. When we woke up this morning, both eyes were matted shut.

We got more eye medication in Cairo, but we finally saw an ophthalmologist in Jordan. The inflection had somewhat cleared up by the time we reached India.

As we flew back to Lagos, Nigeria, it felt ominous flying on an airplane over the lagoon where workers strived to raise pieces of the plane and dead people from the water.

In 1998, Papa Jerry was given the Lifetime Samaritan Award by the International Board. Faraday and Angela Iwuchukwu wrote: "*We are a direct product of Papa Jerry's sacrificial living and enduring faith. We are highly proud of him. We shall write him a personal note soonest.*"

It has been very hard to get and keep a working satellite for our work in Nigeria. Faraday was never allowed a visa to come to the United States, although he applied four times. May the Lord grant mercy full measure and running over to those who have given mercy.

Papa Jerry worked hard and paid for all of his trips. I, personally, had to raise the funds for my journeys.

When we reached India, we had a bed with no mattress, only springs, and no windows and no screens. The mosquitoes almost ate us alive. Our eyes were still matted. The next day, we went to the city and bought a mattress.

CHAPTER 20

THE SACRIFICES

You will find this book full of relationships. It is a core value that we value one another, at all times, and in all seasons. The Samaritans must be linked together for individual protection and for the fruit of the whole.

I am including many letters in this book. They are fresh and pertinent. They show what was important, what was vital.

It would be easy to study the weaknesses in myself, in Good Samaritan Ministries, in the various directors from the various countries, but the Lord has strengthened us, put us together, and His strength is training and teaching each Samaritan to be accountable unto God Himself. We were all corrected. Our spirits were teachable.

In 1997, Jerry and I again found ourselves on the road to Kenya and Uganda. In each country we lived together as mutual and compatible teams. We were all lifted up and not pressed down. There was much for us to learn. You can imagine that Satan had other plans and there was always a battle, but consistently, because of our faithfulness, we saw God's strength in the battle won.

Jerry went home; and I went on to South Africa, where Scott Page met me. **We spent two weeks together in South Africa. This was a very significant journey, for indeed, our relationships were strengthened and the ministry would grow into a healthy bush.**

Scott Page was on staff as a counselor in the Beaverton office. He took the leadership of the satellite for South Africa. Scott had many problems. This journey lifted him up and gave him the encouragement he needed. I was very glad and proud to travel with him.

There was so much to learn in South Africa. We were dealing with many cultures and historic changes in the priorities of a key African country. South Africa is made up of Africans from various countries: natives of South Africa and other African countries, the English, the Asians (mostly East Indians) and the Dutch Afrikaners. Pastor Willie Booysen, a Dutch Afrikaner, had a priority for the integration of all of those cultures and, at the time of our visit, he had the largest integrated church in Pretoria.

I was met at the airport by five vehicles. The driver of one of the vehicles was the man who got us lost on our first visit to South Africa, the man I took three days to forgive. The other vehicles included the Franzsens, where we would be staying. The Franzsens were English. Of the five vehicles, I chose the vehicle of the man I had forgiven, for indeed, there was a deep and powerful relationship through the Spirit of the Lord. We went on to the Franzsen's house in Pretoria and so did many, small black children from our nursery school in Mamelodi.

Now the Franzsens lived in a very beautiful and well-organized home. They had three daughters. In their large living room, all of the small black children from Mamelodi were seated and all of the children were treated with respect. This family enormously brought joy to Scott and me. They were born for this Call and for this work.

David Robinson and Fred Langa were both still active in Good Samaritan Ministries. Although they were on a Mormon mission, they saw the hand of the Lord directing a path that was vital, not only to their own lives, but to the lives of all people. This ministry was something that became so much a part of who they were, that even unto this day in 2013, we powerfully remain friends. Eventually, each man moved to the United States. David Robinson went to the University in Salt Lake, and graduated with a Master's degree. He did not neglect Good Samaritan Ministries. He developed work in Uganda with children, widows and orphans. He makes a trip annually to Uganda, and finances this work by his passion. He lives The Call from deep within by his actions. We all had to learn our lives were to be poured out for many.

Fred Langa came to the United States. He also lived in Utah. Jerry and I visited him and his family. We remain close friends today. Fred is a person who has valued Good Samaritan, and has upheld the work. In 2013, he came to visit me at home. He sat on our living room floor. He said, "You saved my life. I was in a mess and you found an answer and set me free."

In 2002 when Good Samaritan Ministries had an International Conference in Oregon, both David and Fred came from Utah. Pastor Willie Booysen and his brother, Corrie, came from South Africa.

Excerpts and Letters, Reflections on South Africa

Letter I wrote September 14, 1998, to Pastor Willie Booysen, Chairman of Board of GSM—South Africa:

David Robinson and I have had much contact. He was in Uganda for the burial of his father and had some passport trouble returning to South Africa. Upon returning to South Africa, he ended up being deported from South Africa and placed in jail in Kampala. We paid his bail and his situation has been cleared. He is with our key workers now in Uganda; all tremendous men of God, and if it all works together, as I think it will, he's on his way to Continental Training School at Uranga, and will meet with James Opiyo. Our great desire is to see David bear fruit. When he was suffering, he immediately came to the Samaritans. We were his proven family.

Moses Makumanu from Zimbabwe took over directing the work in South Africa. He was a man of integrity, a man who was serving well, and was well liked by the various people involved in the ministry. The ethnic groups agreed that Moses was the right man for that time.

June 23, 1997, Moses wrote from South Africa:

Recently, me and Mama Florence, as we were working out how we can go on with the work out of our poverty, God gave us a solution. Osborn of Uganda said the truth by saying, "A suffering servant brings forth much fruit." We were praying, crying to God how we can get blankets for the children this winter and, fortunately, God heard our prayers. The following morning, Pastor Willie Booysen phoned me to come and collect a donation from our sponsor. To my surprise, it was a sack full of blankets, some plastic chairs and mugs. The other day we received food from other donors. These are just part of the things I can mention. Surely, we did ask for many things from God, and we received them. The other thing, Mama, we have new centers deep in the rural areas, and when you come, I would like you to see these areas.

Letter from David Robinson November 25, 1997:
After all is said and done, the greatest thing for one to do is to do the work of Good Samaritan. Work for that which makes you say "yes."

Of all the people we met in South Africa, Charlene Franzsen made the biggest impact upon Scott Page and me.

April 21, 1998, Charlene wrote:
Yesterday I was at the crèche (nursery) and what a lovely treat it was to see the activities going on there. An organization called Head Start is giving Florah almost free teacher training. Along with this, they supply free toys and games to the school, showing the teachers how to use them properly. For this great help, only 45 rands are paid by the school per month. It is so wonderful to see things happening there now: children drawing, painting, playing games, being challenged and stretched. The adults are also more stimulated as they now have a program to follow and new challenges to meet.

Moses is also doing well and feeling very important as he rides around in our gift from God doing the ministry chores. Note: the gift from God was a vehicle donated to Good Samaritan Ministries. It is such a privilege to work with him and Florah, and see their dedication and commitment. They make sure they attend any community classes going around that the health or education departments are giving without being told to do so. Whatever courses are going around, they are willing to attend and learn from them even if they are in the church. Even David Robinson is starting to click with all of us, and we were excited to see what potential he has and what he is able to teach us. Indeed, God is good to us, as He is faithfully working within each one of us. Slowly, we are making other people aware of GSM work here, and they are interested in hearing all about it. Our own children's school will be having a huge fundraiser next weekend, and I already have them committed to give me all the food that is left over to take to Mamelodi.

During apartheid, Mamelodi was an undeveloped township of blacks. When Mandela became President, he offered each family in Mamelodi a small piece of land to own for building their house. This was a free gift from the government. Most in Mamelodi built shacks on their ground, for the people had little or no money, but they had a great passion to do something with their land.

When Charlene Franzsen drove in her beautiful car out to Mamelodi every week, often by herself, this white English woman was protected and treated well. She experienced the faith and gratitude of all of the people. It was a sight to behold to watch Charlene serve in Mamelodi.

In November, 1998, two members of Good Samaritan Ministries from Oregon and Washington, visited and encouraged the work. James Opiyo also made a second visit to South Africa.

Charlene Franzsen wrote to me:

James Opiyo made a great impression on both Victor and me. We were especially attracted to his humble and sincere personality. There is no mistaking, he is a man led by the Father's wisdom. We were impressed how he handled any problems any of us presented to him. He is a man that can remain impartial, and I enjoyed the fact that he knows we are able to address our own problems and he encourages us to do so. I found that particularly important for our black members here. For so many years, the apartheid system did not let people have a thought of their own or allow them to exercise their own problem-solving skills. Today, they still want others to address issues that they are unsatisfied with. They need to learn that they do have, and need to develop the skills to handle issues that they feel need addressing. We are definitely going to make every attempt to go to Kenya next year when you are there for the Africa Continental Conference. (Special Note: The Franzsens were not able to go, but a representative came from South Africa.)

After his trip to South Africa, Scott Page wrote a report:

We went out to Mamelodi to the two centers regularly during our visit. The larger center had 76 children, the small one, 12. I am impressed with the quality of care the children receive there. Their hours of operation are from 5:30 a.m. to 8:00 p.m. Mama Florah, Evelyn, and several helpers feed, bathe, teach, and give lots of love to the children, who range in age from infants through early grade school. Martha does an excellent job at the smaller center nearby. Many of the children are from very troubled homes, with alcoholism and a host of problems, but they are well behaved and obviously well cared for at the GSM daycare center.

The counseling office at Mamelodi has been re-opened. Mama Dorcas, the landlord, is a very good friend of Good Samaritan Ministriès, and supportive of our work. We now have a larger counseling office for the same price. God is good!

Much training has been occurring with David Wango, David Robinson, Moses Makamanu, and Fred Langa. Two new men, Gregory and Isaiah, are being forged into the team.

Yesterday we had an important meeting with Pastor Booysen, with the aim of getting to know one another better and defining our roles. He is the Chairman of the South African Board of Directors, and a very dedicated and capable man. He teaches at a local Bible college and is completing a Master's Degree in Theology.

This Thursday evening, Vic Franzen is going to fly us in his airplane to Sun City for dinner. Just a short hop. We love the adventure.

We did go down to Bloemefontein, and then we went to Cape Town. Moses Makamanu drove us in the Good Samaritan car. Scott helped drive. It was a long journey. We were very glad to take a closer look at South Africa, and the journey to Cape Town was significant for all of us. Moses had never been there. We went out to Robben Island and saw with our own eyes the tiny cell where Mandela had been held. We saw the conditions for the prisoners on the island, and the distance to the mainland.

From the 1998 Annual Report, GSM-South Africa:

We've had a visit from James Opiyo, who is the African Executive Director of GSM, and we have opened a branch of GSM in Queenstown. Much progress has taken place in Mamelodi. We have been able to feed more than 60 children week-by-week this whole year. We've had training and development programs for the supervisors/teachers to nurture and the care of the children. We introduced a Sunday school, which enjoys an attendance of more than 100 children. In conjunction with our counseling service, we introduced a Sunday morning adult Bible study.

The greatest joy has been fulfilling the central purpose of the ministry, which is counseling. A team of five counselors make themselves available on a rotating basis to provide counseling from 5:00 p.m. to 7:00 p.m., Mondays through Thursdays of every week. 35 people have been counseled since October, and we received testimonies of changes in their lives as they put their trust in the Lord.

June 27, 1999, letter from Charlene Franzsen:
Moses and Joseph come with me on Thursday nights to our church where we are attending a course in counseling taught by a 72-year-old woman with great wisdom and compassion for people. It is a challenging course as she sets high standards (as should be when one is dealing with hurting people), but we are determined to see it through, and to pass the exam at the end of the year. We also have to role play, pretending that one of us is the candidate, and the other is the counselor, and did I mess up my first try! Hopefully, it will get better with time. Counseling is really a very difficult ministry, but also one that is desperately needed, especially Christian counselors.

August 19, 2000, Charlene Franzsen wrote:
Moses was involved in a vehicle accident. This was not his fault, as the other driver, who had been drinking, jumped the stop street and hit the left front wheel of the car, damaging the suspension and side panel of the car. Then, the other driver disappeared without taking responsibility for what he had done. This is such an old car that insurance was not interested in repairing it, but in simply paying us out. In the end, we bought the car from the insurance and they paid us out half of the insured amount. We had the car repaired in a matter of speaking, in Mamelodi, so we still have a vehicle we can use. Moses has accumulated some traffic fines that he has not been paying.

David Robinson visits the school once a week to spend some time with the children, and has now also become involved in some counseling in the middle of town where he lives. I have asked that he submit a report to the Board each time we meet. He is careful to keep reports of his cases. He has decided by himself to attend the board meetings. I am pleased to see at this time, how he is involved in our Lord's work without being prompted to do so. Occasionally, he also comes to visit us at our church. It is always a holy joy to see him there.

John Oundo died in 1997. He had been suffering from a brain tumor. He was so wishing to stay, but he had finished his time and surely he was a great gain to relationship in heaven.

We sent a team to Rwanda. Africans were visiting here, lots of them.

Judith Sellangah of Kenya had tuberculosis. She was extraordinarily ill and had no money. Her husband was a severe alcoholic and the funds they made went to his drinking. **We had to make a decision. Would we pay for the medication to keep Judith alive and to get her well? A Samaritan always makes the decision to pay the price and trust the Lord for the outcome.**

Angela Iwuchukwu came from Nigeria to Kenya and Uganda for training.

Before Judith Sellangah reported tuberculosis, January 20th she wrote:

On Saturday, the 18th of January, 1997, I had a wonderful time with the children in the slums. Several children came. We sang songs together, said poems, told them about the story of Jonah, and it was time to read story books which Gary and Laura Fribbs sent to the children. Many of those children didn't know how to read. I was so surprised and said to God, "Oh God, am I going to start teaching these big children?" But the Lord said to me, "They are very young children. You've been dealing with the multitude, and from today, I want you to deal with the individual child. See them. Listen to them, meet their needs." This is one area I have ignored for a long time, but I've been found out and I can't escape! Well, I taught them about Jonah, but I didn't know it was me God was speaking to. Praise God, the Lord opened my eyes to see.

There's a knock on my door. A lady walks in, this woman with five children, a wife to an alcoholic sobs as she tells me of her problem with her alcoholic husband who mistreats her, doesn't provide for the children, and is now refusing her to go to church. I listened to her, and the Holy Spirit gave me a word for her about the Samaritan woman and Jesus: "God is spirit and His worshipers must worship in spirit and truth." The Lord gave her the joy of her heart and she left for home beaming with a smile. The Lord also taught me of how other women also suffer in the hands of their alcoholic husbands, and that I'm not alone. The Lord lifted my spirit dearly. He has really set me apart for His work.

January 13, 1997, I wrote a letter to John Kajjabwangu, GSM Board Member, Kampala, Uganda:

Your letter is one of the most important letters I have received lately, for there is a great truth in what you said. **People are always looking for what they can get, and we have to teach them what they are able to give. It is an incredible spiritual truth that few know or understand.**

I pray for you, your family, all of you. Papa Jerry and I had a very good trip overseas. By God's grace, Papa Jerry stayed well and came home strong. In fact, when he got off the airplane, he was able to substitute teach the next morning at 8:00 a.m., although we had only arrived home from a 39-hour flight 12 hours before! You know, John K., that is an incredible miracle! Look what intercession did in our lives. There was a 24-hour prayer vigil the whole time we were gone.

How can I thank you enough? Where are the words to thank you for the hours of intercession? The food you do without? Things you don't buy for yourselves that you need because you served and gave in the Name of the Lord Jesus to the glory of His Kingdom into the lives of many.

January 13, 1997, I wrote to Betty Nakiwu and the teachers at Masaka School, Uganda:

Our journey to Africa with Papa Jerry was pretty hard and exhausting for us. We are not so young and it takes a lot of energy. Even coming home, it was a 39-hour flight, with seven take-offs and landings, handling the luggage, moving through airports, different beds every day, different facilities, great changes in climate and food. The temperature range was from 40 degrees centigrade to zero centigrade. With these challenges, I feel we were blessed to be safe. I know much of it is due to the fact that there are thousands of intercessors in Uganda that press in for this work, and its leaders.

Very key:
I was born to teach, and the gift of teaching became a spiritual gift after many years. When I first started teaching, it was really hard to manage the children. I felt overwhelmed with each of their lives. It was only gradually that I could understand that the true curriculum was the child. When I understood that the child was the curriculum, I began to teach in a different way. Oh, would that countries, people, locations and schools would understand the greatest curriculum of all is the child who is sitting in front of us, trying to understand himself, and then to gradually grasp the world around him. It is by the spirit that one becomes a great teacher, even of mathematics or history, for the spirit tells the child that the child is precious as they learn.

January 13, 1997, I wrote to Francis Alex Kabvalo in Malawi:
One of the hardest parts of the ministry is need and poverty. They war with each other in the spirit to discourage the saints. It is the greatest disease we have, and it is easy to succumb to death in this disease. If we are servants along the road, we are giving the same amount. Our people here are giving out of need as well. The need is not as great, but there must be sacrifice in our giving.

February 4, 1997, I wrote to Faraday Iwuchukwu in Nigeria:
As you visit rural centers and communities, are you going to set up good structure, and are you going to train these people as Samaritans with a Samaritan spirit? That is the hardest part. It is easy to take help to them. They love that. It is hard to train them to help themselves and to think beyond materialism and into the spiritual realm. Ponder, how could you train local center's directors, local people, and really bring a change in the way they think and manage.

I know there is a spirit of cooperation in the villages that is greater than in the cities. I believe this work can deeply affect lives in the rural communities, and then gradually, the cities themselves. Remember that you are training children that will eventually be in cities. The training has to reach so deeply inside the spirit, that nothing can remove it. Satan cannot have his way over the mind of a child. This is a deep challenge, Faraday and Angela. It is easy to teach someone for a day or two. Will the teaching you give last in their lives forever, as did the teaching of Christ Jesus? Ponder that and keep it before you until the Lord speaks.

Try to remember to put things of the Spirit before all other things. You live in a culture where materialism is very powerful as it is here. When you are born of the Spirit, the Spirit is more powerful. It will come to pass that people will come to hear the Spirit. I expect, because of what happened while we were there, the airplane accident, that your life will never be the same, Faraday, and God will use you as if he had never used you before. It is what I believe is happening, and if you release yourself from worry and care, it will happen even more. I am deeply moved of the Spirit for the growth I have seen in you.

March 31, 1997, I wrote to Pastor Andrew Kayeski in Zambia:

Andrew, when I came to Zambia, I gave a testimony: The Call I received at Nineveh in Iraq in 1976. The Call is to teach in a new way, to focus in a new way, to reach down inside people and call out what is best and give them the work to do. So many people are looking to the right and to the left. Jesus is looking for those who will genuinely work for Him. He is looking for a thousand times more workers than there ever were. So many come to receive. He is looking to the ones who come into the Kingdom to truly give in His name. Encourage your people to give. I encourage the giving in your spirit.

April 29. 1987, I wrote to Jacob Kugwila in Dar Es Salaam, Tanzania:

Today, Grace Kirya, the widow of Balaki Kirya, the former Minister of State of Uganda, preached at Christ Episcopal

Church in Lake Oswego. In addition, we gave the church the International Samaritan Award. It is the first time we have ever so honored a church. They have saved the lives of hundreds of orphans in Uganda by building them a school, feeding them, and protecting them. It is a blessing, for few churches do anything but talk. Sometimes they give funds, but without sacrifice.

June 13th, I wrote to Alick Malama in Zambia:
I have a word from the Lord for you for the International Day of Prayer, 'They organize at all times. Satan is the author of chaos and depression. You spend too much time fighting Satan. You are to fight for Jesus. Remember His words, those who are not for me are against me.

June 19, 1997, I wrote to Faraday and Angela in Nigeria:
I believe it is a time of incredible grace poured out because you took off your rich clothes and put on your poor ones. Always remember you can never impress someone in Nigeria, because someone will try to impress you more. Faraday, keep that in mind and read it a thousand times a day until you know it more than any. Never try to impress or compete with a society that is in such competition. You must stand out as a man who looks different and is different. The Lord had one suit of clothes. The Lord had simple meals. How complex we are! The Lord had no place to lay his head. How complicated we make it. The Lord did not choose his richness to be in children or in families, but in the needs of everyone. How prideful sometimes we are.

I received a letter written September 5, 1997, from Joseph Ouma Okungo. Joseph served as a Center Director in Kenya. He had greatly impressed me, for I saw his spiritual maturity and willingness to learn.

I thank you very much for your trip that you made in Kenya. I was really blessed in the seminar. Mama, God really brought you to Kenya with a purpose. That seminar changed my life and made me come out to be a holy bold Samaritan. It made me to start training my eyes to see spiritually, and my ears to hear the still, small voice of the Lord. Mama, from what I heard in that seminar, I have come to conclude that I am a man of my own understanding and making. I am responsible to the Lord Himself!

What I know is that Reverend James and Reverend Nicholas are both praying for me, and without their prayers, I can be nothing in this world. There is nothing good that can happen with my life without your prayers, Mama.

As I was called to the ministry in 1990, I had a testimony. I was one of the needy people that you came to visit in Nairobi in the slum area of Gorogochu. God called me to go and serve Him in the rural areas during those days. I was working as a part-time worker in Nairobi. I decided to go back home and I accompanied you up to Uranga. I had a mission to go and do in my local area. In 1991, Gango Center was opened. God has done a lot. So many things have been done in Samia. We have Mama Joan Nursery School (named for Joan Baker), a blind widow, Rosemary Ajiambo receives her support monthly from the ministry, and five other centers have been developed and opened. These are the things God has accomplished up till now. Seven students have been sponsored in high school. I know that what God started, He is going to accomplish.

[Note: Rosemary Ajiambo was given $25 per month for the rest of her life. According to Joseph's testimony, she divided the money with the other widows, and it was life changing for the people of Samia Center. So little can mean so much. The man who gave it here was 100% faithful to his commitment.]

Now I've been transferred to Uranga Headquarters as an Assistant Director of Uranga Center. I am happy with my new post, because it is not by my understanding, wisdom, or knowledge that I am going to do this work, but by the Holy Spirit.

I'm feeling unwell and I am soon going to Nairobi for further medical check-up. Mama, pray for my life. I have not been feeling well now for two years.

Joseph Ouma named his baby Bettie. Joseph Ouma died. He was one who had no greed. His teaching was the way he lived his life.

This letter was written September 22, 1997, to Andrew Kayeski in Zambia.
Andrew, the Lord did many miracles in our time in Kenya. One of his great words was He came to radically love and to radically correct, and that radical love and correction have to be ongoing in the life of each of us, and in the church. This is something to ponder. **Are we willing for radical correction, or are we fighting it or moving from it? What is radical correction? What does need to be corrected in the ministries of each of us?** *If we work in the Name of the Lord Jesus, do we work in the Name of the Lord Jesus, or does our own name and spirit and life slip in there too strongly, interfering with His?*

November 3, 1997, I wrote to Francis Kabvalo in Malawi:
I always consider that a Samaritan is not about something good you do sometimes, work that you do for God occasionally, but a work that you do in many different ways, on any given day your entire life. It is the Spirit of Jesus moving among the people and meeting the needs so deeply, so profoundly, that they are really met. Always remember that in the Parable, there was a second price. Examine yourself to see if you measure up and remember that second price in everyone you see, work with, and uphold in prayer.

November 20, 1997, I shared a story about Nigeria with Majed Alloush, our director in Jerusalem:
Recently, we had to have $2,000 immediately for Nigeria. Norma Jean Partie is the Nigerian Satellite Chairperson. She and her husband are parting because he is a severe alcoholic and she has given up trying to make it with him. Her health had completely broken. She chose to try to sell her home, and she is living with her son and daughter. I said, "Norma, we need $2,000 immediately for Nigeria in order to keep the legalization. If we lose the legalization, we will never get it back as the nation is becoming more and more anti-Christian. What shall we do?" She said, "Don't worry; I will sell all of my furniture." And she did. She brought the funds in and gave them for a country she

will probably never see, and a people she will never know personally.

I am devastatingly worried about attitudes in the world. Where a child somewhere is not in school, or a nation is not making it, or sorrow is overwhelming, do we care in such a way that we would go sell all we have and give to the poor, the lame, and the weak? It is definitely something to ponder in our souls. I am pondering this myself.

CHAPTER 21

WHY GO?

I received a frantic letter from David Robinson. Crossing back from Uganda to South Africa, he ended up in jail in Zambia. He had entered Zambia illegally because his papers were not cleared there.

I immediately contacted Alick Malama, who visited David and assessed the situation and what could be done. In the meantime, when the jail keepers learned that David had friends in the United States, they took him off the floor of the cell and put him on a bed. They gave him covers and fed him much better.

After some time, Alick was able to arrange for David to be released and he went on to South Africa. **Samaritans have strange assignments. They have to be willing to be awakened in the middle of the night.**

1998 was a year of extensive travel.

Passionately believing that Samaritans needed to be developed and that the hardships and rigors of travel would bring about great spiritual breakthroughs, I led two tours to the Middle East. The first tour in the spring we celebrated Holy Week in the Holy Land. We also visited Egypt. The second tour in June we went to Syria, Turkey, Jordan, Israel, and Palestine. Jerry and I led that tour of 50 people.

On the spring tour, we took Moses Ssemanda, Osborn's brother from Kampala, all expenses paid. Why did we do that? Who made that decision? What was that all about?

After horrific torture and imprisonment, Osborn and Moses' father was able to once again function in the ministry. Near Christmas, 1985, their father was leaving on a journey up to Kiwangala, Masaka.

Before he left, he laid hands on each of his 11 children and prayed over them. When he left in the car, they were shocked to see him come back two hours later. He called Osborn in, laid hands on him, and prayed over him a second time.

It was not long before the family received the news that there had been a road accident as Osborn's father was coming home from the crusade. Osborn and Moses' father died in the accident. He was buried on Christmas day in Kampala.

Moses had shared with me, while in Kampala, the story of his father's death, and also that his father had planned to go to the Holy Land that Spring for Holy Week.

According to that information, I personally made the decision that we would take Moses Ssemanda for Holy Week in the spring of 1998 to the Holy Land. Moses was a pastor and the Chairman of the Board of GSM--Uganda. He was passionate about the work. It was an important decision to take him with us.

You will see, as the stories progress, how many times we did the thing that is normally not done. Decisions were made by the heart, as well as by the logic of the head. The Holy Spirit trained our hearts. I can truly say the heart of the Lord ran the ministry. When I would have turned my back, He would turn me toward the very thing that He wanted done.

Good Samaritan Ministries must always have room for a large heart. We must listen, pay attention to the stories, and respond to them from our spiritual resources. We are never to be enablers. We are never to offer goodies. We are to offer mercy, in all its many forms that the LORD of the moment shows us.

In June of 1998, after the tour was completed, I went on to travel with Jackie Wilhelm to Pakistan, Bangladesh, and Singapore. Thus, in the summer of 1998, Jackie and I made a trip around the world.

Joe Cooke of GSM-Beaverton, Oregon, and Nicholas Okungu, our National Director of Kenya, went with our help and blessing to teach and to lead crusades for three weeks in Pakistan. Joe was born of missionary parents in China before World War II. As a teenager, he remained in China during World War II. He was separated from his mother and father from the time he was six years of age on. Joe had a passion for countries, languages, and people. In his brokenness, he became strong.

Nicholas reported to me that on the journey, Joe, who was an old man, got so tired on the long bus and train rides through Pakistan that they gave him a blanket and he laid on the floor.

As 1999 came, Jerry and I made a Samaritan trip into the former Soviet "borderland" called Ukraine with the founding team of the Samaritan ministry there.

The majority of our year was spent sending forth 25 members of Good Samaritan Ministries to 10 different countries in Africa. We all went to Kenya, but from there, teams split off to selected countries. The team visits included Uganda, Burundi, Nigeria, Sierra Leone, Tanzania, Rwanda, Malawi, and Zambia. Taking a larger team was a big assignment; and significantly, the young people who went: Carlene Botts, 13 years old, April Sweitz, 15 years old, Michelle Paine, 17 years old, and Samuel Womack, 17 years old. Each person on the team lived a passion and received a call to be on this journey.

One hour after James Opiyo called to tell me of Bishop Tom Abungu's death, I received a last letter from Tom. While the whole group was in Kenya, we attended his funeral. He had died ten days before we came. James Opiyo sat with him for the last week of Tom's life, sleeping little and comforting him much. While we were at Uranga, Tom's body was brought to the center. The coffin was placed on a bier outside the headquarters of GSM.

As I had soil from the Holy Land with me, I sprinkled the soil on the ground beneath the coffin. There were many prayers, and the ministry participated fully in Bishop Tom's passing into His glory.

Bob Hill and his wife, Alberta, were in their 70s. Bob had retired from public school administration and went back to college to get a Master's Degree in counseling. He volunteered full-time for Good Samaritan Ministries in Talent, Oregon.

Leo Stewart was a Native American who was in recovery from alcoholism. Leo had a great love of God, and his obedience followed his love. He said to me, "I am coming because God has told me to come." His great interest on the journey was the addictions recovery program. He put his passion into his meeting with Charles Onyango, Addictions Recovery Director for Kenya. Leo was so large, dark, and beautiful that everyone was fascinated by him. I believe the healing of wounds from his culture also brought the healing of wounds for Kenya's culture.

We visited extensively in Kenya. Uranga managed to house us and feed us. **I never made money the focus of our visits. Anyone going on a team to Africa was asked to donate $1,000 per country, adjusted according to how long they were staying. We did not wish to be a burden on the people of Africa. In fact, we wanted to add to the funds that their needs might be met also. This meant safer vehicles, gas when needed, and healthy food with clean water.** I believe in our mercy toward the people of the ministry in each country. I believe in our attitude, not just to visit them and use them, but to be with them—all the way. Part of this was in our provision and deep loving care for them. I have never changed my mind. **This is a bottom line: never go for your advantage, go for the advantage of your neighbor. Keep the root of the ministry fully exposed.**

After our time in Kenya, team members moved on to countries of their assignment. I moved on with my sister, Arabelle Fliniau, and Denise Haun, a youth minister at a church in Walla Walla, Washington. We went to Burundi and Nigeria. When we reached Nigeria, two new members of the team joined us: Sheila Hair, Director of Walla Walla, GSM, and John Nichols, Pastor of Athena Baptist Church. After our time in Nigeria, we then moved together to Sierra Leone.

It has been my policy to always send ahead a list of the people coming to each country and something of their background in the ministry. They needed to know us and receive us as part of the whole of Good Samaritan Ministries.

Each team going to a different country was given significant assignments. They were to not only evaluate the role that Good Samaritan might play in the country, but they were also to become a part of the teaming with that country. Sometimes that was easier, and sometimes that was harder.

As we were getting ready to go to Africa, our Beaverton GSM head office was deceived by a local scam. We lost $3,500.

Three members of the ministry went first to Egypt for several days. This was not a tour of Egypt. They worked at the ministry of GSM-Egypt.

I personally spent one month in Africa.

The larger teams and smaller teams functioned well. Each team had an appointed person to coordinate that team. There were some problems. Life is not perfection, but dealing with the realities on the ground.

As Denise Haun, Arabelle, and I went to Burundi, we were fascinated with the beauty of the country. Again, we saw a more progressive people. There was wholeness in the spiritual realm. There was not restlessness on the streets, but a working together for the common good.

For many years, Burundi had lived through a bloody Civil War that was continuing. At any time there would be major gun battles, but people lived life around the problems.

It is always good to meet with the family of the Director and the people called to be staff and coordinators. It was good to watch the graduation of Samaritans who had been in training for a number of months. It was good to listen to them and know where they were coming from and why they had come into the ministry. We saw no games, great sacrifice on the part of our Director, Jeremie and his family. Daily, there were many mouths to feed at their house, open 24/7, a safe place for people who needed to be heard and understood.

In Nigeria, our team now had new members. It is always an event to fly into Lagos, to be met, housed overnight and then be sent on the second airplane to Port Harcourt. With a multi-gifted team, we could do more extensive training. Faraday insisted that all students of the training needed a written test. Sheila corrected the tests by lantern, as the electricity, as usual, was off. Sheila Hair interviewed each trainee. Every team member was part of the training staff. We were all housed in Nigeria in the same location. We worked well together.

The question will always be, "Are they getting it, and if they are, what will they do with it?" There is no easy answer to that question, and much of it depends upon the ability of the leaders to empower the people. The trainees need to be held accountable for the fruit they will bear. There is an ongoing need to supervise trainees far beyond the training, and to keep them linked together in prayer and community.

Since each of the countries have several locations within the country, it is challenging to gather those people. It is workable; make it work.

The question will always remain, throughout the history of Good Samaritan Ministries, "Are they able to do it? Are they able to fully comprehend the Samaritan life when we are no longer there?"

Our journey to Sierra Leone was significant.

As the ferries were not working, we had to take a helicopter into Freetown where we spent eight days. We went to see Arthur and Elizabeth's home, which had been burnt to the ground by the rebels. We comforted Arthur Davies on the loss of his aunt, who, in many ways, was more than a mother to him. We met again with a tremendous number of people, but the most moving part of the journey there was the visit to the amputees' camp.

During Sierra Leone's horrific rebel war, the rebel leader of the fighters had instructed his young fighters to take power by slashing off people's arms or legs. At the amputees' camp, we were confronted by a broken people, men, women and children, vastly slashed, limbs, ears, or fingers removed. The government provided some food for them and an International non-profit was making prosthetic equipment for their needs. **There was a pounding rage inside of most, a deep grief in every face.** They felt they were voiceless, not heard, left there, bereaved, and largely discarded. We saw two brothers. Each had an arm cut off. John Nichols moved the two brothers close to each other. Together, they had one good right arm and one good left arm. Together, they could work the fields. Our job was to inspire the amputees, not just talk in platitudes or religious chatter. The inspiration given in a few minutes can last a lifetime.

I was not horrified. I saw the need to assign them to action. I trained them to go out, speak to the government and get the food and help they needed. When we left, they did as we said and things improved greatly.

The most significant meeting while we were in Sierra Leone was with a little girl who had both of her arms cut off. She was no more than four. Her father was there, and he too had suffered some amputation.

When the President of Sierra Leone met with the rebel leader of the fighters, he took the little girl without arms to the peace table. He sat the little girl on the table and he said, "This is the reason we will make peace."

It has always been my belief, and it will continue to be all the days of my life, that there are too few children at negotiating tables, and adults that don't see them. I was proud of the President of Sierra Leone, and I'm proud of the people and their efforts to get over such horrific shock and step by painful step, try to recover.

While in Sierra Leone, we saw hundreds of children without hands, fathers and mothers with ears cut off, a leg or a hand cut off. We saw thousands in displaced camps and heard of missing children all over the country. We saw that we have 50 counselors working in and out of our office in Freetown, and we thought of all the little places in the world where fellow Samaritans have chosen the hard road.

I want to digress for a moment to say something very important. As a leader, no matter what your position is in that leadership, you are on the line to make a difference where the real need is. During 10 days of the long civil war, there was no communication in or out of Sierra Leone. Even the Red Cross could not get through. From Oregon, I was trying to call Arthur. Finally, on the tenth day, while I was at the hospital visiting my husband, who was recovering from major surgery, my call went through to Arthur Davies. It was then he told me about the firebombing of his house, a house built by his family in the 1920s, and a house that supported a business to provide for the family.

All during the rebel war, Arthur and I had an agreement that on an agreed-upon day, I would call the home of Augustus Davies to speak with him weekly at a certain time. Often, he had to crawl through the streets to get there, and as we were talking, I could hear bombing and shooting in the background. When we talked on the phone for a few minutes, we always got down on our knees and prayed together during that conversation. The two of us became one

spirit in union with the Holy Spirit. This regular telephone call went on for many months.

The rebels used child soldiers. The rebels went into a village, captured a certain number of children, handed them burlap bags, a machete, and told them they were to amputate. When they had collected a full bag of body parts, they would be given an important position. Several of the children were shot in the head with cocaine, and the whole story is horrifically beyond belief.

At the time of this war in Sierra Leone, the western world was concerned about Sarajevo. No help was sent to Sierra Leone. No ship came. No supplies came in. The people looked on the horizon and wondered if anyone would ever come.

We had to come, and we did!

A Word from the Lord

Rwanda, Burundi, and Sierra Leone, the mourning has not begun. Shock hangs appall over the mourners. Who shall mourn so much as those who die by the sword? We must intercede to release the spirits of fear and grief. Let laughter and joy come again among the children.

During the rebel war in Sierra Leone, 20 percent of the people lost their housing. Farmers had their hands cut off so they couldn't farm. Traumatically, 3,000 or more people died in the streets of Freetown. A half-million refugees were left without a home or help. Who led the rebels in the war in Sierra Leone? He was a corporal in the Sierra Leone army who initiated this rebellion, spreading the hatred and the violence against the countryside.

In early 1998, I received word that our GSM-Rwanda National Director died, leaving six children. Osborn Muyanja, our National Director in Uganda, went over to try to help sort things out. We had a trained man to take the deceased director's place, but he needed help. Osborn spent five days in Rwanda. His comment in coming back, when I talked to him on the telephone, was, "We suffered for 30 years, but it is beyond belief in Rwanda. People are lined up all day for a counseling session; mothers, babies. But the saddest were the ones who had been left slashed so badly on their bodies, they were left for dead and everyone in their family was murdered. They were the only survivors."

When we went home, each team wrote a significant report of each country they visited. The most problematic visit was to Tanzania. It was obvious that there was much need for intervention. James Opiyo contacted Samuel Kitwika, and he was sent back to Uranga for training.

Samuel has hung on unto this day. It's been a long journey, and not easy for him or for us. He still serves as National Director of Tanzania. We need to build significant satellite teams that do not discourage, teams who build and inspire others, for each country.

Fair questions when building a team, "Will you inspire the people? Will you see and know the word of correction and inspiration? Will you use it? Will you?"

The hard struggle in sending teams out is the team members tend to talk among themselves rather than using their energies to see and know the people. It is easy for all of us to hide in places that are comfortable. **It is tremendously important that each team member learn to be effective. Each team member has a place to make a difference. Can we inspire, train, and connect the teams going out to know how this will happen and what difference this will make?**

In 1990, I wrote to Faraday Iwuchukwu of Nigeria:

As I see the Samaritan story, it's the story of a small man, who stopped for a small person. I doubt if he told very many people about the stop. I'm sure there were no advertisements about it. In the parable, perhaps, the Samaritan was Jesus Himself. But, surely, He would never take credit. The story would just be left behind.

In September 1998, I wrote a letter to Charles Kayala in Malawi:

You are meek and lowly, a servant of Christ Jesus. As a servant, you might ask Jesus, "Why? What can I do? I am hard-pressed myself and have little."

He might say to you that He had almost nothing. No wife. No home. No funds. But, He changed the course of history because He loved God more profoundly, more intimately than anyone who had ever lived, and He loved His neighbor as Himself. He was willing to suffer any loss for the healing of one person. He was the first of many Samaritans.

January 27, 1999, Cameron DePoe wrote this poem:

Sierra Leone

Oh Father, I pray for Sierra Leone.
I see the bodies and endless bones.
Where is the Sanity? Where is the Peace?
How can I pray this great release?
I feel so inadequate when death still lingers,
children starving with empty fingers.
Mothers wail deep into the night.
Fathers weep from their helpless plight.
So-called men, more like animals, roam the streets,
like beasty cannibals,
Seeking to devour what precious life is left.
How can I pray, Lord? I feel so inept.
Where are your people, Lord?
Are they alive? Are they dead?
We await the news, our hearts filled with dread.

Are my prayers reaching your ears?
Please, Lord, teach me deeper still.
Preserve them, Lord. It is Your will.

Bring me to that difficult place,
where sorrow and suffering walk with grace.
That I might be accepting with joy,
and bearing in love to your great ploy.
You have a plan, I cannot ignore,
and Your hand is on Sierra Leone.

March of 1999, I wrote to the Samaritans in Tanzania:
The greatest danger of any laborer is pride. To be humble is to realize how unworthy you are to even be called to such a

work that Christ asked for when He was here. That our sins would be forgiven is beyond my comprehension.

In May of 1999, I wrote a letter to James Opiyo:

The weeks fly by. Last Monday, a week ago, at 8:00 in the morning, I fell flat on my face: bloody, bent nose, hurt wrist, but nothing broken. I made it through the day. After working a 12-hour day, I got word that Tony Zsoter of men's group was dying, and I had to drive 80 miles round-trip to go visit him, arriving home late. On Tuesday night, Willie Booysen arrived from South Africa to stay with us for three nights and to spend two and a half days with us in the office.

September 2, 1999, I wrote to Faraday in Nigeria:

I would like to make some recommendations, Faraday, and I would like you to follow them. You need to do more planning, and you need to prioritize. You need to understand that your life has been given to Samaritan work, and what the difference is between that and other work. Some of the things you need to address as weaknesses in your work are:

1) You have trouble delegating leadership in significant work.

2) You focus too much on money. Jesus paid none of the apostles. They had no silver and gold and they did His work. Stop focusing on money, and focus on The Call of Christ on all!

3) Remember the words of the Lord, "In the least, I am." Our position must never be anything but the least. If it gets to be more than the least, we cease to reflect the glory of God and begin to reflect the kind of false glory that may be around ourselves. I'm not aware of myself. I'm aware of the Lord. I am aware of the Christ. I am aware of the Holy Spirit. I am not aware of Bettie Mitchell. Break that awareness of self. Break that final stubbornness in your spirit that His Lordship might conquer even the stubborn part. This is very important.

September 2, 1999, I wrote to James Opiyo:

*The Lord has shown me there are four areas of counseling: grief, personal sin, the power of sin, and education. There is one clear thing needed: **AUTHORITY WITH ASSIGNMENT.** You can ponder those words. It is very powerful when you separate* *personal sin from the power of sin itself. I find that the power of sin is not broken in Christians because the conversions have never taken place. Only if you have been totally converted will the power of sin break. Either total forgiveness or none!*

Faraday wrote from Nigeria:

Mama, at times I put myself in your shoes to see how much burden is placed on your shoulders daily. The Lord is your strength. He has the resources and whatever you need to care for the whole world. May He always grant you favor before Him and men. The Lord is your strength.

In September 2000, I wrote to Arthur Davies in Sierra Leone:

When we start handing out things, people always see how inadequate we are. There is a reason that Jesus handed out nothing. I don't believe he ever gave a gift except the healing of someone. That is challenging isn't it? I don't know what to tell you, but perhaps you can pray and consider it yourself.

CHAPTER 22

GOD'S BUSINESS

The choice is between man's business and God's business. May God's business prevail. *"For the love of money is the root of all evil..."* (1 Tim. 6:10).

Over the years, I watched the focus continually shift between money (cost) and the good it did. It is so easy to go to budgets, logic, and reasonableness. When we carry money, giving a little to God and the rest to ourselves, it will be very hard for God's glory to be revealed. Satan uses money to divide and conquer. He uses money to keep our eyes on how much we gave instead of the small miracles across the world. As our love smiles across Africa, we must never forget the children who were changed by the opportunities given for their growth and learning. **When we focus on a bank account, either ours personally, or the ministries, there is danger that we will not be grateful. It was God who saw the needs. It was God answering prayer.**

I have seen the conflict over and over again. Once we were really excited to help and we sacrificed and made a difference in so many lives. But Satan was trying to wean us away from the picture of the miracles. He wanted us to focus on the cost.

What will it cost a child to be locked into endless poverty because the child had no opportunity?

We cannot have our focus on money and at the same time have our focus on God's goodness and mercy. We cannot be free of our own attitudes and ownership of money until we share it freely and delight deep within for all that happened in the lives of others. May our souls delight in the goodness of God to set us free. Our freedom to give in God's name delivers children unto His kingdom, unto the Father's bosom.

There was another temptation. The temptation was to focus on business and lose The Call.

Over the years I spent many board meetings training the board to see. There was never an argument. I just read letter after letter after letter and trained them, thus preventing their eyes from being so focused on business. Their very lives had to experience the realization of the gift of this ministry.

Some boards were more successful than others. Some longed to hear and see, wept, and got down on their knees as board members. Others looked at their watches, became restless, and wanted to complete the business. In the early years, most of our board meetings were five hours long. Three of those hours, minimum, were spent learning to see what God was doing.

One of the greatest dangers to the ministry occurs when a board loses sight of the power of mercy. When a board becomes too focused on business, this weakens the power of our Living Faith.

The miracle in Good Samaritan Ministries was the grass-roots people, the people who came and stayed. The people who helped, knew that this was their home. The people loved our freedom. By their giving spirit, the people participated in the miracles all over the world.

Often, at the door of Good Samaritan Ministries, as someone would come in, either client or member of Good Samaritan Ministries, if I was in the main office, I would say, "Welcome home. It is so good to have you here today!" They could go in the back and play the piano. They could study the photo albums. They learned to understand The Call from the pictures on the walls. They helped if they had a little time when a project was being worked on. **The grass roots, small people of this ministry, gave life to the ministry.**

Often, we had a harambee to raise money for one of the countries, or for the education of the children. Harambee is a Kenyan/African term. It means to work together for the common good, raising the money by giving it freely. It means a community in action, a community that is not afraid, a community that enjoys the spirit of giving. When we had a harambee, we would have an object of some kind; it could have been a rug or a picture. It could be something old. It didn't have to be anything highly significant, but it could be. The rule of the harambee was that whatever you bid, you paid it. The item went to the last bidder, but you paid for every part of your bidding. We started with small money, and moved to places where we got the significant help that was deeply needed. The Kenyan Africans loved harambees. The grass roots of our people loved the harambees here. It was the excitement of working together. Everyone could give a penny. Most could give a dollar, but we were giving together in the spirit of the harambee. We were not looking at the money; we were looking at where it was going to go. Gladly we gave! Gladly Africa was blessed! It meant a lot to Africa that we developed the spirit of harambee. They deeply believed in this community spirit. Engrained in the soul of an African, is the spirit of community.

In Kenya and in Africa, the Spirit of Harambee was the source for all needed community funds. Schools survived by harambees.

When I would return from a journey overseas, I would, at length, train the people in all that I heard and saw. Many of us who journeyed gave reports. Our community would see slides, and learn significant stories. **Our history was daily being developed. It was being heard. The focus was not on need. The focus was on the people and the miracle.**

In the year 2000, Jerry and I led a tour to Jerusalem. We celebrated the high holy days of Passover and the fullness of Holy Week and Easter. We all marched in the Palm Sunday Parade with several thousand people from nations all over the world, each group singing songs and hymns in their own language.

Osborn Muyanga from Uganda was with us.

Why would we do such a thing? Was that not a little bit over the top?

Osborn gave his whole heart and life to children in Uganda. The giving was absolute, the care and fathering of orphans, the keeping of them. He led a small staff with a huge heart, and he made a difference all over the country. His light became a legend in Uganda.

We all went on to Egypt, not only for sights, but for the encouragement of life-giving ministry to the needs of many.

Jerry and I then went on alone to Nairobi, where we met with James Opiyo and Nicholas Okungu. We spent most of the night discussing GSM-Kenya.

The problem lay on the focus of need and money. We did not want to need money, and it was not good for them to need money either. Need and money are dangerous when they're linked together, and they are a destructive force to the spirit of harambee. After many hours, we came to some key agreements.

Here, I want to say, it is very important that we never manipulate nor allow ourselves to be manipulated by others. This sounds good in a sentence on a piece of paper, but the realities of the war of manipulation are the harsh realities of the potential for evil and disaster. It is important to never manipulate a "giver," and never allow a "getter" to manipulate us. It is important to keep the freedom that God is in charge of what happens and we are not. Jesus says you can ask and you will receive, but He did not say, "Manipulate until you get it." Manipulation is a force all over the world. It is not a trait seen only in Africa. It is a common trait of humanity.

I learned to say no, as well as yes. Jesus said, *"Say yes when you mean yes, and no when you mean no. Anything else is from the evil one."* (Matthew 5:37). Swaying people back and forth between yes and no is in the manipulation category. When I said "no," it was hard. I was teaching the Africans to say "no" as well. That word is not easily accepted in the African culture. Hospitality and accommodation must never prevent the strength of our genuine yes or no.

In 1997, Joan Baker and I were led to start recognizing "The International Woman of the Year." We saw so many women out in the field who had great things to teach us. We had so much to learn from them. I want to assure everyone who reads this, GSM is not a women's ministry. It is about the high calling of someone to come and teach. We made a policy that if someone was chosen for the award from another country, all of their expenses were paid, and their way made clear to move freely among us. They were invited to stay for two months in the United States to study and to teach the ministry. An 'International Woman of the Year' received the award for a number of years. In 2000, for the first time, we chose an African American recipient, Dr. Virginia Phillips, founder of Women of Purpose. When she was named International Woman of the Year, we called her into my office. She came with some friends. She had no idea this was going to happen. When we told her, she wept. Her spirit had been longing to go to Africa for many years. Her way was paid to go to Sierra Leone, Nigeria, Kenya, Uganda, and Ethiopia. She encouraged the work of Good Samaritan Ministries.

Another year, we chose Aruna, from India, the wife of Yesu. He came with her, but she had to sit in the front of the car and he had to sit in the back. For the two months, he was to honor his wife. It was life changing in their relationship. Other International Women of the Year were Judith Sellangah of Nairobi, Grace Kirya of Uganda, and Galina Bidenko of Ukraine. In 2001, Joan Baker was sent with a small team to Africa as International Woman of the Year. The horrific tragedy of 9/11 occurred while they were gone. (Read Chapter 24)

The focus of the ministry was on giving. As we kept the focus on giving and we didn't allow that root to dry up and produce less water for the bush, there was a flourishing of the ministry as a whole. There was a working together for the common good. There was joy because we gave enough!

During the year 2000, people came to us from many countries. Each of the visits was significant. When the tour group went to Egypt in 2000, we invited Maqbool Kamal and David Bhatti from Pakistan to join us. We climbed Mt. Sinai together as a whole team.

When David Bhatti finished his time in Egypt, we sent him to Kenya and Uranga to give training there. David was and is very gifted in training Samaritans. He had developed effective centers all over Pakistan. He stayed in Africa for a number of days and his life had an impact on the work in Kenya.

In 2000, Samuel Kitwika sent nine Tanzanians to Continental Training at Uranga. One of the women went with her baby. Some of them were Muslims. At the Continental Training Center, Samaritans never pressure anyone to become a Christian. No expectations are held. They hold the freedom of choice in high regard. All of the Muslims became Christians. It was the freedom that brought them to Christ.

In the year 2000, Judith Sellangah's husband, Josiah, was saved. How it happened is a miracle. 11 Nigerian women were intercessors for Africa. They came to Kenya, met Judith Sellangah, and asked if they could come to her house for dinner. Josiah came in while they were there obviously showing his powerless, addictive life. Right there on the spot the Nigerian women began to intercede for him and they lifted up his hands. He gave up cigarettes. He gave up alcohol. He became a strong Christian, and remains to this day in a strong ministry in Kenya. Judith Sellangah went on to join the Women's Intercessors for Africa ministry. She has a large responsibility for the women of East Africa.

Spiritual breakthrough is the high priority of God's mercy.

When man chooses God's business, he must come to terms with God as a business man. *"As you give, so shall you receive. Knock and the door will be opened to you. The measure you give is the measure you will receive."* **(Matthew 7:7) Our guidelines for business are found in the gospels.**

Do not live with the tension of this world and priorities laid out by circumstances. Live with your face on the ground and your faith risen in absolute trust of the Call of God from above. Jesus said, *"I must be about my Father's business."* (Luke 2:49)

CHAPTER 23

THE STORY OF NEW COUNTRIES

Rwanda -- Francis Ntuyahera, National Director

Francis was born in 1973. He is not a man who dwells on himself, though his formal education stopped after primary 7 because of lack of school fees. He is committed to serving God by loving and helping his neighbor.

Rwanda is a country that is made up of three tribal people all speaking the same language. The Twa were the original inhabitants followed in 1000 AD by the Hutus. In the 14th and 15th centuries, the Tutsis migrated into the area and soon gained dominance over the Hutus, though the Hutus made up the majority of the population. By the 18th century, a single Tutsis-ruled state occupied most of present day Rwanda.

In 1991, the elected president, who was a moderate Hutu, agreed to a new multi-party constitution. In 1993, after he signed a power-sharing agreement, Hutu violence broke out in the capital of Kigali. A new accord was signed in August and a United Nations Peacekeeping Mission was established. However, when Habyarimana, the elected president of Rwanda, and Burundi's president were killed in a suspicious plane crash in 1994, civil strife erupted on a massive scale. Nearly one million people, mostly Tutsi and moderate Hutus were slaughtered. Over two million people, mostly Hutus, fled the country. In 1996, over a million Hutus refugees flooded back into the country. By 1997, there was a growing war between the Rwandan army and the Hutus gorilla bands.

April 6, 1994, marked the beginning of a hundred days of the most intense and brutal massacres of a tribe of people in world history. Not only did the national army systematically kill these people, but neighbor rose up against neighbor, fathers against their families, priests against their parishioners, using hoes, clubs, machetes, rocks, guns, whatever they could find, all in the name of ethnic cleansing. The children were especially targeted in order to eliminate future generations. In the end, one million were dead in a nation the size of Maryland that only had a population of seven million. People continued to be maimed, tortured, raped and terrorized.

Janean Dobos, a GSM Center Director from the northeastern part of Oregon, after travelling to Rwanda in 1999, stated the following: "Rwanda is a nation in recovery!"

Hardly a person exists in Rwanda who was not deeply traumatized by the genocide. During the genocide Francis and his family were refugees in Uganda. After the genocide in 1995, Francis felt called by God to return to his people in Rwanda.

As Francis came from Uganda to Rwanda, he almost starved to death while ministering faithfully to the people. Another Rwandan, Samedi, worked with Francis to found a church in Kigali. Samedi became the Senior Pastor and Francis was the Associate. There was no salary for the associate, but he was able to take some meals with the Samedi family. Francis had to trust God to take care of him.

Francis first heard about GSM when John Kajjabwangu, a member of the GSM National Board in Uganda, came to Rwanda. John was speaking at a church and teaching the basic principles of being a Samaritan. The message spoke to Francis' heart and spirit and he deeply knew he was called to bring this work to Rwanda. A man named Lazarus was with Francis in that meeting. The two men talked to John and were later introduced to the GSM leaders in Uganda. They eventually met me in Kenya at the Continental Training Center in 1997. I appointed Lazarus as the National Director of GSM in Rwanda. Francis shared that even at that time, he knew very deeply that the calling was his, but he said nothing out of deference for Lazarus, who was his elder by many years.

Within the following year, Lazarus died. Francis was participating in the African Continental Training in Uranga, Kenya, in 1997, when he received word Lazarus had died. He left the training and returned to Rwanda. He was appointed to succeed Lazarus as the GSM Director in Rwanda. The following year, he returned to Kenya, and completed his training.

Francis' dedication and commitment were so complete that he served for a full two years without any financial support from GSM or from the church where he was an associate. GSM in Uganda helped him when he was desperate. One time, all of his clothes, which were not many, were stolen, and John K. gave him a suit. The next time John K. saw him, he saw that the suit was gone. When John asked about it, Francis said there was a man who wanted to come to church and he was naked, so Francis gave him the suit.

Francis is forever exploring ways to help the widows earn a living, to help the orphans get an education, to help the street children find productive lives, and to bring reconciliation between people who have been so spiritually annihilated by hate and fear.

Over the years, as Francis has remained faithful to GSM in Rwanda and internationally, he has been given many unusual opportunities to bring forward his education.

Ghana, West Africa–Stephen Adukpoh, National Director

I met Stephen during a trip to Nigeria in 1999. Faraday invited me to speak at a Pastor's Conference he had organized in Port Harcourt. It happened that Stephen was in Nigeria to attend this conference.

Stephen was seated in the middle of the third row in the auditorium, and I made eye contact with him. I sensed in my spirit that he was a man of God. We talked and I invited Stephen to explore whether he wanted to develop Good Samaritan Ministries in his home country of Ghana.

He visited Good Samaritan Ministries in Oregon and stayed to train through the holidays, up to 2000. I said of him at his graduation from Counselor Training in Beaverton, Oregon, in January of 2000, "I believe Stephen has a ministry in this world that we have not seen the end of. He is a person who keeps his word, a man of his word." I said to him, "Anyone in the world can come to you and receive the services of a true Samaritan."

Stephen grew up in a quiet fishing village where they worshipped idols. He underwent serious persecution after his conversion to Christianity, and he was expelled from his family and his village. They refused to speak to him, or to allow him to work. He had to develop strength on the inside to remain standing. He often felt misunderstood, but he persevered, and he did the hard work necessary to be heard.

There was a time a few years ago that his wife, Mabel died. Stephen had been gone, and he returned to find her very ill after the delivery of dead twins. It was with great difficulty that he got her to a hospital, only to have her declared dead. The hospital personnel wanted him to remove the body from the hospital, but he refused. He prayed and would only allow anyone near her who would pray. After three days, she lived, and he took her home. Her recovery was slow, but in time, her health returned. Stephen's faith is strong and he did not waiver. He is a man who can be trusted to stay strong in the midst of adversities. **Stephen said, "The work in Ghana is not a one-day wonder, but a daily walk."** He and his wife, Mabel, had five children. In 2012, Mabel died. She had suffered long illness.

Stephen is one of the most gifted teachers in the ministry. I have heard him teach in other countries, and I have seen how serious his spirit is when he speaks out. He never lets go of the people to whom he is speaking.

Democractic Republic of Congo (DRC) –Dr. Bahati Salumu Mufia Injili, National Director

DRC is about one-quarter the size of the United States. They have been the place of the over-flow of the refugees from the war in Burundi and Rwanda. The country has been attacked with ethnic strife and civil war.

In 1999, Dr. Bahati was pastoring in the region of Goma, in the Northeastern section of the DRC, very near the borders of Rwanda and Burundi. It happened that Bahati had a friend by the name of Pastor Jeremie Ndayishimiye, who was the GSM-Burundi National Director. After hearing Dr. Bahati's testimony, Jeremie told Bahati about the GSM Continental Training at Uranga, Kenya. Jeremie introduced Bahati to me when I was visiting Burundi.

Dr. Bahati reported, "After a brief contact with Mama Bettie at Jeremie's house, she felt in her spirit that I had the spirit of a Samaritan, and she asked Jeremie to send me to the Continental Training in Kenya at Uranga." He felt challenged to be trained to better help his people. When Bahati returned to Goma, he started to immediately call and train other Samaritans in the region of Goma Congo.

He and his wife began to pray for direction that the Lord would have him begin the work of GSM in Congo. They believed that God wanted them to be Samaritans and to help many others to also become Samaritans."

His small team began by training 25 students, some of whom eventually also went to the Continental Training in Kenya. He graduated 30 new Samaritans in June of 2000.

After a death threat upon his life, Bahati and his family fled to Kenya and eventually we helped them move back to Kinshasa, the capitol of D.R.C. Kinshasa is a city of some eight million people. Bahati and his wife, Esther, immediately embarked on developing a Samaritan ministry in that area.

The people who were trained by Dr. Bahati in the Goma region continued the work as trained Samaritans. Even after a devastating earthquake and mudslide, the work has not been defeated. The whole region has been the scene of continual extreme violence.

In the fall of 2013, the rebel group decided to make peace with the military of D.R.C.

The Spirit of a Samaritan is not easily quashed, as it is the manifestation of holy goodness in a man. God creates the work of the Holy Spirit in us and through us. The call penetrates us to action to serve others. Only through merciful action can we fulfill the purpose for which God placed us upon this earth. To walk away from it is to walk into emptiness and deny one's true purpose. Deep within the soul of mankind is a thirst for this trueness to our purpose. Nothing else really satisfies and, once tasted, it can never be forgotten.

Bahati was born in 1972 in Bukavu. His family was loosely connected with the Roman Catholic Church. Bahati's father worked in the administration of former President Mobutu, when the country was called Zaire. The work was hard with little salary. The parents were not able to pay school fees for the children. Bahati says that his brother had to drop out of secondary school because he didn't have any trousers.

Bahati started a small business when he was 11. He and a friend traveled 27 kilometers from Bukavu to Kamembe in Rwanda to buy petrol. They would then bring this back to

Bukavu and sell for a profit. In this way, he earned enough money to pay his school fees.

Dr. Bahati continued his education and acquired a Ph.D. in theology. Later, he also received a degree in law and criminology.

Dr. Bahati has written many publications teaching about Christianity and divinity. He has founded a number of organizations in the Congo. In Kinshasa, there is no public transportation and it is difficult to get across the city. There is unpredictable provision of water and electricity. In the early 2000s, there were an estimated 20,000 street children in Kinshasa, many as young as four years of age.

Liberia, West Africa – Oliver Siafa, National Director

Oliver was born in 1959. His parents were small-scale farmers. He was the second-born child of his mother and the first-born of his father. His older brother, George, had a different father.

When Oliver was five years old, the family, which then consisted of his parents and three sons, decided to move to Liberia's capital, Monrovia, in order to make it financially. The dad gained employment as a security guard with a mining company, but he started drinking up all of his salary and abusing his wife.

Oliver said, "At one time when I went out, a man saw me and asked about my parents. After a week, that man came to our house and asked my parents to allow me to stay with him. My parents were reluctant because this was a stranger asking for their son. After several days of discussion, he took me to his house. A lady was the mediator."

Oliver was only five years old and he lived with that man for a month. He was then sent to live with the man's uncle in Monrovia. Later, he was sent to live with his uncle's brother. After five years, Oliver's father threatened to take the lady who had been the mediator to court and Oliver was traced until he was found and brought back to his father in 1970. Meanwhile, Oliver's mother had left home.

In 1970, Oliver's father was fired because he was not educated and the company wanted educated people for the position. They were forced to move out of the city and the father went back to farming. Oliver was 11 years old when he started school. He would leave home at 5:30 a.m. for the two-hour walk to school each day.

Oliver completed the ninth grade. He was double promoted twice and elected student council president in 1977. He had the highest average grade level in the entire school, and was the graduation speaker for the ninth grade class. Through the intervention of Oliver's brother, George, and through several miracles, Oliver was able to go to high school.

The following year, Oliver was sitting in the yard of his uncle with a gathering of people who had just returned from work. Oliver still had not found any employment for himself. As he was sitting there, he says, "I was overshadowed by a cloud and from that cloud, a voice spoke to me saying, 'You are different from these people. Live differently from them. Get out from among them.' Immediately, I could no longer see my neighbors clearly. When the voice stopped, I got up, went home, and locked the door. I slept well that night. Next morning, I opened my Bible and began to read Genesis."

Oliver read non-stop for many hours. "I was saved that day and I knew it. God gave me peace that I never knew before. I was filled with joy and the view of the entire world was changed to me. For one month, I read my Bible through at the house before going to church or a place of fellowship. One morning, while laying down meditating, I heard a knock at my door. It was about 6:00 a.m."

Someone from the church Oliver had visited was at his door asking if he would be willing to help, under contract for $45, construct the new church building.

He was baptized in 1985, and enrolled at the Liberia Theological Institute in March. One of the requirements for acceptance was to submit three letters of recommendation: one from the local church pastor, one from the applicant's former school, and one from the community. He was unable to get any of these letters. The pastor said he did not know Oliver well enough to write a recommendation. Oliver did not have the funds to go to his former school, and no one in the community could recommend him. Oliver was quite confused and worried about this.

One night, in a dream, a man came to him and asked, "Since you and I have been here, when last did you ask me to recommend you?" I told him, "Before I can accept, a top government official will have to recommend me." The man said to me, "No. If I send someone there, no one can refuse him." I went to that school the following week and was accepted without a single letter of recommendation.

In December of 1989, when the state radio announced that rebels were attacking in Liberia, Oliver, then the District Youth Director of the Church of God, was leading a youth camp. He closed the camp immediately and sent the young people home.

In March of 1991, the National Overseer of the Church of God asked Oliver to pastor a church in Nigeria. While there, he met and married Lucy, a registered nurse and midwife, on April 16, 1994.

A tribal war broke out in Nigeria between Afrike and another village in 1995. Oliver's home was burned and everything they owned destroyed. Later, he was transferred to Port Harcourt, River State, Nigeria. While there, Oliver became a member of the Pentecostal Fellowship of Nigeria, which brought him into contact with Faraday Iwuchukwu, the GSM National Director of Nigeria. With millions in Nigeria, how could this not be a sign of God's favor in The Call?

It was Faraday who used his influence to raise the funds for Oliver and Lucy to return to Liberia. He talked to him about the possibility of opening GSM in Liberia.

Oliver was able to go to Sierra Leone to train with Arthur Davies and John Nichols in the fall of 2000. He also went to Kenya to participate in three months of the African Continental Training at Uranga, Kenya. He earned the honor of being the top student of some 40 participants.

Yes, Good Samaritan Ministries grew in Liberia. It grew and it was blessed. Rooted in profound faith, and great miracles, the first generation responded and obeyed the depth of The Call.

September 6, 2001, I wrote the following letter to Arthur Davies in Sierra Leone:

Arthur,

Work hard on the road. Be a Samaritan. Let me teach you something about the Parable of the Good Samaritan that perhaps none of us fully understand. The man lying on the ground was a Jew. The Jews despised Samaritans. If the role had been reversed, the man lying on the ground would have absolutely not stopped to help the Samaritan. The hearts of the Jews became hard because they would not help the Samaritans. They soon did not help each other. Thus, two Jews walked by.

Finally, the coin was not given to the victim. If the money was given to the victim, the victim would want money all the time. The money was given for a direct purpose to help the victim, but given to someone else.

Now, there is much to be said here, and the story is deep and penetrating. I believe if we look at the story, we will learn much about the way Christ worked, and the way to do Christ's work. He certainly would not satisfy the greed or the needs of people as they present themselves so often on the road today. Everyone is screaming for human rights, but in the background, He would see the one who was not screaming, and he would go to that very one.

February 19, 2001, I wrote to Meshack Mkunda, in Tanzania:

What is a Samaritan? It is someone who faces exactly what all of you have faced. In the midst of evil, insincerity, drought and tragedy, there is a working together of the community, and the coming together of the people. The Samaritans draw people to help one another. The demons separate us; the Spirit draws us together.

September 7, 2001, I wrote to Pastor Victor Suotor of Nigeria:

It is important to note that the Samaritan did not give money to the victim. He gave it to someone who would help the victim, but he did not give it directly to the victim so the victim

would never become a beggar, but would retain his dignity as a man of God.

This story is important. In your country, you have two powerful people who disagree on the relationship with God, the Muslims and the Christians. We must consider that there may come a day that a Muslim will help a Christian, but the deepest question that I ask daily, "Will I be prepared to help him?"

CHAPTER 24

THE IMPOSSIBLE IS BEGUN

9/11 all airplanes disappeared from the sky in the United States. What an incredible quiet. It seemed the face of God was grieving with us, His tears, one with our struggle to do what is right in the face of so many obstacles.

9/11 found Joan Baker in Africa with a team of eight, including Vonda and two youths. As the honored International Samaritan Woman of the Year, Joan and the team visited Uganda, Kenya, Malawi, and Zambia.

They heard about 9/11, but had no way to assess its impact on the United States. Joan Baker's father died while she was gone. She experienced grief, the sorrow of the nations, and longing for rest.

I want to say unashamedly, this work is too hard. It requires the full-time attention of the soul to the leading of the Holy Spirit. We all struggled. We all continued.

In 2001, I was scheduled to go with Kathy Lane (who was a member of the International Board) on a ministry trip around the world. We would be called into the great impact of 9/11. We left on October 2nd. We were heading for London, Spain, Jordan, Israel, Palestine, Pakistan, Bangladesh and Singapore.

Originally, the journey was to include a stop in Iraq. We were all set to go. Everything had been arranged. 9/11 and the country's response to such incredible shock and evil firmly put its hand against this decision.

In Jordan, on the way to Pakistan, I talked to our director in Pakistan, Maqbool. He greatly urged us not to come, and said things were absolutely impossible. It was too dangerous. My response: "That is why we are coming. We will never submit to the Spirit of Fear." Kathy Lane and I spent 11 days in Pakistan. We were kept in hiding. **We had a conference with our leaders from throughout the country. This decision to come greatly changed the personal value that each one began to place upon this ministry. We are a Call of God from above.**

In 2001, I received word from Tanzania, that six Samaritans were murdered in Rudewa. James Opiyo went to Nigeria and

Yassin Hamdan, after years of struggle to find the central call of his life and work, founded Little Blossom Kindergarten in Bethany, East Jerusalem. His passion and dream of working in the Kingdom, where God is truly great, was about to come to pass.

In 2000, I wrote to Cameron DePoe in Monroe, Washington.

Recently, I was talking to James Opiyo on the telephone from Uranga, Kenya, East Africa. His car had been sidetracked for two years because we did not raise the funds to finish the repairs. I asked him what he was going to do about it, and he said, "Well, I think we will probably finish it and sell it. However, I have found that during this time that I didn't have a car was good. Instead of worrying about expenses for the car, I have been able to spend much more money helping others." This moved me very deeply, for James is a man of great integrity. Although the inconvenience and danger has been great, he has always operated in such a spirit that you can see why he is our continental leader in Africa.

April 26, 2001, I wrote to Reverend Callistus Emedobi in Nigeria:

Paul founded the church. Jesus founded the training and ministry of field workers. In the church, the field workers come together. They are grasping the greatness of God in the community by the field work that has been accomplished by each one. If the laborers in the church do not labor in the field, soon, their praises will be hollow, their prayers selfish, and their lives filled with religious spirits, instead of the fruits of the Kingdom of heaven.

Samaritans are field workers! They are the one leper that came back with gratitude overflowing. They are the one that stopped on the road. They are the ones who were grateful for the recognition that Jesus gave them. They are sinners who explode with the gift of praise for the smallest gift of grace.

August 14, 2001, I wrote to Samuel Kitwika in Tanzania:

Samuel, Samuel, it is easy to be busy, but I want you to know this work is not about being busy. It is about a great Spirit, the Spirit of Jesus Himself, who was the Samaritan. He was so despised in his own country he understood the Samaritan life and what it meant to be despised.

When I look at Jesus, He did not do projects, and He did not give money, but He gave each life that He touched, something that changed their life forever. For example, He gave Judas the word, "My friend," in the Garden of Gethsemane. He could have said, "You have become my enemy." He gave Mary and Martha their brother back, and the teaching on the resurrection in such a dynamic way that they were shocked. He gave Peter forgiveness when Peter didn't deserve much after such a game he played. Ponder the Samaritan life of Jesus. Look at the Samaritan life of the people you are training, and the Samaritan life of Samuel and of Tussy. See if you can experience what is too deep for words in what I have spoken here.

In 2001, Osborn Muyanga was stripped of his pastoral position in Uganda. It related to the trip he had taken to the Middle East and our baptism of Fadel Bader, a Muslim. Osborn had been warned in a dream in Cairo that this would happen. He had seen Fadel and Yassin each take Holy Communion. The pointing fingers said, "Awwww, he was baptized before he repented!" The finger of love said otherwise.

Osborn shared:

This was my lifetime's greatest rejection. One pastor stood up for me and was kicked out. I was the head of the marriage department. Some still come to me for counseling. John K. is an elder. They were so broken over this. I have stayed in this church. John K. is a servant in this church. They want our services, but not me, Osborn. As me, Osborn, has meant nothing to them.

The religious spirit is the greatest. Two strong voices speaking into me: God's doing, and the other voice, the attack of the devil.

This announcement about my loss of position went across the churches in Uganda. People said to Osborn, you are stupid. Why did you preach it and tell of the love of God you saw in the Holy Land!?

The voices made me sick, for me, and for the ministry at large.

I went to Uranga and stayed with James Opiyo for a time. We came to know each other. He, too, experienced the terrible culture. James has paid the price.

There are two major areas of great attacks: the religious spirit and men to women, women to men.

I came back and I continued to give to my pastor. During a million attacks of twisting, I keep my wife, Louise, with me at all times to protect me. Funds continued to torture my soul. I knew what it was to give. Would the people know the same? Would they have the giving spirit? Would it change their lives and make the world more whole?

In 1999, I wrote:

Recently I was honored at the Christian Northwest Foundation. There were 42 nominated to receive grants of $5,000 each, but only 12 were chosen. Mine went to Kenya to get a motorcycle for our National Director, Nicholas Okungu, who had ridden a bicycle to do national work, and for the electrification of the Continental Center, which had been long delayed, but finally had come. I was greatly honored and deeply moved even to tears to receive this award. In fact, I sobbed all the way up and all the way back to my seat, knowing that God Himself was hearing our prayers.

November 13, 2001, I wrote to Moushir in Cairo:

I deeply pray for you son, that you keep a central core of His strength, and in the central core of His strength, your emotions are healing and your faith is steady. One of the great problems I have seen consistently in the counseling office is that people have emotional faith. They don't have genuine faith. As the emotions subside and as the storms subside, always remember, your strength cometh from God alone. It is He who has made you. It is He who is testing you to strengthen you. Your enemies are not among the people. Your enemy could be how you respond.

September 4, 2001, I wrote a letter to Linda Tokuta in Nigeria. This letter was a follow-up from our time together in Kenya.

I remember how hard you and Faraday fought all night with Nick and James. Neither side was good, nor right, for the gift of the journey was a gift from God Himself, and your circumstances given by the Lord. This fight was about arrogance. It is easy to see that arrogance comes quickly, but in recognition of who the Master is, and of the whole circumstance, understanding comes very slowly. I pray there will be maturity in the ministry of Nigeria. It is long since due that all of you decide on the path to take.

I will continue to say that this ministry belongs to the grass roots. They are the people who come in, the ones who are longing for something they can't find, the people with hope and tragedy so intermingled in their souls that they struggle every day to find themselves.

An integral part of Good Samaritan Ministries has always been Wednesday Group. What is Wednesday Group?

Wednesday Group was from 10:00 to noon every week, at least 48 weeks a year. The group began in the early 1980s, and it has continued to meet unto this day, now led by Laura Fribbs. Usually 10-15 people a week come to Wednesday Group.

You do not have to belong to Wednesday Group. You welcome it as a time of refreshment: to pause, to catch your breath, and to find, again, what is important and what truly is not.

Sometimes it would seem like Wednesday Group was a women's group. It was a forum for men and women, a place where their voices were significant, a place where they could make decisions and recommend decisions that could influence the ministry all over the world. Wednesday Group was a creative force because the very people who represented all of humanity were always there. You could come once, twice, or always. You were always a member of Wednesday Group.

I always read significant letters to Wednesday Group and other groups that met.

This is why I have given letters for you now to read in this book. You are continuing to be the grass roots of the ministry. You need to hear the letters. You need to recognize that God is using someone a long way from you to speak to you and touch your heart.

Now one particular Wednesday Group made one of the most profound decisions ever made in the history of Good Samaritan Ministries.

As I read the letters and kept the pictures and stories before the people, they became their stories, part of their history, and the greater part of their experience as fellow Samaritans. So let's now speak of the most significant meeting in the history of Good Samaritan Ministries Wednesday Group.

We were meeting one Wednesday in 2001. Everything seemed an ordinary day. I, perhaps, read a letter or two. All of a sudden, Jan Gulacey spoke. She said, "I think we need to bring all of the leaders from the countries here for one great time of meeting. We all need to know one another."

At the time, I could have gasped and very easily said, "We lack the funds even for the day-to-day needs here, and their needs overseas. This is impossible. We'll pray about it, but let's not plan it." I did not say any of these things.

Instead, these words came out of my mouth, "It would be very hard. We have to buy all the air tickets, arrange for all the visas, bring them here, pay for their needs here, we're talking about a lot of people. What do you think? Do you think we can do it?"

At that moment, Tim Baker took a dollar out of his wallet, put it on the floor and said, "We can do it. Here is the first dollar." The vote was final. The grass roots had spoken. Out of their decision, we received the huge amount of funds needed to bring Samaritan leaders here.

Suddenly, there was new life and new energy in the ministry. Everyone was part of the decision and everyone was going to help with the miracle that had to unfold for this to take place. We suddenly all believed in miracles. We spoke like we knew. We trusted. We empowered, and we believed in one another as anointed from God Himself. In the whole history of the ministry, there was never a moment like this one that would include the world, the countries, and represent all the people.

We had a little more than a year to put it all in place. You cannot even begin to possibly imagine how complex it was to do this. First of all, the word needed to go out to everyone, leaders in the U.S., members of Good Samaritan Ministries, and to Good Samaritan Ministries countries. The message had to go out to everyone....and it did! Passion, Faith, Call, we could and did collect the God-given provision for this to take place. Every satellite raised the money for their country leader to come.

To every international, I wrote letters of invitation for them to obtain a visa. These letters were very personal invitations. They were written with the quality of truth, and the knowing of the people we were calling to come. Secondly, we contacted Tim Forsyth, who worked for the State Department. We asked him to contact the countries where the visas would be difficult, and to assure the embassy in each country that the letters were valid and the conference would take place.

Would these who came bear fruit for their generation from the season of this experience? The most important issue for obtaining visas was to ensure that all of the people would go home on time. In each letter, we gave assurance to each State Department.

One day Jackie Wilhelm came in and spoke to me about bringing others. She said, "Yassin Hamdan, a Muslim Palestinian, was the first Samaritan called in another country. Sam Bar-El, an Israeli, has been a covering for this ministry and for you since 1968. We must bring them too." I could only gasp inwardly at the enormity of the project. This would take place.

It is enormously difficult to get a visa to the United States. You must remember this was after 9/11. Our country was radically changing procedures and tightening up on any entry into the United States from certain countries that might not bode well for our safety.

We knew how extremely difficult those visas were going to be to obtain, so intercession began for several months over each person invited to come, over the State Department, and over the people making the final decisions. We knew that God would breathe life on this, but we knew there would be hardship and some would not be able to come.

In 2002, I received a letter from Faraday Iwuchukwu.

Three of us: Faraday, Angela, and Elisha went for the visa interview and we were all refused visas. Reason: the same old flimsy excuse that we have not overcome the presumption of being non-immigrants to the USA. We went with all, if not more than whatever was required, to prove that we intended to maintain non-immigrant status, if granted a visa. The interviews did not last for more than two minutes, each of our passports were stamped no entry to U.S., the usual excuse papers were inserted and given back to us, denying us visas. For me, this was the fifth time in 15 years that I could not come to America to be with the Samaritans.

We slept in Lagos that night and we commenced our long bus journey home the next morning. We got to Owerri at 8:30 p.m., and boarded another bus that was heading to Port Harcourt. We got to Omagwa, about 40 miles from Port Harcourt, and our bus developed a tire problem. The driver parked by the side of the road for replacement of the flat tire. That was done, and all the passengers, about 14 of us, entered the bus again to continue to Port Harcourt at about 9:45 p.m.

Immediately, three armed young men, robbers, emerged from a nearby bush with pistols and ordered all of us to lie down with our faces on the ground. They searched each of us and collected the cash in our dress pockets and handbags. They unpacked all of the luggage, traveling bags, suitcases, cell phones, etc., and vanished into the dark bushy part, ordering us to get into the vehicle and depart. It was like a lightening drama, and we were all powerless in the face of the gun-toting young robbers. We lost all the original GSM land documents, letters of appointments, center contract letters, my counseling certificate from Beaverton, and many important correspondences of GSM International, our Incorporation Certificate of GSM, and my lawyer's papers as a practicing professional. We lost license receipts, law books and Bibles, three international passports for the three of us, identity cards, ordination certificates, cash ($500, part of our BTA, and $30,000 IRA), bank statements of accounts and checkbooks, Angela's wraps and ladies dresses, shoes, the GSM 2001 annual local and international reports booklet, vehicle documents, driving licenses, etc. My reading glasses also, were forcefully removed from my face and damaged.

We left immediately to report the incident to the police at a checkpoint, about four miles away. Having reported the matter *to the police, I asked the police to accompany us, and a few of our courageous men came with them to the scene of the robbery.*

We got back there about an hour later and parked the vehicle while the armed policemen disguised and hid themselves on the floor of the bus. I advised them that we should act as if our vehicle had a breakdown. When the gang of robbers saw another vehicle parking close to the robbery spot, they thought we were another victim they should rob. The robbers immediately rushed to start their operation again, and the armed police crack team came out from the bus and over-powered them. Four of them were arrested and taken to the police station for investigation and necessary process of arraignment. Most of the passengers, including us, were able to identify their faces. We were then asked to write down our complainant's statements. We have been visiting the police station as the investigation continues. Some incriminating items have been found on the robbers, and they have been in detention since awaiting trial and conviction.

Armed robbery is a serious crime in the Nigerian legal system and, if found guilty, such robbers will suffer capital punishment either publicly or privately.

We kept a vigil at the police station, waiting to go to Port Harcourt, but we had no money any more. At 7:00 a.m., we borrowed money from the police to pay for a taxi to go home and come back later.

I have experienced being a Good Samaritan, a lawyer, and now a victim of a robbery attack. I think I have paid my full price for the calling. Let the will of God be done.

As 2002 was upon us, finally, it was clear who would be coming and who would not be coming. We were amazed how much good Tim's letters did in very difficult countries where visas were practically impossible.

It took a people to believe in a miracle. It took the faith of little ones to feed the needs of greater ones. It took Wednesday Group and the satellites to move the hand of the Lord in favor of the grass roots decision.

CHAPTER 25

THE REBIRTH OF THE SAMARITAN COMMUNITY

April 4, 2002, I wrote a letter to Francis Ntuyahera, GSM-Rwanda National Director:

I finally did receive your project proposal. I have trouble understanding how you have come to this conclusion that we are going to build a project like this. I know you desire to do something special in the right place, but I still believe that the greater thing that must be done is to train Samaritans who will be in the field in the right place. We could build 1,000 buildings and have no spirit. If we had spirit, we could send Samaritans along the road. The ministry is much more about the road than it is about the place.

Christian maturity is the issue and both feet must be firmly planted, to carry, as a Samaritan to the world, the power of the cross.

"Building International Community" was the theme of the international leaders conference we were planning.

We held our breath as we received word of those who could not come. We prayed for them to be taught and comforted where they were. The miracle was still unfolding.

One international, David Bhatti of Pakistan, came a month early. He helped with all of the preparations and stayed three months. He was a strength and a comfort.

All the airplanes were met; all the people housed with members of Good Samaritan Ministries, in some instances three or four of them at one house. The structure was in place. Early in September, 40 internationals were at the conference in Oregon. They represented 23 countries. Those countries were Singapore, Egypt, Malawi, Kenya, Congo, Sierra Leone, Liberia, Senegal, Ghana, Cameroon, Uganda, Tanzania, Zambia, Pakistan, South Africa, India, Bangladesh, Thailand, Korea, Ukraine, Canada, Jordan and Israel/Palestine. Nine who were to come did not get their visas.

There were problems, particularly in Pakistan. The embassy in Islamabad was closed due to security issues and it was the only location where visas could be obtained. The embassy finally did open and two of our people went the long distance on the train to try to get their visas. They were denied, although Maqbool had been here in 1994. 9/11 had changed trust from fire to ashes.

Others came: Karen Forsyth and her daughter from Senegal, five from Virginia, two from Utah, who had been founding members of GSM South Africa, two from Illinois, Julia Duin from Washington, D.C., four from North Carolina, two from Nevada, ten from Washington, two from Idaho, and five from California, including Mona and Samuel Estafanos and their two sons. Samuel had been our Assistant Director in Egypt before moving to California. It was during this time he was beginning an international Christian television station that would eventually cover most of the world for the Arab-speaking peoples.

Our first international meeting was a picnic on Labor Day. Jamie and Gail Dall, grass roots Samaritans, put that together.

All of the center directors in the United States spent the first week of the conference with the whole international team. They brought several from their centers. The Samaritans had to meet. We had to be moved by the Spirit to go on.

The first week the meetings were held at Bethlehem Church in Lake Oswego. Bethlehem had backed the ministry for years and they believed in The Call of this work. Why did we make the decision to meet at a church?

Many would like to make Good Samaritan Ministries their church, their Christian life, their Christian work, their Christian faithfulness. This ministry will never be a church. It is a servant to the church at large. It is a servant along the road to the many. The servant daily cultivates the soil that more plants might grow. Thus, the entire first week at the church was a living representation of the clear relationship between the church and Good Samaritan Ministries. It needed to be understood by all!

Many along the road come to this ministry with great needs and vast confusion. Our job is to help them get well and to help them find vital new priorities. With the visitors, most of the people who were hosting, and members of Good Samaritan Ministries filled the auditorium. We were full! We were rich!

We were complete! There would remain the shadow of the nine for whom we continued to pray. We believed they too could be touched, and that they too were present with us.

Meals were terrific. The Samaritans all took turns bringing in food. They helped in every area of the conference. As they studied the crowd and learned of the people, many came to learn where their call would lead.

Those that came from the U.S. were also highly acknowledged and encouraged to share.

Our greatest priority was "The Call" itself. All must understand, this Call came from God alone, not from Mama Bettie, or a committee, or a board of directors, or a person. God spoke out of heaven and The Call from above came. We had an opportunity to trust, believe in, and to know that we were to teach nothing but the Kingdom of God. I showed the slides of the two trips I made to Nineveh in Iraq, one in 1976, the second trip in 1989. We looked long and hard not only at each picture, but at the spiritual depth of each moment. We had to realize the Spirit was speaking to each of us, not just to Mama Bettie. This had to be embraced in order for there to be wholeness, unity, and an agreed-upon purpose in our life's work. IT WAS! BY ALL!

We had to know each other. That meant that everyone had to stand alone, and speak of themselves, their lives, and their experiences in developing Samaritans. For some, this was awkward, but gradually, they took to the assignment. It was exceedingly important.

Sam Bar-El and Yassin were honored and encouraged to continue to cover the ministry; Sam Bar-El, an Israeli Jew, Yassin, a Palestinian Muslim. They were encouraged to cover the ministry as a whole and to speak into our lives if we needed to listen. This was a permanent assignment.

Both men were greatly moved. It was a life-changing experience for each of them. They could see the hand of God that began this work, a hand that was keeping us unto this season. During the week it was Rosh Hashanah, the Jewish New Year. We all celebrated together the Jewish New Year.

From time to time, children joined us. There needed to be more children, but I firmly believe that we have given in to children's restlessness, instead of challenging the development of their greatness. Jesus said, *"Suffer the little children to come unto me for of such is the Kingdom of God."* (Luke 18:16)

Cameroon was a new country. Tangye George Fofungthum was to become the director. George worked full-time for Shell Oil Company in Cameroon. George was a leader who had surrounded himself with very able leaders. Since his job required him to be gone for two weeks at a time out on an oil-rigging in the Atlantic, he needed to share and designate leadership to others.

George and several friends were doing Samaritan work long before he was introduced to GSM. He and his wife, Patricia, took orphans into their home, as is the custom in many countries in Africa; however, George and Patricia learned to do deep attachment work with these children. In addition, he had a profound concern for the widows and orphans throughout his country. He was training leaders from all parts of the country. He also set a goal to establish an addictions ministry, as 80 percent of the population in Cameroon was addicted to alcohol.

Good Samaritan work in Cameroon was introduced by Joseph Nkemontoh, a Cameroonian member of GSM-Oregon. Joseph was the brother-in-law of Tangye George.

In 1996, Joe and his son, Daniel, journeyed to Cameroon where they stayed with Joseph's younger sister, Patricia, and her husband George. Joseph had never met George personally before that time, only knowing him through the letters his sister had written. Joseph said he had not heard George's life story, but that his first impression of him was that he was a man with a heart for the Lord.

Joseph reported that Tangye George had many people in his neighborhood that came for various types of help. We visited a blind man who was trying to establish a trade school for the blind. There was another person who was interested in starting a kids' reading library. When Joseph and his son, Daniel, returned from Cameroon, we talked it over and realized this was a country that had been sent to us, a Samaritan who would keep the covenant and pursue the integrity of the Samaritan life and work. In a short period of time, there was a strong spiritual team of leaders in Cameroon, and the ministry was firmly established.

The ministry in Cameroon was seeking to be fully self-sufficient as soon as possible. It is a strong ministry built by solid and very stable leaders. The ministry in Cameroon would soon become a model for other GSM work, even for those who have been functioning for many years now. George is a great teacher.

George could only stay two weeks. With a guitar, the love of God, and a spirit of humility, those two weeks made a great impact upon all of us.

Pastor Willie Booysen and his brother, Corrie, came from South Africa. Most of their time with us was the first week. They were inspired and a great inspiration to others.

We were so encouraged that four came from Singapore. Three who came had been previously involved in the Good Samaritan Ministries Internship Program here. They also were involved in a Samaritan ministry to one another in Singapore. Each of those who came had training and experience as fellow-Samaritans. They were excited to come.

As many International Samaritan leaders were pastors, it was the church and the Samaritan work that became one. We must gain one understanding. Without faith and action, the church becomes a body of comfortable people pursuing the worship of God, but not raised up into the strength of His call on their lives.

James and Teresa Opiyo were honored as International Samaritans of the Year. It was the first time we had ever honored a couple. This honoring was not only at the conference, but when the conference was over, we sent them to visit the Martin Luther King Center in Atlanta, Georgia, and to visit Washington D.C. In both cities, they were met by Samaritans and cared for during their time there.

During the conference, I found James extremely tired. Not so much physically tired, he was spiritually exhausted from grief. *"...a man of sorrows, acquainted with bitterest grief."* (Living Bible, Isaiah 53:3) By the time he left and returned to Kenya, his grief departed and his life was fully restored. This miracle took place at the Martin Luther King Center in Atlanta, Georgia. After seeing the story of Martin Luther King, he fell to the ground and sobbed much of the day at the center.

I was always looking for ways to extend the training for each of the laborers. Build their character and fruit explodes. Wayne, their host in Atlanta, bought the DVD of King's life and James returned to show it and teach from the story all over Kenya.

There is an interesting story about James Opiyo in the early days of GSM in Uranga, Kenya. We had sent boxes of books for the library at Uranga. Some of the books were the eighth grade textbooks for United States history.

When I went to Uranga and learned that James had read the entire book, I saw the importance of his training. He was willing and eager to learn. His heart embraced the founders of our country, the constitutional government and the spiritual depth of our birth as a country. His training on this extended journey to Atlanta and D.C. was vital to the training that would be offered at the Continental Training Center at Uranga.

Each of the satellites had sent their people to meet the airplanes and they all were involved in the departure of the plane carrying their leader back to Africa. Now the satellites could experience and embrace The Call. They knew what it meant to be satellite members. They embraced the responsibility and the uniqueness of their connection to their country's work. They became co-laborers in Christ Jesus. This became real in the hearts of the whole people.

Several would have to leave after the first week. Therefore, the first week was pivotal. It would set the profound development of community as a bottom line to the Lord's call for us to work together for the common good of all nations.

My personal goal was that leaders from each nation would understand the leaders from other nations, the problems in other nations, the things faced by others. This would draw them to make sacrifices for the needs of one another. If there was a need in one country, such as a natural disaster or spiritual danger, other countries were called to awareness and help. No country would be so self-centered in its own plan that it would not be aware of the greater plan for this calling. Each individual life tends to think in terms of his or her own life, experiences, and the needs they see in front of them. We must learn to think of the whole here and in the countries across the world. **IF WE DO**

NOT THINK OF THE WHOLE, WE WILL NOT THINK OF THE PART!

It is easy to be enthusiastic at a conference when we meet, talk together, and learn, but would this reality hold when they went home? Could we stay passionate for the needs of everyone? How could we learn this, and how could we sacrifice enough to know that we were there for one another? **The Lord arranged that something would occur to build us into a new community!**

The plan of the conference was that everyone who could would stay for the first month. The second month, all of those who had never been to the United States for training would stay for more training. Many stayed: Sierra Leone, Liberia, Korea, Senegal, Cameroon, India, Congo, Zambia, Rwanda, and Pakistan stayed with us the second month. During the second month, they received extensive training, including training that prepared them to be counselors and teachers. They needed to develop the structure and organization necessary for effectiveness. They stayed to study. **They stayed to outgrow themselves and to learn from one another.** Was the training tough enough? Only God knows the answer to that question. The training was tough!

Oliver Siafa came from Liberia. Almost from his first arrival, he said he felt sickly and that he had not been well before he left Liberia. We gave him special consideration, and a nurse to watch over him. Vonda Winkle took responsibility for Oliver's needs for care. Everyone was concerned about Oliver. This began to build among us strong community.

During the first month, we trained hard to develop the community of Samaritans as a whole. During the second month, our focus was to develop effective action in each country. We were constantly emphasizing team building.

The Christian Renewal Center in Silverton, Oregon, allowed us to have a weekend retreat. They paid all of the expenses for the internationals. This was a big gift and a big miracle. I am sure it was hard giving, but they didn't measure the cost. The benefit to others of loving grace was given. So, we had family camp. Not many families came, but we were there, and we experienced what it meant to be honest and to share real burdens.

The goal was not just to appear in some way, but to be who we were. In being authentically who we are, we then can build healthier community in each of our assignments.

All of us, and our families, shared a weekend retreat at the United States Basketball Academy on the McKenzie River in Oregon. This was a gift from the Academy to the ministry as a whole.

Bruce and Eileen O'Neil have been members of Good Samaritan Ministries for many years. When Bruce and his team built the United States Basketball Academy and they were about to dedicate the Academy, Bruce asked me to be present and play a pivotal role in the dedication. The people present were leaders in the basketball world from all over the United States. I was shocked and gladdened that I could be with them.

At our retreat there, many Samaritans came from all over. Each one present stood and spoke to the whole. Each of us was developing poise and character, wisdom and integrity.

This was not the final event. For the whole of the experience was an ongoing lifetime event!

At the end of the training, for those who stayed on, we went to a nearby Presbyterian church to worship and pray together. They gave us lunch. They welcomed us and encouraged us. Here, I anointed each one of our internationals with oil, and spoke prophetic words over each life. We closed in an act of worship and prayer.

David Bhatti of Pakistan later said:

I saw this conference in two ways: it was the greater commission of Jesus Christ our Lord. It was the greatest commandment in action. This ministry is not about America it is all about mutual respect. Christianity is not a qualification for volunteering or receiving help. I experienced the words, 'Go. Come out of your comfort zone. Go to the world.' I saw growth of faith in the whole ministry. It was a surprise that so many meetings were held in different places. We sat and ate together, shared our vision, empowering everyone's voice. There were no walls of hatred or divisions. We were building each other.

America seems to show more love. Sometimes we don't see the price America pays. ***We were building a bridge among nations. This is the kingdom of God.*** *At the conference the first* *week, I, a Pakistani, had India sitting on one side of me, and Bangladesh sitting on the other side. **There was no nationality.** All were in the kingdom of God. We were one!*

Three of the international directors are part of a twelve-person intercessory prayer team that covers the work all over the world. Faraday was praying in Nigeria. He was interceding. David Bhatti and Osborn Muyanga taught about intercessory prayer. Prayer is key to a person's life. **Jesus entered into prayer. He never taught his disciples how to preach, only how to pray.**

What was the action after the conference? When David went back to Pakistan, GSM-Pakistan began building bridge schools for Muslim and Christian children. Each school had an equal number of Christian and Muslim children. In Pakistan, only 3 percent of the whole population is Christian. At the bridge schools, Christian children were never the minority.

David remembered something I said in Pakistan years before, "I am not an American, I am from the Lord!"

David, as a field director in Pakistan, went to each center with a vision of building the community. He summarizes, "I trained them all."

David Bhatti saw himself as one who has no home, "I have 30 countries."

MUTUAL RESPECT

The situation in Pakistan became so difficult and David's health began to break. He decided to move his family to Canada. He developed GSM-Canada. He built the website. His goal was make impact and give effective actions. This past Christmas, Hindus and Muslims from Canada, and 20 countries came together in celebration in 2012. David said, "The world is on our doorstep. We must take down the barriers!"

Raymond of Senegal wrote:

The gathering was one of a kind, where one could not help but picture heaven as a place where all people, irrespective of their race, gender or religion, comes together to pray, praise and worship the most high God.

The GSM International Conference and training in 2002, with Jesus in attendance (Matthew 18:20) positively saved, molded, and shaped our lives forever. I, Raymond, personally thank God for being part of such a godly historic event.

Raymond of Senegal, a former Muslim, was called out, during his prayers at a mosque, by the Lord, Himself, to become a Christian.

Many airplanes were leaving again. All of us would go with each of them.

CHAPTER 26

TEST AND TRAGEDY BUILDS THE WHOLE

Oliver Siafa of Liberia was very ill. As the weeks went by, we didn't quite know what to do. You see, no one had health insurance, and of course, we had no money. We had to decide what to do and how to manage. We finally got Oliver to a hospital where he was diagnosed with serious liver cancer, but the process was arduous.

During the International Conference, Vonda played a key role in health care for each of the International attendees. She arranged that all would have their teeth and eyes done, free of charge, by dentists and eye doctors around the area. If there were major problems with their teeth, they were fixed. If they needed glasses, they received them.

Vonda looked for a doctor who would be willing to see Oliver free of charge. We found one, but we had to pay for all of the labs.

Oliver kept saying, "I don't want to go to the hospital." Vonda did have to take him to a hospital for lab work. She shared that while she had him waiting on a bench in the hospital, she suddenly had a severe migraine headache and ran to a bathroom where she did projectile vomiting all over the bathroom. Grateful of heart were we all for the personal cost so many willingly paid.

While at the hospital for two hours, Oliver received x-rays and blood work. The doctor called later and said Oliver had Hepatitis A. He gave us instructions for treating him.

Oliver always wanted to be where the training was. We brought in a couch. Oliver could lie down during all of the meetings.

Oliver shared with us that he was concerned before he left Liberia that he might have a serious illness. His wife, Lucy's words to him were, "God has something for you. You must go."

As Oliver was not improving, Vonda took him back to the doctor for more tests. They called and apologized, saying they had misdiagnosed him. He had Hepatitis B.

Dr. Victoria ordered homeopathic IVs for Oliver. His stomach was bloating. There was edema in his legs. We had to get him to the hospital. When we went into Emanuel Hospital, Vonda filled out all of the papers and signed them that GSM was personally responsible. Eventually, after long weeks, the hospital rescinded that decision and Emanuel Hospital said they would be responsible.

Within the first 24 hours, Oliver was diagnosed with Hepatitis C and liver cancer.

The internationals were shook up. Oliver was one of them. He was important to them. The Internationals decided to rotate and sit with Oliver 24 hours a day. We knew by this time that Oliver was going to die. Oliver asked Vonda to call his brother, George, who lived in Chicago. George came within 24 hours. At the time, he said, "I had to come so quick because no white person could take care of Oliver as well as I could." While here, George learned, we all could. Yet, George never left Oliver's side.

I came to the hospital with all the International Directors who were still here. Vonda went daily and was a bridge to the doctors. I will always remember, as I walked out of Oliver's room, a day or two before he died, I turned at the door and said to him, "I will see you soon, Oliver."

We were worried that Oliver would die here and we wouldn't know what to do with his body. It was decided that Oliver and George would get air tickets for both of them to go to Liberia. The tickets were purchased. Oliver kept saying, "I want to go home." George and Oliver never made it to the plane. The morning they were to fly out, he died. We had reassured Oliver, "We will make sure you go home."

The burial of Oliver was a tough decision for the whole ministry. At first, we thought we would bring Lucy here for his burial. Rock Creek Church donated a plot. The African National Directors spoke firmly that the whole culture of Africa is against cremation. We had told Oliver that he would go home. We priced what it would take to send him home and what the process would be. He had to be embalmed three times, put in a wooden casket and then in a metal casket. He had to be sent naked. His body would have a significant layover during the flight home. The cost of sending Oliver home was $20,000.

Funerals of testimony and decent burials are very important in Africa. It was a profound decision to gasp and then decide we would raise the money to pay for Oliver to go home.

The funeral was held at Bethlehem Church, where we had spent the first week of the conference. George and his wife flew in from Chicago for the funeral. The church was full. Many African Americans came. They noted what we had done, the decision we had made, and they respected this community for that decision.

Oliver's brother, George, Vonda, Osborn, and I, the four of us, spoke at the memorial service. We gave much testimony. As I look back on it, it was a time when the fire of the Holy Spirit, and the electricity in that room of people who knew that Oliver was a saint, so filled the atmosphere, that it was life-changing to have been there.

Vonda had met previously with Oliver in Kenya at the Training Center in 2001. They already had a strong relationship. Vonda met Oliver's wife, Lucy, in Uranga at the Training Center in 2007. She said, "Lucy amazed me that God had prepared her. She had a dream that the roof of her house was blown off. Oliver was her covering."

Did we make the right decision? We had choices. Did we make the right decision to send Oliver home?

On the part of the ministry here, it was a grass roots decision and a profound act of courage. There was a powerful effect within the African community here and among all of the directors who said words from many countries during service. It was noted that love had been defined once again, love and respect held as sacred. Before a living God, as the decision was made, there came a living presence of the Holy Spirit to remind us of the value of just one laborer in His Kingdom. In a short length of time, God brought us the $20,000 by the sacrifices of many.

George flew with his brother's casket to Liberia. There was much confusion when the casket arrived and they discovered that Oliver was naked. The Liberians had trouble understanding the decision. They did not understand that it was international law for shipping a body.

One year after Oliver died, George came from Chicago and we had a remembrance service for Oliver. In the group room at Good Samaritan Ministries, there is a painting of Oliver done by one of our grass roots members. It will remain there as a testimony of a miracle.

Oliver was buried in Monrovia, the capitol of Liberia. I and a small team have been to his grave with his wife, Lucy.

Lucy Siafa took up the cross and followed Christ. She was named National Director of Good Samaritan Ministries in Liberia. She has borne the burden of the care of their five children. Lucy found temporary housing in a Christian compound. She was managing.

May 10, 2005, letter to Lucy Siafa:

Dear Mama Lucy,

I appreciated your prayers and the depth of your honesty! How well I understand, Lucy, desperation in a woman's heart and spirit: longsuffering, breakdown, breakthrough.

What your problems were, they are no different than mine have been. We are definitely sisters. We understand that The Call always wins, even in our greatest level of weaknesses.

I am glad you told me that you have been lonely all your life. Let's start a journey of breaking it. I don't know how this will be, but I believe it is the beginning of something very important.

I was lonely too, but when the Lord came to live inside of me, it was different than just accepting Him. The key for me was not me accepting Jesus, but Jesus accepting me. He willingly dwelt in me, in the whole inner realm of my life; never to depart.

All of our training has been "Accept Jesus, Be Baptized, Be Saved." It is all wrong, Lucy. The good news was "Jesus accepted us! It pleased the Father to give us His Kingdom." We are anointed and we are brought home. No one can take us out!

Christianity has been filled with bad news that has caused tremendous suffering, and the hell of competition in the religious realm. I beg you, my sister in Christ Jesus, to come with me into His joy.

I don't think that anyone is going to come to Liberia this year. We have suggested, instead, to help pay for the ones who are going to go to Nigeria. Would you give me the amount that is going to be needed, as soon as possible, so we can make arrangements for the money for your flights? God bless you, Lucy. We love you.

I want to remind you, Mama Lucy, if the church never tells you this; the truth is: our sins have been forgiven, eternally. The blood of Jesus covers our past, our present and our future.

Mama Bettie

A small team and I went to Liberia in 2006. Liberia was still a disaster area. The civil war, the evil and the violence that had been committed in the country, left a profound effect on all of the people. The grief in Liberia was like the grief in Rwanda. "God help Liberia to rebuild. Give them the courage to face the grief and live beyond it!"

Lucy went on to be a great laborer, one of the most amazing women in the ministries overseas. She developed an office in Monrovia, and gave vast amounts of counselor training. People had to stay in training for months and they had to be serious. She sent each of the trainees out with assignments. We visited one of those assignments. It was a rehab center for those who had committed great violence. It was a place for their lives, their souls, to somehow be rebuilt, and for them to be trained enough to earn an honest living. Good Samaritan Ministries in Liberia has played a significant counseling role in the rebirth of a free Liberia.

Oliver's death was the seed that fell to the ground. Weep no more, it is the rebirth of the ministry as a whole!

Chapter 27

SUFFERING, LEADERSHIP, AND TRANSITIONS

In the last few days, I have become more aware of the importance of the content in my conscience, and our conscience as a ministry. Conscience can be full of information, confusion and chaos.

Many years ago I put the Parable of the Good Samaritan in charge of my conscience full-time. The ministry would not be a victim. We would not be robbers, and we would not walk on by. In all things, my own conscience was personally weighed by the words, "Go and do likewise." This kept the ministry and I sensitive to the needs we saw and faced every day. I had to remember, without ceasing, our decisions would affect the lives of many. **I did not have a situational conscience, led by the Holy Spirit, I had a full-time conscience!**

July 9, 1993, I wrote to James Kabvalo: He was developing our work in Malawi, and at the time I wrote, he was attending the Continental Training in Uranga.

Do not be afraid to suggest to me changes that you think need to be made, corrections. Do not be afraid to challenge me, or James Opiyo, or any of us. For we don't consider you less than we are, we consider you as His servant with all of us. The Holy Spirit moves among us all, and through us all, corrections must be made. We can only be comforted and healed by His Spirit moving among us. I firmly believe that one of the great weaknesses in modern Christianity has been that the Spirit has not been really set free to move among the people. It often has been controlled, and used to manipulate people in power. It has often been taken away from the common man as his way of expressing the truth. Feel free to express the truth as you see it, James Kabvalo. Feel freedom in your spirit, son. We are a voice for the Lord, Himself. We are a voice declaring respect for the needs of our fellow man.

December 29, 1994, I wrote to Harry Gama, the Chairman of GSM-Malawi:

I can say to you quite honestly that I found no guile in James Kabvalo. I found a simple man trying to understand his duties He was recovering from the slaughter by those who thought they were more important. God always loves the one who is less, and as James has become less, God has loved him more and raised him higher than many others.

February 6, 1996, I wrote to James Kabvalo:
There is very little understanding in the Christian world that Jesus did not come to start a new religion. He came to start a new sacredness in all relationships, sacredness that would force us daily to look in the mirror and weigh whether we loved our neighbor as much as we loved ourselves. Hear these words; heed them.

One of the mistakes that I have seen in many people in the ministry is they begin to think they have a ministry and it belongs to them. I want to say to the entire ministry of Malawi, "If this ministry belongs to GSM or to you, you have missed the point and have seriously walked away from the Lord Jesus." The ministry belongs to our Lord, and it is only for that purpose that it was called into existence. When we use His name, we must humble ourselves and empty ourselves of guile and pride. I know you hear my words.

March 27, 1996, I wrote to James Kabvalo in Malawi:
I was sorry not to do anything about the vehicle. As Joan shared with you, it was not possible, but I want to say something else to you, James, that is really, really important. I believe that you are praying for the needs that you have for the ministry in Malawi, but I do not believe you are praying for the needs of your brothers and sisters in the other countries. I believe that you are looking for the things you need for the ministry there. Are you looking for a new vehicle for Nigeria? Are you looking for a vehicle for South Africa or Pakistan, or another nation? Are you saying, "Lord, give the vehicle to the one who needs it the most and let me wait until my need is in your hand, Lord."
You have to remember, James Kabvalo that you are not just in national ministry, you are in international ministry. Your

concern for others is as important a lesson as anything you will ever learn from your Father in heaven.

May 7, 1997, I wrote to James Kabvalo:

You tend to write stories of victimization. You have not learned how to turn every story of everything that happens to you into a true Samaritan story. According to the Word of God, all things are working together for good in order to conform you into the image of His Son, Jesus Christ. The victimization stories of robberies and difficulties that you have had are true and honest, but you have left them as victim stories, and you do not bring the victory through. You did not mention the Samaritans that helped you. You did not mention the work of Samaritans that is continually being done. **For example, as you wrote about the robbery in the bathroom, you did not write of the miracle of the Samaritans in Lilongwe when Samaritans helped you with the money to get home. It is amazing if you start to turn these victim stories over to the Samaritan story. You are going to find a great change in the way you respond to difficulty and tragedy.** *Since you are a leader and a teacher of your nation, the Lord would require you to rethink everything you write about, and every way you present victim material. The main point I got out of this story is after the robbery you decided to never travel alone. Yet, the Lord Jesus commended the Samaritan who was on a very dangerous road, could have been killed instantly and traveled alone. He was helping someone else who had been hurt. There is a time to go out by twos and there is a time to lay down your own life for others.*

October 28, 1997, I wrote to James Kabvalo:

I want to really warn you, James, to not be bound by logic, but be wise in the balance between a good mind, a good heart, and the extremely important direction given by the Holy Spirit. If you do not hear the Holy Spirit directing you in strange and mysterious ways, you may be missing the balance. The Holy Spirit is our teacher, and He will call us to significant action beyond our minds and simple hearts. Our minds are finite and our hearts are limited. God's power, His grace, His wisdom, and His movement through us are unlimited. It is easy, over a period of time, to build a system, but it is the creative power of the Holy Spirit breathing on us that creates the life of the Spirit in this ministry.

December 22, 1998, I wrote to James Kabvalo:
I have great respect for you, James Kabvalo. I believe that the team that was to be has settled in, and the others have departed. It is amazing how many come into the ministry when they think they might get something for themselves, but when it is all finished, and the dust is shaken off the feet, the goats and the sheep are separated, and then the good fruit comes. The attacks come. Now, they will be less, for Satan has seen that he can do little to change your mind. As you know, James, this is not a temporary call upon your life and the lives of your team.

September 22, 1999, I spoke to James Kabvalo on the phone. At that time, he said, "This is a ministry of the people. GSM is a symbol of peace and reconciliation."

In October of 2004, we were aware that James Kabvalo was in very serious physical condition. He had cancer of the throat. At that time, we sent James Opiyo from Kenya to Malawi to spend significant days with James Kabvalo, and to meet with him about the transition that would need to take place. James Opiyo and I both considered it important that the transition decision be made by James Kabvalo himself and that no one would challenge that transition decision if it were made on his deathbed.

By July, James Kabvalo could swallow at least liquids, but since August, he couldn't swallow anything, not even his own saliva. He was being fed through tubes for the last four months of his life.

At the time of James Opiyo's visit, James made a thorough survey of the ministry at large in Malawi. He met with many of the people. **It is important to clarify in this book that the Continental Director of Africa must play a role in decisions that will come about as countries go through transition and change.**

James Opiyo was effective in deciding how those transitions would take place, and how God could bring about a new season and a new hope in GSM-Malawi.

With James' visit, others were being trained to be effective in roles that would hold the ministry together. Justina Msofi played an important role, and continues to do so in the transitions of GSM.

Here, Jill Hartzell, took the Satellite for Malawi to heart. She took the lifetime assignment to be there for them, and for Malawi. She and her whole family became part of the transition, a part that played a vital role because the people would feel the safety of their relationship to the ministry as a whole. Since 1998, to this day in 2013, Jill and her family continue in this assignment.

At this point I want to say a word to the whole ministry, and to any who would consider that they might like to be Samaritans.

A satellite can weaken God's work or strengthen it. The people here, the people who support that country, must develop a passion that does not wane when things are difficult. Finding leaders who would not walk on by has been one of the big struggles in the ministry. The countries that have had passionate leadership partners from our end have born the greatest fruit along the shared Samaritan road. Any satellite member who experimented with the assignment, came to meetings once in a while, and lacked vision and passion, created harder struggles in the countries they were called to serve.

Jill and her family have made annual trips to Malawi. They have raised the funds to do this. They have been passionate to help make a difference. They co-labor to make decisions that will create effective actions for the ministry in Malawi.

A satellite leader must never work just for a project or a ministry. They must work for a country. We are living and breathing for the good of the country, and for the breakthroughs needed for people to be well.

God knows the frustration that I have experienced. Many put their toe in the water, but did not immerse themselves in The Call.

I will continue, until my last breath, to challenge Good Samaritan Ministries here. We must teach people who come

in to give their last breath. Covering, protection, and positive suggestions instead of negative criticism are vital to the strengthening of nations beginning to grasp the work of Christ Jesus among the whole. I say these words passionately. I do not hesitate to say, "We need to stop thinking somebody else will do it, and learn that doing it is a profound obedience. We are to be a servant to a nation as Christ was a servant to His."

Over the years, I struggled in my conscience. Was I faithful? Were our people faithful? Would we encourage faithfulness? I struggled with the needs being fairly met among the nations.

Most of the national directors in Africa received a monthly stipend. As the years went by, James Opiyo received $400 a month. Some of the national directors in larger countries, where the situation was more active and required more movement in their work, received $300 per month. The rest received $250 a month. They were never given a raise. After a time, I never personally received from the ministry more than James. God provided what we all needed. The wants were sacrificed by all of us!

The purpose of the stipend was not only to provide for survival of the family, but also to provide the money for the leader to move and do the work. Leaders could not just sit in an office or sit in a house. They had to be able to move, and they had to be able to be effective in the bigger picture.

I say these things because they are important for everyone to know. As the ministry transitions, do not consider this to be a light issue; it is a profound issue that the Lord would provide enough for the servant to do His labor, to give his labor to the work.

January 2, 2005, James Kabvalo had left the work in the hands of the Holy Spirit and with the people who were capable of keeping it as a sacred trust. His life here was finished. His intercession in heaven would continue to help make an effective ministry in Malawi.

Samson Meleka was chosen by James Kabvalo and James Opiyo to be the national director of GSM-Malawi. The appointment of Samson Meleka was not coming by my direction, but by the full direction of James Opiyo and James Kabvalo.

Africa must be empowered to make decisions, and we need to believe that the Lord will check and work with the Africans to make their decisions. Samson Meleka had been sent to Kenya for the Continental Training in 2001 and again in 2003. He received the full training. He was a man that was highly respected. He had been the pastor of 12 churches, and the chairman of five zones. When he became the Director of Good Samaritan Ministries--Malawi, empowerment happened and the Holy Spirit helped him build healthy teams that could make a difference in Malawi.

On July 5, 2005, I wrote an instructional letter to Samson Meleka:

No skimming is allowed in this ministry. When someone gives us $30 for a nursery school for Malawi, we do not skim money here and keep some for our general operation costs. In like note, if $30 is given for a nursery school in Malawi, you may not skim for your personal expenses, but all $30 must go to that nursery school. All funds are to be 100% accounted for to go for what they are earmarked. The end of the year, you will have to send in an annual report and an annual financial report. Jill will give you the training needed.

When you work in the ministry and people think you have funds from a foreign source, they will come around with many stories and pretend many things. You are saved from embarrassment by the fact that we send the budget from here for the money. Skimming is not allowed, therefore, it cannot be given to them.

This is not an easy lesson for Africa. In Africa, you are used to feeling that all things are held in common, but in the long run, it provides that a great deal more can be done. The bills are paid on time, and the ministry has ethics. People will then trust your word.

August 10, 2005, I wrote a letter to Pastor Samson Meleka:

Build a good team and be a good team player. *In Africa, too often, the tribal leader has too much pride and the little people do not spiritually grow and develop. If you are a good team leader, everyone will grow and develop, including you. It will be very good!*

I have included this story of transition because it is an important lesson for each country, and a very important lesson for us who must be strengthened by the passion of Christ to do His work.

As you can see by the progression of letters, I was encouraging, training, building, and providing lessons that could be shared with many.

I have said in another place in this book, in addition to the letters to the national directors, I wrote to many of the local center directors and others who had the Samaritan spirit, but needed to have it developed and encouraged. We need to believe in the little person, and consider their work as important as our own.

This is part of the root of Good Samaritan Ministries. How easy it would have been to flail around and not know what to do. How important it was that the roots of the ministry in Malawi were protected and they were able to grow a healthy bush. We must never lose sight of the roots of The Call and the greatness of the simple work that draws us all unto Him.

CHAPTER 28

THE VISION OF JESUS

In 1994, I wrote to James Opiyo:
According to Osborn Muyanga's account, President Museveni asked the entire nation to become Samaritans. He told them that he was a Samaritan.

Osborn's spirit groaned and wept when he realized what 45 minutes did with their President. The President never forgot the little Good Samaritan pin I gave him in 1992.

May 11, 2004, letter to Rajabu Mziwanda:
We come as profoundly called to be in your midst, to speak of things that are more important than entertainment or socialization. Indeed, the words must be few, and they must come from above among us all. I asked the Lord to draw you together with me at this time. It is one thing to follow ministries, and something entirely different to follow our Lord Jesus.

September 7, 2004, I wrote to Pastor Alfonce Lubarati in Dar Es Salaam, Tanzania:
There are big churches full of lots of activity, but this is a profound work along the road. It must not be lost. Please empower and encourage one another for the sake of His Kingdom.

In July and August of 2004, a small team of Samaritans made a profound journey to Africa. The team included Rose Slavkowsky, Jennie Mitchell, Nike Greene, Kathy Lane, Carol Chapman, Stanley McKenzie, and me.

Stanley McKenzie made a deep impression on me. He was a very humble spirit and he said he only went to learn. While we were in Kenya, it came about that we began an extensive training for caretakers of senior citizens. Stanley, who had much experience in that field, and Kathy Lane, a former nurse, developed and conducted the training.

Why did Stanley make a deep impression on me? He was poor, and yet he gave unto God for this journey. He was living in

California, and had not connected with the ministry for quite some time. On this journey, he was preparing to tell the story of this journey to every single member of his family.

How Stanley did this was unique. He e-mailed every family member, each month, in the time that followed the journey to Africa. He told them a different story each month. Soon, many in the family were supporting Good Samaritan Ministries' work in Africa.

The purpose of the journey in 2004 was to gather the national directors of Central and East Africa to the Continental Training Center at Uranga, Kenya, for training, and to gather the West African National Directors at the West African Continental Training Center in Port Harcourt, Nigeria. In Nigeria we were to develop the curriculum and the unity of those who would be sending trainees in the years to come.

In 2004, I was 70 years old. It was an awesome responsibility to travel, and to guide and protect the ones going on the journey with me. We met with so many people on such key and important issues. I knew my time directing the ministry would end when I was 75, if not before, due to illness or death. I knew this was a very important decision to get people together who would hold, protect, and guide the ministry in the years to come.

Each person that traveled on our team played an important role. We were not just going through the motions; we were living with the Africans in the most personal manner possible. Together, we were living the Samaritan story—all of us.

I had been seeking the face of Jesus a long time, that he might truly be the teacher of this ministry. In the year 2004, He revealed that. **Three revelations were given as the journey progresses: We may have only one Father and that is our Father in Heaven. We may have only one teacher and that is Jesus. We may have only one culture, the Kingdom of God.**

We were all in a battlefield with Satan, and Satan's goal was to knock us off hard. Each of us present in the training, throughout the journey, would have to learn we are the ones who must never forget we have only one teacher and that is Jesus.

Gradually, the word "vision" became a huge part of the whole training and the whole experience, guided by the Holy Spirit and the Scripture, *"My people perish for lack of a vision."* (Prov. 29:18)

All Uranga was a disaster area when we first came in 1987. Few had vision or energy to fix a roof. They would just get a bucket for the leaking water. They had been taught religion, but no one had ever received the Vision of Jesus.

How was this training different? You're baptized as an individual, NEVER an assembly line!

Samuel Kitwika shared with Jennie during Sunday dinner. He had learned to look at a simple question and rethink, "How to comfort his people?"

In the meeting at the Uranga African International Conference, the attendees were our directors from South Africa, Tanzania, Congo, Uganda, Rwanda, Burundi, Kenya, Zambia, and Mozambique. In addition, most of the center directors from throughout Kenya were in attendance. We were studying the ministry as a whole: the emphasis needed, the things they had seen, and the possibilities of empowering the people.

I said, "Go back to the seniors and get them involved in the WHOLE work of Good Samaritan Ministries, AND THE VISION. Change the hearts of children. Look for the lost children in your country, but also look for the lost children of Africa. Children are not just saved or unsaved. They must be developed!

Train Bible teachers. The teachers were not just to teach the Bible. They also needed to develop their own skills of learning as they taught.

Osborn Muyanja related an incident with the GSM school up in Masaka, an incident that was life-changing for both he and the children. This incident occurred on July 17, 2004. Now, three weeks later, he was with us in Kenya.

They had rented a bus in order to take some of the high school children to a football match in Kampala. 69 people were on the bus, including five teachers. They left at 5:00 a.m., and they were on their way back to Kiwangala at 10:45 p.m.

The road from Masaka Town up to Kiwangala is narrow and rough. At 10:45 p.m., all on the bus were attacked by six thieves who had torches, guns, and a panga. The thieves pushed the bus to the side of the road, down a hill, and into a ditch. Someone on the bus felt they were going backwards and that there could be a terrible accident. One of the boys went up to the front of the bus and pushed on the brake. He saved the lives of the children, otherwise they would have turned over in the deep ditch. The thieves emptied the bus. They ordered all the teachers and children to the ground, told them to undress, and empty themselves of any belongings. Eventually, the thieves left after taking all they wanted, but now there were 69 people, 64 children and five teachers, all naked. This was a primitive area, but there was a house fairly close by. By God's grace, the man at the house was awakened and came out. He allowed the girls wait for help inside his house. At 7:00 a.m., Osborn arrived from Kampala. At first he found three children hiding in the bush and one teacher. The teacher said, "Thank God for my life. He had a gun and he was going to hit me, but he didn't." Two men from the house took him to a clinic and gave him a shirt and a blanket.

Students ran out of their hiding places in the woods. They were all in shock by what had happened. Margarita was unconscious. Justin was bleeding terribly. Osborn said, "I couldn't recognize the face of one teacher; he had been hit so much. Another teacher shook all over when she sat down."

After Osborn arrived, he had everyone singing. Those who had been sitting near windows sang less, for glass from the bus windows had cut them.

The police had been called, but they said they had no fuel to come and help. There was no help from the police, or the hospital. Osborn made sure the nine injured students were taken to the hospital, but there was no one to take care of them.

George was unconscious. Osborn said, "Wake up. Let's go home." Meanwhile, in Kiwangala, church members thought the students were dead. When they finally arrived at the village, Osborn marched them all into the church. He didn't say, "Sorry, sorry, this is a terrible thing that has happened to you kids." He said, "Monday I'm going to call and make sure all of you students are in school."

Now the children fully understood the Parable of the Good Samaritan. They fully understood why they were Samaritans, why they were in their school, and what the training meant.

Later, after the conference at Uranga, we came to Uganda and met with the students and teachers. All were still in massive shock. Some were recovering from injury.

There is always the haunting question in this ministry: "Will we provide and pay for the medical care needed? Or will we walk on by?"

You who are grown up are born ahead of children. Remember children are not dumb, they know. Children at our schools in Uganda receive the same training as all of the center directors. They understand as they take the training, and often they do better than the adults, for they grasp the action. They have far less fear of doing the work. "Treat me the same when I am five, ten, or 15 years old." Remember, kids grow every day, every hour. The teaching and experiential training given each child grows the child on the inside. Emphasize to the children they are the future leaders.

A better way to teach children is to put them among us. Give them a voice, and use them to help make decisions. At the meeting at Uranga, in silence, we sat stunned by the story. How easy it is for us to forget the lives of the children and their vulnerability to danger. In this tragic event, we encountered the great possibility of learning. They can act on behalf of God!

During the training given on the journey, everyone was reminded: **Jesus helped people in their own home, and their own environment. He came to them.**

As leaders, we get the feeling people have to be paid for Samaritan work. It probably comes from the devil. I don't think the apostles were paid. **The first thing often thought of is money, not how will I do this as it must be done with little or no money.**

Osborn further shared, "If you see a child who wants to play his own game alone, then the child does not have leadership quality. Yet, I would add the child always has the possibility. Therefore, every Thursday, I, (Osborn) went to school to play with the children." Again, all of us quietly sat there, with another question, "Did we play with the children?" James Osewe spoke up, "Yes, we must play with the children!" No one else responded. Are we lost in our adulthood?

It has been a blessing that our daughter, Jennie Mitchell took extensive notes on the journey. By God's grace, she found her notes. I share these notes with you.

**NOTE FROM JENNIE MITCHELL'S DIARY:
VISION GIVES US HOPE AND HOPE GIVES US FAITH**

WORDS FROM THE TEACHING:
1. We must understand our attitudes and our knowledge.
2. Do we know our community in detail?
3. You must know your personal self to build genuine community.
4. Long-term vision should be self-supporting and self-sustaining. Create this understanding among the people.
5. Questions are the most important teaching method. A few words—vital questions, "Who influences your life?"
6. *Our freedom is our greatest asset, use it wisely!*
7. I shared a story about Martin Luther King. He knew which way he was going. What kills us is the business. What heals us is knowing where we are going.
8. Sandy, our National Director from South Africa shared, "It is vital that we each pass on a vision or the vision dies with us."
9. Do we know God's passion? Do we know the intense desire of God to change this world?
10. Integrity was defined as one who does not talk behind someone's back.
11. **We may never teach anyone before we know them. Jesus knew each one. Always remember, you must teach the person, not just the material.**
12. **Until Jesus comes, we are His substitute teachers. We are to draw attention to our teacher, never to ourselves.**

During these meetings at Uranga, all of the training and our experiences were shared. Each of the leaders, who had become fieldwork teachers, brought the group together into fields where they could see, learn, and know.

Questions that I asked during the teaching: "What is your story? How did you find Good Samaritan Ministries? What do you remember about your teachers, the good ones and the bad ones?" Above all things, we were educating by experience, actions, parables, the Glory of God and the Kingdom He gave us.

We helped each other establish priorities. First, we had to see the present priority to come to grips with the future priorities. It is key that we empower the people. Tell the people you believe in them and God believes in them. **Communicate, Communicate, Communicate!**

In the vision of the ministry, we each go to our own churches. However, when we go to the fields to work, we are all together in one group.

It cannot be said too often, don't mix up vision with projects. The most important call upon each of us is the real inspiration shown in our work. **Jesus' work was inspiring.**

We discussed two New Testament visions. The vision of Jesus for field workers, and the vision of St. Paul for church workers. It was urgent that we understood this.

Don't start projects without the vision of where you want to go. Vision must always challenge us to ask, what is the end result needed? This must be clear.

Understand the Vision of Jesus. He took less than 100 people and trained them. St. Paul decided to make tents for a living, never taking dollars from people. He supported his work himself by hard physical work.

Jesus begs for us. He talks to God about our prayers.

You have to be willing to learn what it truly means to be a servant to others. Speak no evil of anyone for we do not know the day of their salvation.

Above all, our job is to train children to be lifetime Samaritans, and to keep the faith. This will always sustain their actions.

When our team went on to Uganda, by far the most important visit was to the children at Kiwangala. We came in as one with them, and as we left, we were still one team with them.

It would be easy for this ministry to forget that education in Uganda was a vision. When we lose sight of the vision and we focus on the money, the vision fades, and the Kingdom of God grieves.

I asked the directors, "Who do you call into the work and will they make a remarkable difference?"

One of my clients at the Beaverton office came back one day and looked at our bulletin board of pictures of orphans in Sierra Leone. He said clearly, "I have no problems." Always remember that if a client is still selfish when they leave, they are not better! They are not Samaritans until they are no longer inclined toward selfishness.

A core value of this ministry: It is not my vision or your vision; it will always be the vision of Jesus.

As we traveled into Rwanda, we saw a very beautiful country, the hills, the houses, and the people. We were entering a holy place. The genocide changed Rwanda. Classic tribal divisions brought wholeness to the country. There is an agreement in Rwanda that you may no longer ever speak of your tribe. You may only say, "I am Rwandan."

I taught: **Evil stole your family, your children, your generation; you MUST be about the Father's business! You must not be a nation of victims and survivors; you must be a nation of people who never walk on by.**

Know Jesus because you are living and breathing in His Name.

We went from Rwanda over to Goma, Congo. We obtained a day pass at the border. A volcanic eruption had destroyed over half of Goma. Even today, vast evil is at work in Congo, torturing the people for some hazy importance in the minds of those committed to living a life of rebellion.

What I remember most on the journey into Goma Congo was the survival of people who knew they were in the Father's business. Suffering had created strength.

As we had to be out of Congo by dark, we stayed in a hostel on the Rwandan side of the border. I will never forget that night. Several of us sat outside by the light of a lantern: Our team, Bahati from Congo, Francis from Rwanda, and Jeremie from Burundi.

This was one of the most empowering moments I have experienced. It is one thing to think we know the vision of Jesus, but it is something else for heaven to pronounce it. On that night, heaven pronounced the vision. He cut all the bloodlines in the world through His blood, making us of one blood. *"You must call no one on earth your father, since you have only one Father, and he is in heaven. Nor must you allow yourselves to be called teachers, for you have only one Teacher, the Christ. The greatest among you must be your servant."* (Matthew 23:9-12)

"You may have only one teacher and that is Me."

"It pleases the Father to give you the Kingdom of God."

The final word uttered by us that night, "We are one."
We have one mouth and two ears so listening is twice as important. The actions of Samaritans are important. They are seen by God and experienced by many.

Jesus surely taught us a society must be changed. We only have to change a small group of people. This is a core value of your vision and a must in your actions.

I want to say very frankly, the church often did not follow Jesus, but their mistakes.

When Jesus spoke to me at Nineveh, it was like Jesus taking us back to His very words and His teaching.

"This Call is from Heaven or you wouldn't see me here today!"

Carol Chapman of Lowell, Oregon, went to Goma and her heart and spirit has never abandoned Goma. Her life is a testimony of keeping the faith.

All over Rwanda there are genocide sites. Rwanda, before the genocide, was a Christian nation without a vision.

We all do field work as a single team. We all help. We visited two genocide sites including the public graves in Kigali.

Jennie Mitchell described the other genocide site we visited:

It had been a technical school. Now, we visited the classrooms, 24 rooms of bodies. There were six tables in each room filled with the bodies of those who died. They were preserved in such a way that you saw everything they had been wearing and what they had experienced.

There, we also saw a mass grave where 50,000 were buried. We saw that the babies' legs were tied together and their heads hit against the wall. We walked to the classrooms with four survivors. One man had a bullet in his head. He came every day to the sites. He talked to us.

The countryside was beautiful. I nearly threw up and had to run out of the first room. The smell, the site; it made me feel incredibly sad and sick. I decided I needed to capture the individual body and face so that others could understand the tragedy and why we should never have ethnic discrimination. I took several pictures of individual bodies and faces so that one could recognize the horror on the face and relate to the individual pain. There were several rooms with just babies and children. When I came out, I saw a poor, dirty girl on the other side of a barbed wire fence looking at me. I went over and held her hand. I don't know what she was saying to me. I asked if I could take her picture and I did. This poor face behind the barbed wire fence faced the mass graves and bodies. The beautiful countryside was on my side of the fence.

We got in the van and drove down the bumpy dirt road to the bottom. The driver lost a tire again, so we had to stop. A lady came up to my window. I touched her hand and the hand of the small child she was holding. I saw another child and reached out to touch him. She pointed at my water. I grabbed my empty bottle and poured water in from the larger bottle, my allocation for the day. I give about half of my water so we are now sharing the water supply. She smiles and is very grateful.

Now, as the graduation of GSM students was to be held shortly, we went to lunch at a hotel with a pool. It nearly made me sick to see the pool and the people drinking beer and laughing at the bar right after we had just come from the genocide center. I am not super happy that we are stopping to eat lunch at some fancy place after I just shared my water with a woman and four children. The waitress came and took our soda order. I felt sick. I ate. The food was good.

During this experience, Pastor Jeremie of Burundi was filled with compassion and grief. The full impact hit him. Rwanda and Burundi were forever tied together in the experience God had allowed to happen to heal man and to bring about a better world.

The teaching was put before many. But was the choice understood? This is the hardest part! Much of the team left for home. Kathy Lane, Carol and I went on to Tanzania.

Finally, Kathy Lane, James Opiyo, and I flew to Nigeria to meet with the West African leaders.

CHAPTER 29

THE WEST AFRICA CONTINENTAL TRAINING CENTER PORT HARCOURT, NIGERIA

February 17, 1999, from a letter written from Bettie Mitchell to Faraday Iwuchukwu, Director of Nigeria:
Faraday,
One of the things I see in your ministry is that you ask for a great deal, but you don't ask the people for very much. Perhaps it is out of balance. I think you need to ask the people for a great deal. The Lord will show you how you hold back from asking, and how you make them to be stuck and paralyzed in their true giving. Don't let the board or anyone else convince you that God's funds are not in Nigeria, because that is not the truth. God's funds are everywhere, and among God's people, they can be raised on any given day in any community. People need to share what is hard to give, and you need to challenge them. Sometimes, as intercessors, we develop timidity with the people, but if we don't teach them to give, we have failed in our mission. I teach everyone to give sacrificially and I teach it without shame or fear. I teach it humbly.

In the third quarter of 1999, Nigeria GSM was publishing their own "Along the Way" newsletter. A new building was a possibility. "The Lord has helped us purchase a piece of land at Mgbuoba—NTA Road, Obio Akpor, LGA, recently. The stage now is to lay the foundation and commence building. The architectural design was for a two-story building. We estimate it will cost $100,000 to complete the building and move in."

This center shall serve as the Nigerian Administrative Headquarters and the West African Sub-Regional—Training Center for field social workers, missionaries, counselors, instructors, and road crusaders, as well as a rehabilitation center for released offenders, widows, orphans, the disabled, and converted prostitutes.

In the article, they appealed for people to donate either cash or building materials toward the construction.

On August 10, 1999, a small team that was with me visited the property and laid the cornerstone for the building.

Another article from the newsletter:

Key Concepts in Relationships.

1. You are responsible for how you treat others.

2. You may not always be responsible for how others treat you.

3. You are responsible for how you react to those who are different from you or your philosophical persuasions.

The Good Samaritan story is one of conscience. What is good in life? Did the lawyer ask his question with an evil intent, or just a desire to have a discussion or argument with a great celebrity like Jesus?

It is not enough to inquire or know about godly things, but we must determine to do the work, and obey the will of God. It is not enough to know God. We must know God intimately in the realm of the Spirit. In Biblical times, the Jews believed that anyone who was not of their nation, religion, or sect, could not be a neighbor.

A very crippled man lived at the Christian Renewal Center in Silverton, Oregon. Leroy Thompson was born in Congo, Africa. He gave $10,000 for the development of the West African Continental Training Center. He had a passion to help in Africa.

It was one thing for us to lay a cornerstone. It was a far greater task to fund the building.

May 30, 2000, I wrote a letter to Faraday and Angela Iwuchukwu in Nigeria:

I want to deeply remind you, Faraday and Angela, that I am not very interested in form, but highly interested in substance. As you know, often Nigeria has been stuck in form and been stylized by posturing religion. I want to see the center built and I want to see your hands raised in a far greater faith through the movement of the Holy Spirit. With a clear vision, a pronounced vision, this will not fall by the wayside, but will, indeed, come to pass. It is easy to have lofty ideals. It is hard to have practical common sense with them. Chew these words, for we must examine the lofty ideals of faith against the limited use of that faith in our own actions. It is very tough! We have very hard assignments.

I am profoundly concerned that we all, once again, submit our lives to Christ Jesus. There are many ideas that can take our minds, but it is only Christ who can conquer our minds. I ask that he conquer the minds of all of us, that we may not be consumed by our own selfishness, our own desires, or our own input. We must not reach the point where we miss entirely the greater call and the whole point of this ministry.

May 17, 2001, I received a letter from Faraday in Nigeria.

Faraday reported illnesses and how they managed them. His wife had been in the hospital for seven days but she was then greatly improved. She was now in Abuga, attending an International Conference for women empowerment. She was invited by an official to attend. The conference had both leadership and socio-political women empowerment undertones.

The conference was sponsored by the Nigerian government, especially the office of the first lady, Mrs. Stella Obasanjo, under the African Leadership Forum. Participants were drawn from the State Governors' wives, federal female administrators, state female commissioners, accomplished female educators, activists, and NGO women leaders.

To us, it was a great privilege for Angela to be invited and accommodated in the most expensive hotel: Sheraton Towers, Abuja, at government expense. Angela will be worshipping at the first family's ASO Rock Chapel on Sunday before returning.

God gave us an unusual miracle of U.S. $900 last month. A Nigerian Christian young man sent in a check for this amount in appreciation of our selfless services to humanity, and as his support to the GSM West African Center Project. This was unusual and came to us as a surprise because some Africans, or rather Nigerians, seem to think we are rich because we used to have white visitors from time-to-time, who give us a lot of money. Hence, they often say, "We should rather help them, and should not ask for financial support for our projects." We often find it amusing and difficult to argue unnecessarily with them because they would hardly believe otherwise." The donation of Sheila Hair's awards and Celestine's gift point to the fact that

God has a special interest in this project. We ask the whole GSM International to consider this project with us.

This ministry, our GSM, has tremendously blessed me spiritually, socially, significantly. It has grown, produced and is still producing in me a cherished life experience of integrity, reverence, and brokenness. I often cry each day to know the Lord better, and become a better Samaritan. I see the humility, pragmatism, purposeful and dynamic leadership, compassionate and sacrificial love and care, out-reaching personality, tolerance, and holy boldness in you each day. I feel unworthy to lay claim to anything except the cross of Christ that brought us thus far.

I WOULD LIKE TO MAKE A SPECIAL NOTE THAT ONE OF THE TEACHINGS I DID IN NIGERIA WAS ON HOLY BOLDNESS. This teaching got Faraday's attention and dramatically changed the level of his faith. He spoke of it many times over the years.

August 9, 2001, Faraday wrote:

Mama Bettie,

The Lord gave me a vision on the third of June, 2001, at about 2:00 a.m. In that trance/vision, I saw Mama Bettie with the poster, having the cross of Jesus Christ on it, and she was pasting it on the face of every Samaritan around the world. I pondered for its interpretation. The Holy Ghost told me that it was the evidence of Christ-centeredness, GSM, and its leadership. Thanks, Lord, for such insight.

I replied to that letter:

Faraday,

I loved your vision. I agree. I'm pinning down the whole ministry to the cross of Christ Jesus. It is the only reason we are in ministry, and it is the key to what is in our hearts. If greed and competition are in the heart, the cross departs and is not with us. It is the way you look at a man, and it is the way you know a man, by whether this is deep within his heart. It's the same for a woman or child also.

Faraday had recently received his law degree, and had been appointed to the Bar. I commented on this:
May God be with you. May He comfort and challenge your spirit. Congratulations on your accomplishment. You are now a Samaritan who became a lawyer. Be careful for it may strip you of what you really are, which is a bondservant to Christ Jesus, broken before the cross of our Lord. I know you know! But, it is easy to let it slip as men fawn over you and think you accomplished something. It is the Lord who accomplished something for all of us!

I love you, and I passionately pray for your peace, your energy, and a completion of the training center. Remember, you are going to do it on half the money. Not what you budgeted, but what you received. You must do it well, and you must call the people into accountability. You must bring about the building of this school, for it is as important as the wall that Nehemiah built in ancient Jerusalem. It is a symbol of the Samaritan work in the world.

Faraday wrote in 2001:
The GSM West African Training Center building project has been on course. We are using the ground floor for offices. I sold some personal family properties to raise some funds: $1,500, and added it to the loan of $4,000 from the money lenders at an interest rate of 7% just to continue with the building. I also took some building materials: iron rods, chippen cement (on credit worth $2,300). These steps may sound outrageous and foolish, but I am sure I acted on divine instruction.

September 24, 2003, I wrote to Faraday Iwuchukwu in Nigeria:
I absolutely have a deep and profound relationship with you, Faraday. One that has never been broken, fractured, or ever been cut in two. But I cannot allow you to not look at some things and understand that you need to develop a healthy structure in this ministry. You are caught among too many problems, too many forces, illnesses, family problems, needs, a ministry flung all over, and none of it is going well. I don't think it can go well until it comes to the size that Nigeria GSM can

manage in a healthy manner. I urge you to pray a prayer of surrender. Surrender your opinions. Surrender your feelings. Surrender your priorities. Surrender your lists, your urgencies, and your requests, your health, your children. Surrender your need to be right, your ambitions, your lack of money, your having money, your vehicle, the ministry, surrender all of this to Jesus. That prayer of surrender has to be so powerful that it is life changing. You will live in His hand, as one who is nothing. At that point of surrender, He can begin to work with you to bring the healing and structure He wants for your life and your part in this ministry in Nigeria.

One can see from all the letters that our relationship to the national directors must be one of inspiration, correction and empowerment. It is always personal because each director is a person. I always remember the stresses in their lives and understand that it is a miracle they accepted the assignment. It is important, in the years ahead, for personal empowerment to continue. They want us to understand their work. They want to do the work with us. They want us to be friends and fellow Samaritans.

It took several years to build the West Africa Continental Training Center and to develop the structure and the community of the West African countries. It was a high priority that they work together and keep each other as a full team, always aware of West Africa and The Call upon each life to receive, obey and give.

Finally, in 2004 we dedicated the center permanently. Kathy Lane and I came from Tanzania, and James Opiyo came to Nigeria from Kenya. Teresa Stroup, representing the West Africa satellites, came from GSM--Keno, Oregon.

We decided the directors from the West African Samaritan countries had to come, for if it was going to be a West African Continental Training Center, they would all be responsible for developing the curriculum needed. This meant that we paid the expenses to come to Port Harcourt, Nigeria, for the following: Stephen Adukpoh, National Director of Ghana, Arthur Davies, National Director of Sierra Leone, Lucy Siafa, National Director of Liberia, Tangye George, National Director of Cameroon, and

Raymond Tipson, National Director of Senegal. In addition, Peter Ayafor, National Coordinator of Cameroon, and Reverend Benson, National Board Chairman of Liberia were there with us.

In the last chapter you saw the experiences of this 2004 journey in East Africa. Can you imagine the responsibility in Nigeria to provide our integrity to meet with their integrity. We were creating a work that would benefit all trainees. This would be a work of all the nations, keeping common purpose. Together, we did the planning of all of the curriculum.

James Opiyo gave a comprehensive talk about the work of Good Samaritan in Africa. He was reporting to them. He was not a "teller," he was a "reporter."

Together we created a list of classes and specific trainings that had to take place:
- Introduction to GSM
- Samaritan Ethics
- Samaritan Concepts
- Abuse Recovery
- Addictions Recovery
- Demonology
- Level I Counselor Training
- Level II, The Professional Ethics of Counseling
- Attachment and Attachment Disorders
- Inner-Healing
- Loneliness
- Anger Management
- Ask the people in training to write a paper on the Samaritan Call

It was decided that the West African Continental Training would occur each year in July and August. People would come from the countries of West Africa. We would be largely responsible for the needs of the trainees.

We worked on proposals, projects, and management. I emphasized fund raising in Africa. Other thoughts that came: man's logic, or will of God. We had concern for Biblical education. Trainees must be taught that you might know a great deal about the Bible, but Biblical action is the point of this ministry and, in fact, it was the point of Christ's life. We emphasized concepts of Christian healing, the healing miracles of Jesus, and rural outreach.

The curriculum was agreed upon, and it was also agreed that annually one or two of the national directors would come from the other countries to lead a portion of the training. This was a big assignment, but it got Nigeria not to be the central location focus. The true location was all of West Africa.

Faraday was very pleased. All of the directors agreed to be hands-on and to participate in preparing those they would send each year. Those directors from other West African countries would not go for the two months. They might teach for a shorter time, but in the process, they got to look over the trainees and understand the development of this work.

I emphasize these things in this book because we must understand, we as a ministry must comprehend that this is a work among us all. They are among us, and we are among them. It is a creative work, bringing out an education from the grass roots to the grass roots.

During this time together, Lucy Siafa was confirmed as National Director of Liberia. Teresa Stroup, with her team in Keno, Oregon, took the assignment to develop the satellite covering Liberia. The satellite would give provision for the work.

The second continental training school was opened and commissioned while we were there. Faraday was appointed the Principal of the Training Center. It was officially decided the training center would be known as West Africa Continental Samaritan Training Center, Port Harcourt, Nigeria.

During the time I was there, I taught some classes: notably one, Learning Through Ministry Leadership. We worked together to develop healthy financial reports, by-laws and successions.

During the time we were there, two national Nigerian board meetings were held. In those two board meetings, many issues concerning the work in Nigeria were discussed and some problems were resolved.

James Opiyo remained in Nigeria with the trainees for one month. James did a great deal of training. 20 people received that training. James trained in the morning and in the evening. He held individual counseling sessions. Sunday evenings they all participated in group therapy.

James Opiyo reported that it was key that he give the introduction of Samaritan work, how to develop a vision, other basic counseling skills, and taking case studies. During the training, they had many Biblical dramas, including the Samaritan story. Faraday and James held a final board meeting before James returned to Kenya. They reported a major resolution about how to solicit funds for the completion of the training center. The board was much encouraged by the establishment of the West Africa Continental Samaritan Training Center. The process for fund raising was put in gear. Pledges were to be tracked. This board meeting was also used for summing up what God had done for that period of one month that James was in Port Harcourt.

In 2004, the first and second levels of the training center were complete. The second level housed the trainees. The third level of the building provided housing and much-needed space for the Iwuchukwu family. There were several bathrooms and showers throughout the building. The cooking for the whole center was done outside and on the third floor.

When Kathy Lane and I returned to the United States, we were fully aware that something of great importance had taken place.

The final decisions during this period of time: the Continental Training Center in Kenya would be responsible for Africa as a whole, but the sub-training for West Africa would be conducted by the West Africa Samaritan Training Center. Each side would monitor and encourage the leaders and the trainees. There would be consistency and quality in the development of each trainee. We saw the trainees as the future trainers in West Africa.

We sang songs, prayed, and encouraged one another. We all departed to empower the decision we had made.

FINALLY, THE SIGNIFICANT JOURNEY TO AFRICA OF 2004 HAD BEEN COMPLETED. Can you imagine the work that lay ahead for me personally in returning home? Not only weeks of mail, clients waiting to see me, board meetings to be held, satellites to be further developed, enormous amounts of correspondence. My greatest assignment was to have the faith that could move the mountains.

The leaders in West Africa have continued in the work. One exception is Raymond Tipson, who married and moved to the United States. In his place, one of the trainees from Port Harcourt Continental Training School was appointed Director of Senegal.

Perhaps you'll be bored with the level of detail in this chapter and you will wonder why it is so important, but those in Africa know why it was so important. Their lives were given over to the greater work of this ministry. They went home with the blessings of each of us.

Finally, June 1, 2005, I wrote a letter to Faraday Iwuchukwu in Nigeria:

As you saw, we have outstanding directors in West Africa! They are focused and understand the deep seriousness of The Call. It has broken your isolation and broken you into a deeper understanding. The inner development of work beyond religious service will occur. I think you know what I mean. If we cannot bring healing to the individual, if we cannot bring breakthrough from the demonic world, then all of the praises of God have failed because we have not followed Jesus, used His Name, and done His work.

CHAPTER 30

THE FINAL STRENGTH GIVEN
JOURNEY 2006

I was 72 years-old. My strength was waning. West Africa was heavy on my heart. The final journey must be made there. As I left with a team for West Africa, I had deep sorrow over a situation at home in the ministry in Oregon. I had reached a point where I slept too little and gave too much. There was no doubt that this was the end of my travel overseas. I was glad, for I had done the fullness of what the Lord asked.

This journey was from August 15 to September 21, 2006. The participants on the journey were Bettie Mitchell, Matthew Barber of Walla Walla, Washington; Denise Haun of Spokane, Washington; and Kathy Lane, representing the International Board.

There were other participants in various parts of the journey. Maria Macias from Lake Tahoe, California, came with us to Nigeria and Cameroon. Teresa Stroup and Lisa Angland, from Keno, Oregon, joined us in Liberia. Melba Adamson and Sarah Hansel spent two weeks in Sierra Leone. Karen and Christine Forsyth and Tom and Harriet Beck met us in Senegal. We were all traveling as one team.

I want to speak about some of the participants. Matthew Barber of Walla Walla, Washington, was a young man of much talent and ability. He had high energy, great curiosity, and a willingness to learn. Wherever he went, he took in more than we could see, and gave out what he had to give. He was heading to an international career that would span most of the globe.

Teresa Stroup was the Liberia Satellite Leader from Keno, Oregon. Keno's assignment had been to cover Liberia. She knew of the hardships. Now she saw them.

Melba Adamson visited Sierra Leone because she had been the Satellite Director for many years. It was a hard journey for her. She was challenged spiritually. Karen founded GSM-Senegal, when her husband, Tim, was working for the U.S. State Department at Dakar. Tom and Harriet Beck were the Satellite Leaders of Senegal.

The purpose of the journey was to evaluate our work in West Africa. The West African Training Center at Port Harcourt, Nigeria, was a high priority. We needed to look into the quality of the development in each country in order to make recommendations for the future of GSM in West Africa. We also purposed to understand in each country the conditions, goals, staffing and plans for continuity. During this journey to West Africa, we visited six countries. In each country, there was strong purpose and much need for us to know and to seek deeper understanding among us all. Could I make it? Could I hold up? It was very hard!

REPORT FROM NIGERIA

The West African Continental Training Center was 99% complete. It was really a very miraculous accomplishment for the ministry. We were very pleased at the set up, and the kind of work that was being done there. It is a West African Training Center, not a Nigerian Training Center. The staff reflects the West African nature of the training center in that they have come from other West African countries, as well as from Nigeria.

While we were in Nigeria, we attended the West African Training Course. The bulk of the work falls to Faraday and Angela Iwuchukwu as directors. Stephen Adukpoh, of Ghana, spent ten days teaching at Port Harcourt. Tangye George of Cameroon, with his wife, spent several days there as trainees. There were nine students from other countries. Those countries included Congo, Sierra Leone, Senegal, Ivory Coast, and Benin. There were men as well as women in training, and several Nigerians participated. The spirit of the trainees was good. 12 completed the full two months of training and graduated.

The school was well-managed and the curriculum well-developed. The students were very grateful for the training. Our team of five was present for five days at the training center, and we participated by doing a considerable amount of teaching. We gave Christian sex education called "The Marriage Bed." Maria taught about addictions. Denise Haun did a lot of training bringing the concepts we are using to develop young children in the Kingdom of God. Kathy Lane and I presented to develop an effective use of an Abuse Group. We gave them personal experience as participants in group therapy. We broke through our own learning barriers and came to effective community among us all.

On this journey I carried a large picture of the prophetic call on the Walls of Nineveh. I consistently gave testimony in each country, and urged that our passion and our call be "to teach nothing but the Kingdom of God."

The Iwuchukwu's were quiet and well-focused during the training. They attended most of the training sessions while we were there. They needed soaking prayer for physical strength. They had four children in college and one near the end of high school. They had two old, but running, vehicles. The beds and cooking facilities were sufficient for the school. A generator had to be used for electricity, as the whole of Nigeria has extremely unreliable power sources. Faraday Iwuchukwu wrote the following:

REPORT FROM FARADAY IWUCHUKWU:
Why is GSM training essential in West Africa?

We must praise and thank God immensely for what he is doing in West African Samaritan Training School, Port Harcourt, Nigeria. This training was passionate, in-depth, intensive, strict and challenging to both the students and staff teachers. Everyone learned new things. The students were eager to learn, and more serious about their training. All of the students from Nigeria and other countries in West and Central Africa were overwhelmed and broken by what the Lord did during the training, and it was revealing and reassuring to the teachers who spent their lives training others. Most of the students regretted that they had been in ministry for too long, with little understanding of what the real ministry is, and what constitutes the Spirit of Jesus in practical reality. The training was, indeed, an eye opener for all the trainees. They were very happy to become part of the global work of GSM. Each year we have been able to improve students and staff discipline: strict compliance to school vision, rules and regulations. We had quality teachings that yielded tremendous results in both staff and students. No one was more important than the other. Even as the rector of the school I did morning manual labor with the students, Angela did the cooking and equally taught her classes.

The teachers complimented each other as there was immense cooperation and humility among us.

The Lord provided our basic needs through local and international support. Arthur Davies of Sierra Leone sent us $100 support, and Raymond Tipson sent $160 to assist in logistics. Our local church Redeemed Brethren Mission and one or two former clients also gave us two sacks of rice. The U.S. Samaritan team greatly assisted financially and spiritually.

The training really produced wonderful Samaritan counselors and results. We did not allow distractions from phone calls, e-mails, frivolous movements, or unhealthy relationships among the students. It was such a serious affair with commitment. There were many sacrifices here and there. The students were, perhaps, the best set we ever had with a widespread representation. We had two students from Senegal, one from Cote D'Voire, one from Benin Republic, two from Congo, one from Sierra Leone, and 13 from Nigeria.

After the two months intensive training and feet washing, 12 students graduated successfully on the 30th of August, 2006. The arrival of the U.S. team on the 19th of August was an outstanding boost of the content and context of the training. I decided to surrender the whole week to Mama Bettie because I needed to learn better. Both staff members and students became privileged students together as God extraordinarily used Mama Bettie, Mama Kathy Lane, and others to train us in key areas of ministry beyond our subject areas. I spent more time this time to learn deeper and better from these vessels of honor in God's hand. I had several personal sessions with our International Director.

The U.S.A team was a splendid blessing to all. We had good periods of sincere interactions and intercessions. Two center directors were formally appointed after prayerful consideration to take care of and develop the work in Cote de'Voire (Prince Senyo and Benin Republic (Felly Kinsama.) They were commissioned for The Call.

We had a period to dance and sing cross-culturally, great fun indeed. We worked and ate as a family and enjoyed each other's company.

I want to speak of the Directors of Cote D'Voire and Benin. Each of them went home determined to take the message and develop the work. Tragically, Cote de'Voire went into a civil war. Felly had a major health issue while he was in Benin, and financial shortage. It was hard, but I trust the Almighty that He sent them to bare the fruit into vessels that would hear the testimony.

October 31, 2006, Faraday Iwuchukwu wrote a letter giving a report from one of the students:

Joseph Solah Rasaq wrote, *"****THE TRAINING CHANGED MY LIFE FOR GOOD***. *I was converted from Islam to Christianity several years ago. I grew spiritually and enjoyed my new life in Christ. I later received divine call to be a pastor. For quite some time, I went through several challenges in the ministry, especially in my former church station, where I had pastored Christ Apostolic Church in River State. I was later transferred to another church station.*

I passed through severe spiritual attacks, especially after we had bought a piece of land for the church building. Surprisingly, I found that the land in question had a lot of demonic ancient covenants that can only be destroyed through powerful prayer. The land in question had been under dispute between two families in that community. Our church was known as a praying denomination. I applied my faith and encouraged the outright purchase of the land and development started on the piece of property. Thereafter, the satanic attacks increased on me as the devil became more furious on me for taking the bold step of faith. I believed there was a big trouble in the kingdom of darkness.

At one of our mid-week fasting prayers, a woman walked into the church and confessed that many other pastors had been there before trying for 35 years to start a mission work to no avail, and she wondered why I, as a young man, should succeed at doing such a great work. She rounded out her confession with a stern warning, "Young man, be prepared to receive the most deadly blows from forces of evil."

The church engaged in serious prayers. Truly, the storm arose after the confrontational open confession and all manner of illnesses took over my whole life. I became very uncomfortable and fearful to the point I was about to die the next moment. One fateful day, as I was traveling to Port Harcourt, I saw the signpost of Good Samaritan Ministries West African Training School. There was also a banner for the two-month Samaritan Intensive Training Programs July and August 2005. Along the line, I came down from the bus to verify the information. On getting to the West African Samaritan Training School premises, I met Pastor Angela Iwuchukwu and narrated my ordeal and life to her. She conducted powerful counseling with me and I was assured that GSM, indeed, is dedicated to helping my fellow man. Thereafter, I obtained the admission form for the Continental Training and Dr. Faraday conducted a screening interview on me. I finally gained admission to receive the training and the passionate and in-depth teaching started. **I found out this is the only Nigeria school of this status that does not charge for the students.**

I was very happy because I could not have been able to pay school fees for such quality lectures to heart training. The more I attended lectures, the more my healing and deliverance increased. As the training continued, I decided to open up to Stephen Adukpoh from Ghana. I explained my experiences to him and he prayed with me and counseled me further. I became totally delivered from satanic blows. I had been praying all alone to no avail. The reason was that God wanted me to pass through Good Samaritan Ministries in order to perform great miracles in my life.

I am now more successful and comfortable in all my focuses and doings. As one of the pioneering students of this great school in West Africa in 2005, many miracles started pouring into my life and ministry. I now have absolute victory in Christ's name. **Praise the Lord, this is a life-transforming center! May others discover this and be blessed as I have experienced.**

LIBERIA

During our time in Liberia, the Good Samaritan Ministries office was robbed for the second time. We did three days of counselor training in the office and graduated six students from very advanced training that they had been participating in for a number of months.

We were particularly impressed that Lucy Siafa chose the counselor training Level Three internship be done at the LOIC, a training and counseling center that has been developed by the United Nations to train ex-combatants from the war. There were 354 trainees, 34 female, in the training center at LOIC. Some of our counselors were doing their internships there. We provided gospel counseling. We addressed every class of trainees in the LOIC program. Many will be receiving our Monrovia counseling services. Lucy believed they were going to be overrun with clients as the country was a major disaster area.

Lucy Siafa is an effective leader. She is still learning. She would like to attend training this next year either in Kenya or in the United States. I recommend we send her to Kenya because that is where Oliver Siafa received his training.

We found the people participating in the training to be of fine caliber with teachable spirits and good focus on the development needed to make Liberia a safer country. We visited the grave of Oliver Siafa and we left the future planning in the hands of the Liberia Satellite representatives, Teresa Stroup and Lisa Anglin.

Lucy, in 2006, was 42 years old. She was dealing with some fear and insecurity. She felt a desperate need to have a place of her own to live. By God's grace, after this time, Good Samaritan Ministries was able to help her build a home. She built the housing on the property that GSM already owned. Lucy had graduated from a university nursing program. She said, "People look at my life and gain courage."

We loved Liberia. There was something special about this nation that was in recovery from the vast evil that had nearly destroyed it. The terrorists were being helped and retrained. Many were counseled by GSM. You felt a quiet rebuilding spirit in Monrovia. We sensed this from the time we arrived until the time we left several days later. We visited other centers and met with widows and the children's program.

GHANA
We stayed several days in Ghana, and had a chance to evaluate the conditions in the country. We visited Stephen Adukpoh, his family, his work, and the centers he had developed. We explored his vision and direction for the ministry and sought to understand his real passions.

One of the best parts of our journey was spent in Ghana. The team and I have become convinced that Stephen is ready and doing substantive work in the ministry. He is obviously a gifted leader and many people listen to him. His passion has become counseling, inner-healing and the Kingdom of God. Some pastors shake their heads and say, "Stephen is crazy." But, we met with many pastors who said that Stephen is the first person who has any answers for us that work. He is training more and more people and making himself more available in several regions of the country.

While in Ghana, we visited a Liberian refugee camp. They were housing 45,000 refugees who were not allowed to work in Ghana and had no money to return to Liberia. Stephen shared he would go the first part of October to do a one-week training of the leaders there to help them develop trauma counselors needed in that camp.

Several key pastors in Accra, the capitol, were going to receive training. They were really convinced that this call has come from God.

As I preached at the church in Denu on the book of Jonah, all present became a part of the story. The pastor, Stephen Adukpoh, sat in the dust on the ground as the King of Nineveh. All the people representing Nineveh sat in the dust of the ground repenting. Together, we saw that Jonah, representing Israel, was the only one in the story who didn't repent. He had anger towards God that God was not as exclusive as he had thought. God was merciful to people outside of Jonah's interest. It was a very, very telling moment to look at Jonah sitting outside the building, having a tantrum with God while everyone else was in repentance. It was one of the clearest visualizations I have ever seen in my life of what has happened to Israel. It fulfilled the words of St. Paul in Romans, "Israel will be the last to be saved."

The work in Denu is effective. There was a very adequate counseling office, an effective Board of Directors, and many workers.

Stephen Adukpoh had a very fine family. His wife, Mabel, was still taking psychiatric medication. Stephen was very close to her, and there was genuine tenderness and consideration for her life. Mabel is a fine woman. We can respect the job she has done with Stephen to raise their children, who were servants to us the whole time we were there.

In addition, Stephen and Mabel Adukpoh had been raising eight boys for the last 10 years. They lived at the Denu GSM office. Those boys were in need of vocational apprenticeships. They were stuck, and Stephen had been stuck with them. He didn't quite know what to do. He recommended we send $100 a month to cover those eight boys for vocational experiences as apprentices. When they do apprenticeships, a small monthly fee is required. Our support of that decision has been a good one, as I met with the boys and saw their capabilities. One of his great burdens was that he could not send them away until they finished the training they needed to survive.

Stephen worked out a very good system, with a school in Denu, who willingly received many of the Good Samaritan Ministries children without tuition. 200 elementary and 68 junior high students were allowed to go free. The school was called Amazing Love.

While in Ghana, we met with John Douvon, our representative in Togo. He was with us in Denu for the duration of our time there. In addition, John brought over the nearby border several Togolese on the last day we were in Denu. We had a significant meeting with them. We are doing no funding in Togo, but we are definitely encouraging the call. They asked if it might be possible to have some small sponsorships for some students. I found John to be a person who might be developing and improving. According to Stephen, he has come a long way. He did complete the West African GSM training last year. He was sincere and obviously, able to draw people together and bring them to the recognition and call of the ministry. Stephen Adukpoh will provide supervision of John's work.

SIERRA LEONE

Our time in Sierra Leone was short—just three days. Melba Adamson and Sarah Hansel from Los Angeles stayed two weeks. Sarah was given our names by Pastor John Nichols of Athena, Oregon. She wrote and asked to go as she felt a call to travel with Melba. It was a miraculous decision. Melba had just been diagnosed with very severe osteoporosis. The doctor said she has the body of an 80 year-old woman. She is a cancer survivor and works as a vocational and physical therapist with very handicapped children. This ministry needs to seriously intercede for her life. She has been the Satellite Director of Sierra Leone since the beginning of our work there.

We found Arthur quite burned out. He is a man of great integrity and his spirit is willing, but there was a deep, deep inner-exhaustion in him. The country is still devastated from the civil war, which ended in 1999. There has been some rebuilding, and there have been efforts, but there is still this profound loss everywhere. We sensed it all along the road.

We met with the board. We were deeply impressed with the Chairman, Phillip Taylor. He is an educated and wise man. We met with some of the center's directors, and we particularly admired the Director, Rosalie Cole, from a town called Bo in Central Sierra Leone. Her husband died the end of June, leaving her with seven children; 19 to three years of age, and an entirely new situation. She is very brave and strong; someone to admire She represents what is very best in Africa, inner-strength we have too seldom seen in the United States.

There was a church service on Sunday afternoon for the 11th Anniversary of Arthur's church. During the service, there was an absolutely miraculous breaking-in of the Holy Spirit that will affect me for the rest of my life, and, I believe, will have ultimate effect on the ministry as a whole.

The question had become **"Who is this Jesus we are following?"** All over the world I have found a perversion of His character. The Lord spoke very strongly through the spirit and said, "My character has never changed. I am who I am."

SENEGAL

My main team stayed in Senegal only two days. One of those days, I was quite ill. The others stayed a week or more.

Raymond had located a very adequate space for a large work to be done in the ministry. He had purchased a car, but still owed $3,000 to pay for it. Dakar is a large city, and good transportation is an important issue.

The work being done in Senegal and Dakar at that time was advanced computer training, with some Biblical education, and group therapy.

CAMEROON

We arrived fairly late at Doula, and then had to make the journey to Limbe, where the headquarters of Good Samaritan Ministries is located. Limbe is a medium-sized town along the coast of Africa with a lovely beachfront. They were renting a very adequate counseling and training center. Since our visit in 2006, Cameroon has built a central headquarters of Good Samaritan Ministries, Cameroon.

We found Cameroon to be a lovely country. It was the only country where electricity was adequate. All of the other countries had drastically inadequate electricity. I was able to spend a lot more time developing the teamwork in Limbe, which was the central headquarters of Cameroon.

In addition to the Limbe Center, others came from other parts of Cameroon, and we did considerable training. The training was very well received by over 50 people. Initially, each person gave their testimony as to what Good Samaritan training had done in their lives. The testimony was clear and concise. Tangye George and his staff in Cameroon have the gift of teaching, counseling, and deliverance. They are following the call very closely. They are committed to helping with the West African Training Center. They were encouraging Angela Iwuchukwu and Stephen Adukpoh to come to Cameroon and do a conference for them in December. This took place. They are very relational with other countries' leaders.

The last 48 hours of the journey were spent in Lagos. I asked Faraday to spend that time with us. At that time, I gave him an extensive report of the journey and we had much time to discuss some of the spiritual issues in West Africa. We were closely bonded through the Holy Spirit, and we had a profound trust relationship. There were times when I had to really press into the corrections needed, but this man has been faithful to the call without exception since 1987.

We were hosted in Lagos by Tunji and his family. They had a very large condo and very comfortable facilities. Tunji is willing to meet in Lagos the airplanes of trainees, get people on planes to Port Harcourt, and help them fly out of Lagos. He wanted to make sure the trainees coming into Lagos had their needs met along the road. Tunji was a Muslim who received Christ, as was

Raymond Tipson of Senegal. It is to be remembered that they have been called out. They have paid a price for their faith. Faraday Iwuchukwu describes our visit in those last days in Lagos:

> My visit to Lagos, lastly, on Mama Bettie's request, was an unusual divinely arranged event. The two days and the few hours I spent with her alone, powerfully and supernaturally transformed my whole being. It was the greatest experience I have had since I became a Samaritan. It was too deep and melting that I lack the strength and wisdom to explain. I am extremely grateful that I made it to see her off in Lagos. My initial weakness and reluctance would have robbed me of the rare opportunity and spiritual blessing. None of us bargained for it, but God did. Thanks, Lord!

SIGNIFICANT LESSONS FROM THE JOURNEY

1. The Holy Spirit is not the Spirit of gifts, but the Spirit of Jesus. This is a deep and profound issue when we teach nothing but the Kingdom of God.

2. I found few in the world who know the Jesus they are following. They have been perverted in definition by modern Christianity. The Lord made it perfectly clear to me that He has never changed. His character is the same, and we must find the truth of the Jesus we are following.

3. A key teaching on the journey was the "Marriage Bed." All profaning of the marriage bed must be broken. Marriage must be a relationship between man, woman and God. Even children cannot violate the marriage bed, for the marriage bed belongs to the marriage. There was profound training in this area that was new and very empowered by the Holy Spirit.

4. The Lord clearly and deeply spoke into my spirit that He is going to cleanse all of us from any pride that we keep. We can take pride in nothing. Anything we take pride in will be taken away from us. It is a time of change and purification in the world; an era of self-examination that the Holy Spirit might remove the last of what separates us from the love of God.

My journey was complete. I was finished. Now the task ahead is for us to develop the next generation of Samaritans here.

We must encourage each of the countries to remember they must develop the next generation. Keep The Call alive!

Thoughts on My African Trip, by Denise Haun:
When I would see an African person surviving who should be totally in defeat, I have to step back and ask why? Well, they are using their God-given talents and skills to be creative and caring for others. They have learned the secret that to help themselves simply means to help others.

Givers and Takers of Partnership, by Teresa Stroup:
I recently went to Liberia to strengthen and encourage the Samaritans, meet with their Board of Directors, and to establish a partnership between the GSM ministry in Liberia and our Satellite. What I found is that the work is going very well. The GSM center is training people to be very skilled in counseling and the ministry is significant in Liberia. I also found that after the death of Oliver Siafa, there were some who had become discouraged.

The board was not meeting often enough, and there were too few members. There needs to be a concrete plan for the future. Out of our meetings, we began to understand that **the U.S. could not be the givers, and African, the takers. Rather, we must become partners in the work of the Kingdom of God.**

This led us to consider building a school to teach children that Americans are not the givers, and they, the takers, but rather, they are students whose school is GSM Liberia's work. Teachers are paid for their work to the Glory of God. We then, are partners in this Kingdom work, and there is a balance in our relationship.

To begin this work, I (Bettie) challenged the Liberia GSM Board to raise the first $1,000 for the school. At first this idea was startling until we considered some possible ways they could do that. In a country where University Professors are paid 20 U.S. dollars a month, one can understand what an enormous request this is to them.

Liberians are a proud people who truly do not want to form a dependency on Americans, but on Christ alone. They do not want to train children to look outside their own country for help, but to find it by relying on a faithful God who gives His creativity in their own country.

Developing the Samaritan spirit in people must take precedence over our projects and even over the needs that are present in the countries where we are working. Both sides can easily be side-tracked by our own ideas of what we perceive is needed.

Our visit was life-changing for us and for those we met. We are all stronger and have a greater sense of vision and purpose for the Liberia Satellite. The Liberians are now members of our Satellite and we are members of their Satellite.

While in Africa, I fell four times; twice were serious falls. Once, I fell around the toilet in Nigeria, and the other time on my face across the floor in Sierra Leone.

Many reading this book must be strengthened. It is a long, hard journey, but it leads to life.

CHAPTER 31

THE EDUCATION STORY

When someone asked, "What is Good Samaritan Ministries?" it was always a difficult question to answer. The deepest answer is the Spirit of the Samaritan lives in this organization and, indeed, it is what keeps us alive and well. We live lives of faith in action!

On our first trip to Kenya, it was obvious that education was a high priority for them. Would it be a high priority for us? It did not seem possible to take on anything else.

It would have been easy to say, "We'll stop doing this, and we'll do that...." It was not where the Lord was leading us. He was leading us into paths of faith that would test the very limits of our compassion and our relationship with children, with teachers, and with our fellow Samaritans. This would be a lifetime test. The education story is about why we educated and what happened.

Throughout this book you have seen mention of children going to school, and what we learned when we tried to do student sponsorships. It is important at this time to review. We learned that student sponsorships should not be done by a named individual. The relationship between the sponsor and the child could be harmful. The sponsor may gain pride, and the child may gain a sense of entitlement and a manipulative relationship with the sponsor.

All things had to come from God alone. The ministry was a vehicle to move, to teach, to keep, to train up, and to develop. The first to develop were the Samaritans here. The last to develop are the ones who don't hear what the spirit is saying. As fellow Samaritans, we were challenged.

The school and student sponsorships began in Kenya, and developed in Uganda, Tanzania, Nigeria, Malawi, Zambia, South Africa, Ghana, Sierra Leone, and Liberia. This had to develop slowly, or we would have been overwhelmed. We had to develop Samaritan children who would go and do likewise. The true issue was greater than money for school fees. Our motivation and commitment had to come from above. The educational call of the cry of the Father reached beyond money for school fees. Our passion was called to develop the lives of the children and the teachers we helped.

Over the years, the number of children we put through school increased. By 2009, there were almost 10,000 being sponsored by Good Samaritan Ministries. The majority of those children were from Africa. In Beaverton, we had a staff of five. They were paid little and worked hard. We were developing centers in the United States. In many countries local centers were being developed. Our own eyes stayed steadily upon the children. **We could always work one more hour because our eyes stayed on those children who needed us to protect them in the dangerous world of abandonment.**

When we began school sponsorships, we tried to get sponsors for individual children. We knew something of their stories. From many of the countries, we had lists of children who needed help with education. We, the Samaritans in Africa and we here, learned as all of us worked together. We had to keep the children's eyes on God and His mercy. We were all called to trust Him absolutely, that needs would be met and miracles would occur.

In the early years, there were some instances of manipulation of sponsors. We had to keep our eyes on the children and learn to keep, but not to judge.

We carry the passionate concern of God who was demanding The Call be pronounced again over the whole ministry. Never forget the question received at The Call, "Here are the children! Where are the teachers?"

As we would send a little to a country, I want to clarify that the money was sent to the National Office in each country. The money was budgeted according to agreements we had made for amounts. As we sent the amount for education, the National Directors and their staff had to decide what they would do. If we sent, for example, $25 per child, they saw twice as many children as we saw. If we saw 25 children, they would see 50, or 1000 who needed help. They worked with the local schools and found ways to give to the needs of the school. In exchange, the school would not charge school fees for some of the children. There was great creativity.

We kept an enormous amount of faith that what we were doing was in the eyes of Jesus, "Do you see this child?"

Pakistan bought a lot of material for school uniforms for Kenya. We sent books and started libraries. Gradually, the Samaritans built schools, paid teachers, and fed children. As we looked across Africa and saw the need was genuine, each day we would be more challenged. **Here we built an International Education Satellite, and a Widows and Orphans Satellite. We assigned them the impossible and they found the possible!**

When we were short of funds we needed to send in order to keep the children we were sponsoring in school, I would go to several satellites of the countries and I would say, **"This is the situation....This is what you need to do....We cannot send less. We must send enough. We must send enough!"**

At least twice a week, Papa Jerry and I took a long walk through our neighborhood area. We spent all of our time on those walks looking for cans to pick up for bottle returns. That nickel would feed an orphan or a widow for a day. 30 cans would feed them for a month. We picked up coins in the street for widows and orphans. Even today, I picked up a penny lying on the ground in front of the Good Samaritan Ministries office. We did this year around—even if it was pouring down rain. It was a lesson for us and it was a lesson for the ministry as a whole. At one time, Laurie Masenhimer's garage was full from the cement floor to the ceiling of pop cans to be turned in. It became almost a full-time job. There were many other fundraisers. We went to the people and talked to them. We kept the need in front of us all. It was the Father saying to us, "Do you see the children?"

As I looked at the ministry here, year after year I said, "Where are the children here?" It is so easy to let children have a good life and the advantages they need; but, are we spiritually developing the children here? **Are we developing our children to be true givers? Are we developing their sensitivity to the needs of others? I passionately believe that the parents, the teachers, all of us, must gather the children here and in Africa to bring about a new time for the ministry of children to children.**

I have so much joy when I think of what the Africans have accomplished through Good Samaritan Ministries in Africa. Their eyes looked into the eyes of the children and saw them. Their eyes met with them, their eyes kept them, their eyes did not waiver from their lives. The Samaritan countries that were passionate about "Where are the children?" prospered. The ministry flowed like living water. All of our eyes must have heart. We do not teach by words, platitudes, or even by prayers. We are all to teach by the pouring out of our lives for the help of many.

When people thought of Good Samaritan Ministries sponsoring children, they were always thinking about, "Oh, the poor little orphan, or the child of that widow..." They were always looking at sponsoring the very, very poor children through a basic elementary program. It was hard for us to conceive that this call was to truly educate the child, not just sponsor them for a little while because they were needy. In Uranga region, where several thousand people lived, not one child had ever gone to high school.

Educate the children. Educate the teachers. Educate the community. We must develop a spirit of giving among us all.

Look into the eyes of each child and say, "You are learning. I am so proud of you! Your life will make a difference in this world!"

As the years went by, particularly in Kenya and Uganda, high school education became part of the essential for the children. If they didn't pass, we sent them back. Maybe they took an extra year, but it made a difference because we were there for them.

Where are the leaders in Africa? We had to provide for the effective leadership of many, leaders who would make a difference in their country! Gradually, this began to take place. We sent 40 children in Uganda into higher education fields: teachers, accountants, social workers, sewing school teachers, caterers, artists, information technicians, four nurses, and two doctors.

Yesterday, I spent the whole day with Osborn Muyanga, our National Director of Uganda, who was staying at our house. We talked at length about the children. I wanted to know them more.

When one of Osborn's adopted sons, Moses, graduated in IT, he couldn't find a job, so he worked for two years as a Samaritan volunteer. He finally became the manager of a hostel in Kampala.

Osborn said our school in Masaka provided dormitory and total care for 300 orphans and K-Senior 6 education for 1,113 children in 2013. Nambirizi School, which is in a very rural and hard-pressed area, is educating a multitude of children as well. In 2013, Nambirizi educated 312 children.

Josham and Stephen were teenagers in Kiwangala in 1990 when Osborn first came to that area. Both of the young men went through all of the Samaritan training and both became directors of local centers in Uganda. Josham lived in a very poor area where most of the people were refugees from Rwanda. They had run to escape from death. With his heart, hands, love, and care, Josham began to educate the children of Nambirizi. He and the children built a school room by room. I was there, I saw it.

Always, our leaders are looking for vocational education so children can develop skills in order to take care of themselves.

This morning, Osborn shared that the first time I came to Kiwangala, he was already facing the fact that the children were wandering in the streets as total orphans. He gathered them and taught them mathematics, and how to read. There was no school for them to attend. From the very beginning, the passion of this ministry has known it must focus on this question: "Here are the children, where are the teachers?"

Osborn also shared, his sister, Sarah, is now a lawyer. She is a trainer at all of the centers, helping people with their legal issues, and the legal issues of GSM. For example, at all the centers in Uganda, she teaches how to write a Will. These are not things she does as a fundraiser for herself; these are things she does as a pouring out to many. She sees the children and the widows. She willingly visits the 13 centers in Uganda and trains many.

We sponsored the first student into high school in the Uranga region of Kenya. He was the first ever to go to high school in the whole region. He became a high school teacher and we became lifetime friends.

TESTIMONIES FROM SPONSORED STUDENTS

The Story of Erick Owino in Kenya

I was born the 23rd of May, 1975. I come from a polygamist family, with a total number of 18 children. I grew up in Uranga until the age of four. At that time, I left my mother and moved 20 kilometers away to be with my father. My father had settled in this area, trying to do business in odd jobs.

At 10, I was doing my laundry and learning how to prepare meals. At 12, I was cooking for the whole family. My other five brothers and three sisters and I were sharing a single room. Since both of our mothers were never around, all the household chores had to be shared. In 1982, I joined Grade 1 in an over-populated school. Class 1 had over 300 pupils. When it came to class work, being in the top 150 was a great achievement.

In 1984, when I was in Grade 3, despite all his troubles and difficulties, my dad took it upon himself to check our books every Saturday morning before leaving to cycle 20 kilometers to be with other members of the family. This was the day one dreaded, but at the same time, looked forward to. This was the day dad was to be away until Monday, so we would get to play and go places with our friends. **But, the sad part was that if you missed school, or skipped an assignment, this was a chance to pay the price. Despite the punishment you had at school, dad had his own: missing bread ration for two to three days, several strokes of the cane, banned on playing soccer for the whole week, or destroying all the toys you had.** *I'm glad he did all of this. He gave us a foundation. Since there were many children, the only way one was respected and recognized was by performing well at school.*

In 1986, I was in Grade 5. My dad was taken ill and went to bed for five years. Freedom was there, but the pain of seeing my dad suffering was unbearable. My mother was always on the run trying to put things in order. My second mother, my step-mother, is mentally unstable. Therefore, all of the family affairs were for my mother to decide. **I began to run with a bad crowd and my grades started falling. Since my father was down, nobody could punish me. By the time I was in Grade 7, my grades were at their worse. The best grade I had was a C.** *One night, my father called me by his bedside and talked to me in a way that* *awakened my conscience.* At this time, we decided that I was not prepared to proceed to Grade 8, so I was to retake Grade 7. I got so mad that I ran away from home for three days. This was the turning point in my life.

In 1990, my grades improved so much that I surprised even my teachers. By the time I was doing final primary exams, I was among the best three students in the school.

I am really glad that my father took that tough stand. Now, I do appreciate that it was out of love, not punishment.

Because my grades were so high, I was admitted to one of the top high schools in the Nyanza Province. My father gave me 50 Kenya schillings to last for a whole term of 14 weeks. (Note: 50 Kenya schillings were less than $2.00) The school was in a very dry area. Water was a problem. For one to bathe and do laundry, it was a trek of over three kilometers. I could bathe, but by the time I got back to the school, I was sweating.

Coping with life in boarding school became a problem. My class work flopped. I was in position 103, with a mean grade of C-. It was devastating. I vowed never to go back to that school. My father pretended to understand my problems, but when the time came for the school to start a new term, I was forced back. Thanks be to God, I survived, and improved my performance. The family source of income was lost. My mother started selling locally made strong brews to supplement the family budget. I started pedaling bang (marijuana), working on construction sites, peeling potatoes in restaurants, washing cars, to raise part of my school fees and pocket money. Life was very hard for all members of the family.

I could stay at home for up to two months out of three months due to lack of school fees. Good Samaritan Ministries gave my father a relief when they sponsored one of my stepbrothers through high school.

I made a vow to finish high school and make it to university. No one believed me since my performance was dwindling after being on and off school. When out of school, I worked during the day, but studied deep into the night. I got very bad stomach ulcers. In 1993, my hard work paid off. After being away from school for one and a half months, I managed to be at the top of our class. Teachers were amazed. I, myself, was surprised.

Teachers advised me to seek help in the counseling department at school. They began to award me some financial aid for the school fees.

In 1994, I was doing my Grade 12. The fee was so high, my balance shot up to 12,000 Kenya schillings. The head teacher/principal wanted to ban me from sitting for my national final exams. My father went to school and pleaded with him to give me a chance. He agreed on condition, to withhold my result slips and other testimonials until the whole balance was paid. I gladly accepted. I was rewarded. I emerged among the top ten students in the school.

<u>In 1995, I joined Good Samaritan Ministries</u>. After completing my high school, I moved back to Uranga to stay with my mother. I could do nothing further until the balance of my school fees was paid.

The late Naboth Omondi, may the Lord rest his soul in eternal peace, was my cousin. (Note: Naboth was the first director of the First Aid program in Kenya. He was almost totally deaf, and dying of sickle-cell anemia.) I must admit I didn't like the ministry then and the whole fraternity that used to go there. I was not inclined to join. Naboth never gave up. Reluctantly, I joined the counseling training, which was on from January to April 1995. I counseled myself that I could always walk away when I wanted to. Instead of getting bored, I made new good friends from different countries. I got hooked up into the program. After graduation, I was assigned to assist Naboth in the First Aid section. After some time, I was moved to be a messenger at the continental office. Along the way, the officials of the ministry realized I had a special talent that had to be tapped.

October, 1995, James Opiyo sent me to Nairobi to learn how to operate a video camera and other electronic equipment, most of which I had never seen. I was received at a bus stop by the late George Okendo, Chairman of GSM Board, and they took me in for two weeks. After staying with another pastor of GSM, I finally settled at Judith Sellangah's house. This is where I stayed comfortably like a family member. I was well cared for, but I missed home, so I left her place without Reverend James' consent. He was furious.

After being home for two weeks, Reverend James realized I didn't have my certificates and testimonials due to outstanding fee balance. He took the issue up. He told me, "Erick, be brave. Always focus, looking upon the Lord, and everything will be alright." Since then, he took me in as his own child. All this time, my mama was still brewing and selling traditional liquor to youths and old men who could get drunk and make a lot of noise in our house. One night, the Lord talked to me and let me know what was happening was wrong. So, in the morning, I went ahead and talked to Mom. "You know, Mama, selling alcohol to these young men is wrong. Their future is getting ruined since they spend a lot of their time and money taking this stuff. Imagine if somebody could have been offering me the same. How would you feel?" She got touched, and that was the last time she did that. Initially, she was afraid of how she was going to care for the family, but she took the heed and realized that all of our help comes from God. Things were not easy. We survived. That is when I got to buy my first fixed-focus camera. I could take photos for a fee to supplement the family income.

In 1996, I got my admission letter to the University of Nairobi. My mama was delighted. She couldn't believe it! Another problem got started in our family. Jealousy and enmity was the devil. I couldn't understand. Our family was breaking apart. I started counseling with Reverend James. He told me one thing that helps me a lot. He said to never return hate with hate. What God has in store for you, nobody will take away.

Another blow occurred. James Opiyo was involved in a bad accident in 1996. He was in an intensive care unit for three days. When he came to his consciousness, he requested that I be brought to his bedside. I didn't know that for a whole two weeks, I was going to stay there next to him in the hospital. I could do all he wanted, and keep talking at night when he couldn't sleep. He was really agonizing. The pain he was undergoing was unbelievable. He would wake up in the night from very bad nightmares, screaming and crying, but after a while, the effect of the trauma died down.

When he was discharged from the hospital, he insisted I go to stay with him at his house. So, through his healing and recovery period, I was by his side day and night. It was a real

trying time for me. We became much closer. We talked a lot at night. I used to ask myself, "Why me?" I was young, only 21. There were so many things I could have done, like hanging out with my friends.

After his recovery, the day I was to leave for the university, Reverend James applied olive oil on my forehead. As he prayed for me, he told me, "You have a special purpose in life. Continue trusting in Him."

I realized that the whole episode had humbled me, and had taught me to be a servant. Above all, it had made me mature.

October, 1996, I left home for the admission at the university. I didn't know what to expect since money wasn't coming. The government was supposed to give me a loan and it didn't come. The total fee was 48,000 Kenya schillings. Reverend James gave me 10,000 Kenya schillings from Good Samaritan Ministries. I didn't get admitted, so I stayed with the Sellangah family and worked on sorting out the fee problem. Before the end of the first month, a student leader was found dead in his room, half burnt. Most people suspected foul play from government security agents, since he was an outspoken leader and the country was getting ready for the second multi-party elections. There was such student unrest, the college was closed. I stayed with the Sellangah family.

Gradually, Erick began to look around and realized that there were many disadvantaged children. All of this became less about him and more about helping the other students and the young children around him.

In 2002, Erick graduated from veterinarian school. He went on to take some training in community development and rural project management. He used the time to put all of his thoughts and vision about a children's home on paper as a proposal. He had a heart to take in the children and make a difference in their lives. All along this journey, Erick was becoming a Samaritan.

Erick said, "*In January, 2003, university students could not go back to college due to lack of fees and pocket money.* ***I called a few fellow students sponsored by Good Samaritan Ministries to my house. We resolved to help each person. We would all contribute to solve the situation. That was the birth date of Good Samaritan Sponsored Student Association (GSSA). Since*** *then, it has grown from strength to strength, encouraging those still at school, organizing private tuition for those with various problems in career counseling. God has been working through these people, glory be to Him."*

In 2003, Erick led a team of GSSA members to the Good Samaritan Ministries Children's Camp in Uganda. It was a special moment for self-realization and to be with the Lord.

He said, *"I learned how to wait upon the Lord, and above all, to be honest. A small boy taught me that. On September 10th, after being in the camp for three days, I lost my wallet while watching a soccer game. After the game, the rain poured. I knew it was going to be bad. With all of my money in my wallet, plus all the identification papers, I was not going to be lucky. But, Osborn was positive it would be found. After the rain, a young boy, about 11 years old, brought the wallet intact with all of its contents to me. It was touching. I have never met such honesty because with over 700 children at that camp, he could have gone with the wallet and nobody would have noticed. I was amazed and into tears. On September 11th, the following day at 7:00 a.m., all the college and university students were packed into a classroom. I couldn't believe it that we were so highly regarded in Uganda, that a special session had to be organized. Osborn and the Ugandan leaders thought that GSSA was a superb idea, hence they wanted us to share how we began it, with the others. He wanted us to engage them because they seemed to be taking sponsorship for granted, and they were too materialistic.* The Holy Spirit led us and the impact was great. Hence, another seminar is being organized for all students in Kampala. Kenya GSSA members will be the main speakers. May the will of God be done. Amen.

I hope my story may mean something to the people who will read it. God bless us all!"

What did it mean to you?

THREE STORIES FROM UGANDA:

Testimony from Diana Nampiima
"I was born in 1989, the eldest of three children. My father abandoned us when I was very young. I grew up seeing my mom take on all the responsibility of the parent and what a father would have done, such as provide school fees and feeding. Having started school at Mother Care Kindergarten, then to Bat Valley Primary School, it was not easy for my mother to continue paying my school fees."

"Good Samaritan Ministries Uganda decided to sponsor me. I went into Good Samaritan Primary School in Kiwangala, Masaka in Primary 3. I was there until Senior 4, and they later took me to St. Mbuga Vocational Senior Secondary School for my high school. Since my childhood, I had aspired to being a nurse. I was able to pursue my dream at Nsambya School of Nursing for three years. On the 27th of September, 2013, I graduated with a certificate in nursing."

"I am currently working as a school nurse at a primary school. I want to show appreciation to Good Samaritan Ministries and all the people who helped me. It was an unbelievable birthing for me to be able, not only to be a Good Samaritan, but to live and see what that Good Samaritan is. It defined and molded my life. I wouldn't be what I am today. Above all, I wish to thank God Almighty for the loving kindness shown to me.

Long live Good Samaritan Ministries worldwide. "Your labor of love is not in vain." 1 Corinthians 15:58."

Testimony from Beatrice Kulabako:
"Every morning when I wake up, the first thing I have to do is to thank God for the gift of life He has given me, and the rest of the people in the world who still have strength to cope with life along its length. Just look at me now. **I am no longer the other small girl who used to sit on the Veranda early every morning just to admire those kids who had the opportunity to go to school. Hardly, I had ever thought that one day I would too get the chance to go to school.** All of my good dreams melted each day, which passed for I had no hope for my future. I was staying

with my aunt who had just lost her husband, and his death led to the end of my education.

"One Sunday, my aunt told me to do all of my housework so I could go to church early. It was a special Sunday because we were expecting some visitors. **I had no shoes, and never wore any in my life, but quickly, I went to church where I met the Good Samaritans who uplifted my life."**

"I went to school and from that day, I never looked back with my studies. I finished my primary, and had to join high school at Good Samaritan High School in Kiwangala, Masaka, where I completed my studies and went to the institute to do the course of my dream, which I completed in 2009. A month later, I got a job, and now I live a happy life. I share with others. I can now smile, though the road to my success has not been easy, but someone was there always to support and encourage me. I can now support my family and have enough to share with others who need my help. I thank God for Good Samaritans who played a big part in brightening my future."

Testimony of Josephine Bouchard Namukasa:

"Hello my lovely parents of Good Samaritan Ministries!!!!! I am really so happy that you came into my life ever since I was a kid, five years old. You played a big part in my life. I am what I am today because of the Good Samaritan Ministries, but not only me, many children in Africa can stand up on their own due to the great work you did unto their lives. May the almighty God bless you according to all your hearts' desires."

"Mama Bettie Mitchell, you really played a big part in your group. God used you and you followed him spiritually. That is why Good Samaritan Ministries is exciting all the way from America to Uganda and other countries. How amazing this is!"

"Papa Osborn Muyanga and the Good Samaritan staff in Uganda raised me up since I was five years old."

"We were many orphans in Masaka, but I was the one chosen among them. Really, God knew me before I was born. My dad died when I was two years old, and left seven children with mom. Mom wanted us to go to school, but she had no way to get school fees for us. Our lives were like one plant without water. Then, Mama Betty Nakuru, our Director at Kiwangala, Masaka

School, came back and asked my biological mom to be with her. Mom was happy to hear that. She took me and stayed with me up to the time I finished my studies, providing me everything, for example: love, food, school fees, all school requirements, healthy cloths, and taught me how to cook, dig, and do domestic work."

"I completed primary and O level at the Good Samaritan high school. Then I went to the college called Nateete Community Development Center in Kampala. I have received a diploma in information technology. I finally got a job at a certain school called K Garden Grove College, Buddo, Kampala. I have been working as a bursar for five years."

"All my lovely parents from Good Samaritan Ministries were there for me until I finished my studies and got a job. Now, I'm married to a Canadian man, whose name is Gilles Bouchard from Niagara Falls. If it wasn't for Good Samaritan Ministries, it would not have happened."

"Therefore, glory be to God, the One who used all members of Good Samaritan Ministries to do such a gorgeous work to needy people, especially children of Africa. I also thank our beloved director, Papa Osborn, for counseling me. He has been there for me and **he still talks into the lives of all the children.**"

Testimony of Moses Kaggwa:
"I really thank God for He is a loving God. He knows and plans for us. We don't choose Him, but He chooses us. I have witnessed this in the whole of my life from the time when I was a little boy, up till now, when I see myself grown up."

"But in whose hands have I been raised? Many years back when I was left at the landing site with no one to take care of me, many people counted me dead, but they were not my God. My grandmother picked me up and took care of me; and thereafter, my uncle, Pastor Josham Serwanja picked me in 1995. He began taking care of me. Life was not good at all. We were living in a bush. **We could go for days without a meal.** There was no treatment when we got sick, apart from natural herbs. It was hard to get clothes, and one time, I wore a multi-purpose t-shirt that worked as a trouser and shirt at the same time for almost three months. During that time, the church was the source of my food, treatment, clothes, and my uncle was my mother and father."

"It was during that time that my uncle started a simple school where I was his first student, using charcoal as chalk and sticks as pencils. What an education! What a teacher! What a student! I did not know how far my education would go because there was no nearby school where I could go and there were no funds to facilitate my education in other schools. Nevertheless, my uncle did not stop teaching me until when other pupils from the community joined us. None of us knew what was next after Nambirizi. **In the village, I met Pastor Osborn, who came for the visit. He asked me a question that I will never forget in my life. It has inspired me until now, "Moses, what do you want to be in case you proceed with your education?"** I failed the test the first time, but on the second time we met, I told him, "**I want to be a health worker because there is no hospital here. Neither is there a clinic apart from the witch doctors.**" He told me, "**You will become one.**" **I marked those words. I walked with them until now.**"

"Through Papa Osborn, I joined Good Samaritan Sponsorship when I was in Primary 2. Since then, I have seen myself excelling in my education; I have never been chased from school for school fees until now. This Moses from Nambirizi, never expected to be in any boarding school. Good Samaritan was the first to educate him at a boarding school (Good Samaritan High School) where I finished my Level O, I was sent on to St. Mbuga Vocational Secondary School, where I did my A level through 2008. I never forgot to carry science subjects, however tough they were, and through all of these levels, **I have seen the hand of God. I received the best love from the Good Samaritan family, nationally and internationally.**"

"However, there is a moment when I shed tears asking God what will happen next when I was called to the GSM office and told that GSM could not support me anymore after my Senior 6. Richard Zziwa told me to believe God more than before. He will make a way for further studies. I did not know how that would be, but waited to see God's plan upon my life."

"I went back home and began serving (volunteering) as a science and English teacher for nine months at Good Samaritan

Primary School at Nambirizi. Thereafter, I joined Good Samaritan High School, where I volunteered as a laboratory attendant, helping students in science practicals."

"The only option I had by then was to get on my knees and ask God to provide the way He provided for Elisha. But all-in-all, Papa Osborn encouraged me. "Moses, God is faithful. He will answer in a time we do not know. Let us serve Him faithfully."

"In June, 2010, he asked me if I was willing to join the solar light team. Not knowing what would happen, I met Mama Charlene and the rest of the team members, including my brothers Will and Scuyler, who became my great friends."

"Through these brothers (not blood brothers) I got a mother, the mother of Will and Scuyler, Lane Anderson. She decided to take care of my university bills. Since January 2011, I joined Uganda Christian University, pursuing my Bachelor in Community Health. Since then, God has transformed my life spiritually, mentally, and more so, socially. I am so thankful to the Lord for the great success."

By now, Moses has graduated with a Bachelor's Degree in Community Health. He believes God will provide a Master's degree in Service Management and Public Health because he believes and trusts that he is called to run health programs and projects, including hospitals. This made him the first person to graduate with a degree in this community of Nambirizi.

Moses continues:

"These simple successes I have attained in life are of great benefit to my community and the world at large. Right now, I am heading a youth ministry called Gospel Team International Ministries, where we are reaching out to lost souls all over the world."

"At Nambirizi I started a demonstration farm, where we raise pigs and poultry. The purpose is to teach community members modern ways of farming and to give them start-up capital on top of creating job opportunities. In the projects, there are two people already employed. I am running another program called Come Out of Poverty. I'm dealing with health, promotion and sensitization, and I am also working with Enterprise Uganda, to sensitize the community about development. In addition to this, I

am volunteering at Nambirizi Good Samaritan Primary School. I am looking forward to starting health programs and projects both nationally and internationally."

"Therefore, I thank God for this great success He has put in my hands, where I was seeing His plans really coming to pass upon my life. I thank God for Good Samaritan Ministries for having brought me this far. You picked me from a point where all other persons and ministries would have bypassed me to the stage where I can now benefit the world. Since then, I can see the plan of God coming to pass every day."

"I will always mention this one major thing I have learned from you: "Go and do likewise." We must remember this ministry has to continue. Therefore, whatever I can do, I will do it."

Good Samaritan Ministries has educated approximately 12,000 students in Africa. Some students were sponsored from nursery school through university. With Africa, we have developed 24 nursery schools, 16 primary schools, and five high schools (three in Kenya, one in Uganda, and one in Tanzania),

In addition, we have sponsored children individually. This has been up to the Director of Good Samaritan Ministries in each country as to who will be sponsored. We considered that the most important children to sponsor would be the children of the directors in each country, as they were given so little income, and expected from the call upon their lives to give so much. We have done individual sponsorships in Nigeria, Cameroon, Burundi, Congo, Liberia, Sierra Leone, Senegal, Ghana, and Rwanda.

In Kenya, 58 students were sponsored through university; 25 were put through teacher-training colleges, and two students were trained and are working on the police force. In GSSS (Good Samaritan Sponsored Students Association) 80 students who graduated are working together to make the program more and more a program given by those to whom much was given. As they give to others, we have seen the hand of God training all in this ministry to be true givers.

Only one of the Ugandan students came to the United States. She was Osborn's adopted daughter, Betty. Robert and Alberta Hill of Talent, Oregon, offered Betty a chance to go to nursing school, but her primary call in coming to the United States was to live with and help take care of these senior citizens. Now, for several years, she has helped meet their needs. They legally adopted Betty to be their daughter.

As the years have gone by, it has been urgent to provide sponsorships for qualified teachers and to provide help for children called to go to boarding schools. **We live under the call to be accountable and compassionate. Jesus taught his disciples the value of each child's life.**

IS THE EDUCATION STORY ABOUT MONEY? NO. IT IS ABOUT THE CHILDREN!

CHAPTER 32

THE FINAL WORD

TO AFRICA:

Each country in Africa that received The Call of Good Samaritan Ministries had a unique experience. Leaders faced their local and national needs, and their limitations of freedom to move due to finances. They saw needs everywhere they looked. But the great challenge was The Call itself.

It is easy for everyone to say "Mama Bettie was called." This is not the truth. The truth is heaven spoke, and through this Call, we have accepted a lifetime assignment. All of our decisions through this Call will be challenged and cherished throughout our lifetime.

Each of the Samaritan countries in Africa is uniquely under the authority of The Call. You in Africa are all challenged to live a life blessed with faith, filled with miracles and the increase of laborers in the fields. Your work is to challenge the lives of many!

When we sit down at a table, we are all fellow-Samaritans. We break bread with one another. We do not compete with one another. Above all, we must never compare our story with another story!

Each of you in Africa has experienced the joys and the hardships of this ministry. Each of you is human and you will always have your human struggles. As your problems over the years were extraordinary, there were days that this Call seemed impossible. The Lord greatly thanks you for your faithfulness along the road. He saw how difficult it was, and how valiant were your efforts.

I want to say to Africa, stay together! Do not think just of your small area, but think of the whole. Think of every laborer out in the field. Think of the people. The Lord desires you to always remember in your life's work you are part of the greater picture of His whole Kingdom.

Be an encouragement to one another. Write each other often. Listen to the cries of one another from the Holy Spirit.

In the early years, we had primitive communication. Now you have e-mail and possibilities of great communication.

When you feel absorbed in your own problems, you lose sight that God called you and that He knew you would rise above your circumstances to a life of faith.

I know the crowds cry for money, and some of those cries are true and desperate. The needs confront your eyes daily. The situation is not easy for any of you!

We, as fellow-Samaritans, respect all of the meals you didn't eat, all of the food you shared with many, and all of the nights you kept before the Lord to sustain the lives of others. **We must carry in our spirit the most profound respect for one another. The Call is sacred. It creates in us the sacredness of all life.** Daily, you will be reminded of the profound sacredness of others.

I say to you, integrity, integrity, integrity! Let our lives be found among those who kept integrity. Integrity means giving and keeping your word, even to yourself. For example, if I said, "I'm going to write my annual report on Friday." Then, I must write it on Friday. If we do not keep our word in small things, we will soon find we keep our word about less and less. **Keeping your word always involves giving your word.** Let your word be your honor to God and your blessing.

I say to you, communicate, communicate, communicate! Those who did may find their letters in this book. Those who didn't often waited with empty hands. **When you preach, it is from your pulpit. When you listen to the people, it is from His pulpit.** Never think your monologue is communication. **God desires communication to be dialogue! Did He not dialogue with many in the Scriptures? All the people must know you hear them! Do you?**

Does your heart take your communication as a divine command? It still is!!

At times I know you have been tempted to promise others things that did not take place, needs you said would be met that were not met. It is important that you weigh the needs of everyone, not just the needs you see. **You may have great ideas, you all daily have great challenges, but do you see ALL of the** people? Are your eyes clear? Are your eyes sound? Will your word be kept, or just a word given to please the crowd?

As we have all aged, the mission now is to train three generations. We have the profound mission to pass The Call to future generations. **We have the mission to find the ones that are called, and not be disappointed in those who were truly not.**

I know many of you have experienced people who came wanting things, and later they brought betrayal by their actions. This could create wounded spirits in any of us. May we be changed by His healing and the renewal of our vision. We must be tempered by God's mercy.

Let go of those you are to let go of. Keep the ones that passed through the fire and were refined. Always let people leave with a blessing. None of us must allow expectations, disappointment, or anger to control the coming in or the leaving of anyone.

Be prepared at all times to turn the work over. Continue to prepare people for the harder tasks. Don't just make others your servants in the smaller things. **Challenge others to the greater things that must be accomplished. This Christ firmly taught us all, when he sent out the 12.**

Some of you have had a very hard time keeping teams together and keeping your eyes on **effective teamwork.** This is not an activity that is a good idea. We are divinely appointed to acts of obedience. If you are not trustworthy to your word, teams will always fall apart. Each team member, even a child, has equal value in God's eyes.

We will let the Holy Spirit break each of us until there is nothing left but the grace of God to pass on to those coming!

Do not fear about money. Some of you hang on to Good Samaritan because of money. It is hard to let go of money, but you must not fear the loss of income, or the loss of help. You will not fear anything. You were born to do the will of God.

These words sound easy to say, but hard to do. **It is hard for each of us to see our own weaknesses and fairly judge our individual strengths. We must take the plank out of our own eye first. This is a daily assignment in all circumstances.**

Let yourself be evaluated daily by the Holy Spirit. He will always tell you where you are right and where you are wrong. He will quicken your conscience, and he will remind you that you are not free, but linked together with Him as an integral part of the whole.

Over the years, I have been very proud of most of you, indeed, of ALL of you! There is always the temptation to manipulate for a legitimate need and to argue for that need. As you've shown gentleness, you have argued less, and we together have accomplished more. God has chosen to meet the needs in His time and in His way. He says to you, "Well done my good and faithful servant, you that waited upon the Lord."

If it is time to lay down the work you are called to do, it is time! It is time to not consider our leadership to be the most essential part of the ministry, for the leadership is entirely in the hands of the Holy Spirit, and the Holy Spirit is available through many. If it is time for you to lay down your task and let go of your position, then you must do it. You must do it willingly, and you must do it in the eyes of God your Father.

The stories in this book are not favoring one person over another. They are parables of struggle, stories of anguish, and challenges along the road. Indeed, the stories represent all of us.

It has always been important that we provided as much as possible for the education of your children. It is a gift from God to grant you freedom from that fear. Be grateful for this. Be in awe, for it comes only by His hand, His mercy, and His Word to you.

Be in prayer and intercession for the whole ministry, each country, and each Samaritan. Do not look more at the problems you carry, but look at "The Call" we carry together. Jesus walked this road and He told us to follow Him. This is the prayer request of our LORD!

Those of you who have weak teams, face this. Look at it, and deal with it! It was a high priority to Jesus to have a strong team. He worked to strengthen those called daily. Deal with this, face it, and develop team integrity. The team members work with you and with one another.

As you develop centers in other parts of the country of your influence, really develop them! Listen to them! Pay attention to them. In the night, intercede for them. In the day, be watchful for ways that you can be an encouragement.

I have visited many of the centers in Africa, the small communities where this ministry has been held in sacredness. I have watched teams come to consensus and work with and for one another. I have seen integrity that is incredible.

I never found anyone in Africa who was trying to impress me as a leader. This is a grace from God! We all know we must never try to impress one another. We must be who we are, and who He has called us to be.

We bless God that your families have been sustained. Time and again, in great danger, your lives have been sustained. We have watched the passing into glory of Oliver in Liberia, James Kabvalo and Samson in Malawi, and most recently Nicholas Okungu in Kenya.

I have known many of your sacrifices to remain comforters. You have often traveled great distances to help one another.

The final word is integrity. Follow Jesus.

CORE VALUE

The greatest decision that Africa needs to make is whether they will continue the West Africa Continental Training Center in Nigeria, and the African Continental Training Center in Kenya. Do you believe in a central place to send key trainees? Will Africa have the courage to make sure these roots are cared for, and continue? Will you work together to make sure that effective training continues? Will you fight for this training and give it your highest priority? **God will provide in Africa when Africa believes the provision will come from Him in Africa.** Bring the training to maturity! I challenge your faith and your actions to maturity.

Over the years, we have sent funds for all of the trainees to come to Continental Training. This was very hard. It was about integrity among us. It was about keeping our word. **Now it's time for you to meet together, and truly develop the quality of training that will reach the distant years of those who hunger and thirst for righteousness.**

Do not let what you receive from America influence what you do in Africa. Do not let lack of funds limit your vision. The grace of God is sufficient, and His ways are found. We then can place our deep trust before Him. Please, keep the integrity of the training of Africa in Africa. Do it!
We greatly love one another. Most of us know each other very well. **We know our weaknesses and our strengths. We know our blind spots and our vision. We will always represent the first generation that received The Call, held it sacred, acted upon it, and passed it to the next generation!**
We are all replaceable. It is tempting to think we are not. It is tempting to think of what we want to do. But I tell you solemnly, there is a time to be born, and there is a time for the death of self. Do you agree, Africa? Do you agree to this time? Will you keep your integrity? Pass The Call to the next generation!

Two years ago, President Museveni called the entire country of Uganda to return to God, and at the national stadium, he repented before the people. He spoke these words, "We should forgive one another, and ask God to forgive all of us."

President Museveni and Uganda worked for peace in Somalia, Southern Sudan, Burundi, Congo, and Rwanda. *"Happy the peacemakers: they shall be called Sons of God."* (Matthew 5:9)

Pass The Call to the next generation! **THE FINAL WORD IS INTEGRITY. FOLLOW JESUS!**

TO THE SATELLITES:

I have included, in this part of the book, drawings that are very important, for the term "satellite" came from God alone. It was nothing that I could conceive. It is something He saw when He looked at us.

What is a satellite? It is something in the heavens that travels around the earth. It travels in an orbit that God created in the planetary system. It is a moving vehicle and it is in God's hands.

First and foremost, I must say to you, it is a privilege to be on a satellite team that works from above. It is a privilege not to take this word of the Lord lightly. It is a joy. It is not a responsibility. It is a life! Satellite leaders are ones that know that the satellite is in the heavens. Only as we move our help and prayers through the satellite to the place where a gift will be received, will we be completely satisfied with the work itself. Our work will come to others through God's own hand.

I thought a lot about the teams that have been built over the years, these teams of satellites. There were some that were long-suffering and steadfast. Others were less ignited by The Call, and therefore, limited in willingness to show up and complete their faithfulness.

As I have been thinking about this, it has occurred to me that it is a privilege to be on a Satellite, a privilege given to few. Only when it becomes a privilege, will you become effective.

I want to boldly suggest that before a person can join a satellite, they must be interviewed and trained as to what is expected.

We could speak about the satellites that have been successful, and we could speak about the satellites that never took hold because nobody wanted those countries. We could speak about the grief that happened because nobody wanted that country and that country became an unwanted child. We could speak about our history in satellites and we could speak about our experience. **But, above all things, let us speak about the heavens and our fragile gift that goes through the satellite unto a nation, unto the people who are hungry and too often terrifically desperate.**

When I look back on the development of the work in Uganda, we must ask ourselves, "How did they sustain the schools?" I would say to you, many of the Samaritan people ate only two to three meals a week in order to feed the children. If a satellite does not understand this, if they begin to think in terms of personalities, or aggravations, then that affects the whole.

Again, I say firmly, make it a privilege to belong to a satellite. Let us leave no unwanted children (countries) out there because no one cared to select them.

When I was in school, for many years, I was always the last one chosen for the sports teams. Never in my lifetime have I been able to get a volleyball over the net, or throw a softball overhand. But, the Lord, Himself chose what was weak in me to make this Call strong in you. **Never live a life of limited vision to your own opinions. Live a life of integrity to The Call.**

If you are called to go to Africa, go. But, when you come home, you're not called to finish you're called to begin. As you come home and begin the work, with your heart, your integrity, and your sacrifice, then your journey will be pleasing in the eyes of God.

Sometimes, when you have travelled to Africa, they have made us more important than we really are. They've touched us, followed us, and asked us to speak here and there. Always remember, we were there to listen to them speak. Often they have weaknesses that can only be strengthened and healed by us choosing them to be on the team.

I want to say to the satellites, don't meet too seldom and believe that everything is being done. For, when you meet seldom, and pray seldom, what is being done? You are not reaching the heavens, you are only reaching for your own needs.

Over the years, when I was awakened by the phone during the night, night after night, there was a fragile voice on the other end of the phone. I never made them pay for the call. I called them back, and sometimes it took three to four hours to get through on that call back. When we talked, it was sacred. It was not practical. It was sacred. It was holy. It was divinely ordained that we would speak to one another!

All the work you do to alleviate suffering in this world and to encourage growth is sacred. Every meeting you have, every conversation you have, every story you will ever tell….all of your life's work to help others is holy and sacred.

You can only be satisfied if you have paid the price. The price will never be convenient, but it will be sent through the heart of the Father, the Son, and the Holy Spirit.

Never let your focus on money or problems detach you! Focus on miracles. Remember always, you are interceding and keeping a whole nation. You keep this firmly in your heart. The nation will change, but first we must change. We have asked the Africans to focus on their entire nation. Surely, we must faithfully join them!

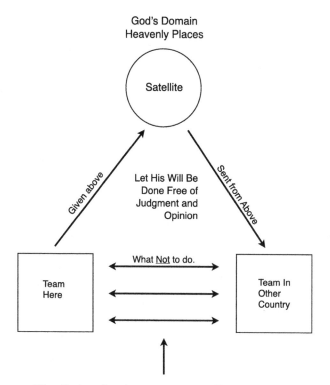

Dangers In Working Across

- Control
- Manipulate
- Limit Sacrifice

- Dying Satellite Team
- Burn-out
- Our definition of Mercy Replaces God's mercy.

"Satellite" was a word given by God.

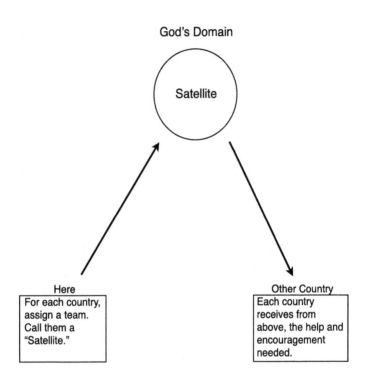

We Move In And Through Him!

Finally, to the satellites, I want to tell a story. I had forgotten this story, but Osborn Muyanga was here in the last couple of weeks, and he, himself, told the story at a meeting we attended together. The story was this:

It was the night before Osborn was to marry Louise. He was staying at his mother's house, and sleeping on a mattress on the floor. Without his knowledge, or any sense of danger, a candle had tipped over, falling on the mattress, and the mattress was burning. At that moment, he was deep in sleep, but he was awakened because I telephoned him from the United States. I said, "Osborn, fire!" He was not burned. The marriage took place with joy, and a very tired servant of the Lord was heard through the satellite from the heavens. Unto us a child is given. Unto us a child is spared. Unto us is all there is or ever will be. In Jesus' Name, Amen.

TO THE SAMARITANS:

We all admire greatly a new story of courage and brave action. We have heard the words, "This person was truly a Samaritan." We may eagerly listen to new Samaritan stories and we might keep one or two of these stories in mind for a lifetime.

Jesus told one news story, the Parable of the Good Samaritan. He told it to us. He spoke intimately to us. It was a word of the Lord to us, and it challenges us where we are weak. "Am I being a thief? Am I ignoring the problem by walking on by? Am I one that stole and took everything they had? Will I stop and pay the price? Am I willing to pay the second price?"

We may study the story from the standpoint of the lawyer, watching the story, listening to the story. By not taking this parable to heart as Jesus' training for our personal conscience, we will not hear the words, "Go and do likewise." Ponder this. Keep this in mind. Let the words of Jesus speak into your conscience. Let them dwell in you to help you find the truth about yourself as a Samaritan.

Over the years I have seen many people spend a lot of money foolishly. I have seen all of us do it. It is hard because there is that temptation to put our needs ahead of others and give what we have left. It is a very great temptation, and we must grow in the realization, "May we have less, that others may have enough!"

I am proud of us because we work together for the common good. There are those who break out, find fault, and criticize. That is alright, because they are being called out of this work until they are ready. We must stay faithful on the road we chose.

Each of us needs many intercessors over our lives. I would say, a minimum of three, and better for 12. It would make a difference in our actions and our health. We must seek and find who those intercessors are. This is a dangerous road and intercession will make the difference. Over many years, John K. of Uganda was a daily intercessor for Papa Jerry.

On every trip I took to Africa or to any other country, I notified people all over the world to pray for me and those going. I said to them, "You are to begin praying a month before we leave, and you are to continue to pray for a month after we come home. We must be covered. Have any of you ever asked with authority and been so specific? It will make a huge difference. It will be a life force for you—the saints praying for you.

The ministry here needs our consistent help. Many depend on us. We must remember the sacredness of our giving. Jesus pointed out the Samaritan paid the price and was willing to give more.

Several years ago, a woman paid for her trip to the Holy Land. She was excited to go on the tour, and then one day she called me and said, "I'm not going. You are to use the money to send whoever is to be sent."

In your daily life, wherever you are, watch for the Samaritans. The Lord will show them to you if you are looking. He will not lead you to those who make false claims or seek fame. He will lead you to true Samaritans, and He will breathe on you to breathe His life into them.

The Samaritan life is not about tasks it is about life and death!

This ministry has given much to many, and carried the cross with you. We have been faithful.

Now it is time for you to examine your faithfulness. Many like to volunteer, but not give. Others like to dabble and give

when it is convenient. Many like to come. Do they help others to come? Do they pay the bus fare of someone who cannot get there any other way? Many think that somehow the leadership of Good Samaritan Ministries will solve the problems. I want to radically say to each person who reads this book, the grass roots people will solve the problems when they know the problems of this ministry are in their hands.

Even today I received a call from a woman named Eva who lives in another town. She was radically broken, confused, destroyed, and terrified. Our daughter, Laura, asked her to call. We can be a calming effect on the raging storms. **Do we realize who brought us together, and who the Master is of this ministry?**

Over the years, Jerry and I looked at our financial giving to the church, the ministry, and to other needs. It was my personal policy to read the newsletters that were sent to us from all other organizations. If I could not give, I prayed. I encouraged. I listened, and I saw. If I could read all of those newsletters, can you read the Samaritan newsletter you receive? Can you be glad of receiving and holding it sacred in your hand? Please realize the hours, the labor, and the enormous effort it took to put it into your hand, even for the postman delivering it.

We must pour out our gratitude, focusing less on our problems and far more on our gratitude for this ministry. You see there was another Samaritan story. There was the story of the ten lepers, and only the Samaritan poured out his gratitude at the feet of Jesus. The others took the healing, but never responded to it as a precious gift from God. You will know you're a Samaritan when the whole of gratitude is quickened in your spirit, and when tears flow from your eyes when you hear of the genuine needs of others. **You will know you are a Samaritan when your spirit of gratitude is so overwhelming it lessens every trouble you have, and increases every gift you give.**

One year, I was so worried at the end of the year because we were short in funds and we were not in the black. It was New Year's Eve. I always went to the office and collected the mail. If the office was closed and the mail was delivered, I never failed to go get it. I opened an envelope and there was a check for $15,000. I sobbed and sobbed. Someone was listening to the Lord and paid the price.

You have friends all over the world. You know people by name and by experience with them. Your stories mingled with their stories have made a great testimony, a great symphony of our actions and works of faith.

When new ones come into the ministry, we must welcome them with all of our being. We must express the kind of gratitude when I sobbed over the check for $15,000. We must sob inwardly our gratitude when we see them and know that their presence is a miracle.

It is hard to keep track of people. I know I was worried about Dean Pontius. I hadn't seen him for quite a long time and I was really worried about him. Finally, I wrote him a letter. It was really important that I knew where he was. He was still alive and still a Samaritan. I was so glad!

About three weeks ago, I received a letter from Mary Elliott of Kanab, Utah. It was a letter telling me the story of her husband's death.

Dear Bettie,

I want you to know that Hardy went to his new assignment in the third heaven according to the angels that talked to him all the time. His assignment is to be the Secretary of State.

He made it to his 95th birthday. He wanted to live until our 50th anniversary, April 25th. He bargained with the angels, but he missed the mark, so they took him October 11th. He was in the hospital from 1:00 p.m. Thursday, and I stayed with him all day and that night. For several hours, he kept calling me. He only suffered a short few hours, and left at 8:30 a.m., Friday. Thank you for all you did to help him find peace with God.

The pallbearers were clowns. They honored his clowning and the joy he brought to the people.

Hardy didn't have much money and he didn't have much health at all. He wanted to go on the tour to the Holy Land in 1981. He and his wife, Mary, worked hard to make that happen. I'll always remember Hardy climbed Mt. Sinai to the top. All along the way he expressed unlimited gratitude that he could make this journey with us. I haven't seen Hardy since, but with this letter Mary sent me his picture. You see, Hardy was one of those Samaritans out there, one of us, one with you, one of the faithful ones.

The ministry needs a great deal of energy from each of us. I have watched our daughter, Laura, at Lincoln City, blossom into her lifetime's work as a Samaritan. She is a Samaritan at large for all of Lincoln City. She loads her car and often another car with people who are in all stages of lack of recovery from addictions. She takes them to Celebrate Recovery. They call her many times a day. She is there for them.

Each of us must examine ourselves. Did we do all that was needed? Did we give all that we had to give, full measure and running over? Was our gratitude poured out in front of our fellow man and our testimony alive?

Never take this call for granted. Don't rush on by and never think you are finished, for indeed, for many of us, we are just starting.

THE FINAL WORD:

It is the Lord Himself who must speak the final word. He is the author and the finisher of our lives. His words will bring us life and truth.

Here is the story of the words He spoke a few weeks ago. I was in my counseling office at home seeing a client. He and his wife had been problem-centered clients. As he was presenting his problems, his case, suddenly the Holy Spirit burst through my mouth. I slammed my hand on the table, and the Spirit said to him, "You have only one problem and that is you are not born again! Furthermore, you must be born again every single day!"

I was shocked at the power that came from these words. They were commanding an absolute. The Spirit continued to speak to the man, "When Jesus carried the cross, He carried no baggage. When Jesus died on the cross, he gave us the power to forgive. All of your problems are baggage!!! You cannot carry the cross of Christ, which is the power to forgive, when your focus is on pain and suffering. You were told by Jesus, Himself, to take up your cross and follow Him. The cross of Jesus cannot be defined by suffering and hardship. Our cross cannot be defined by suffering and hardship. When we focus on the suffering, we lose the power to forgive. You are to carry your cross. **Follow Jesus, and with no baggage, YOU WILL BE GIVEN POWER FROM ON HIGH, THE POWER TO FORGIVE!"**

Through the Cross of Christ Jesus we are receiving **The Power to Forgive.**

Do not center His or your cross on suffering, as this will become your baggage. To be born again daily is to let go of all baggage and each day live a new life in Christ Jesus.

The man left stunned. I was stunned—shocked! It was, indeed, the Lord who had spoken.

Six weeks later the man came back and said that he and his wife had talked about nothing else since that day. The Holy Spirit said, "Oh, there is one more thing. You must give up your ethnicity."

Again I was shocked as the man began to rejoice and willingly give up his ethnicity. Again, these word came from the Kingdom, "You will choose the Kingdom of God or your ethnicity!" He immediately replied, "I choose the Kingdom of God."

He laughed. His ethnicity that had been so important to him for so many years was gone. There was hope for his adopted gypsy daughter born in Romania. She could be healed. She too could give up her ethnicity.

What is your ethnicity? What is your own culture in relationship to the Kingdom of God?

Even your culture, within your religious beliefs, can weaken your joy at being given the Kingdom of God.

These words about ethnicity are very big. **We can become ethnic Christians carrying identification papers but not carrying in our body the Power to Forgive!**

There is one more issue. I have seen Christians taught to put their problems at the foot of the cross—to just leave them there. Jesus never taught this. It makes us weak and keeps us in bondage. He said, "Take up your cross and follow me!" Baggage can only be relinquished by the Power to Forgive. There is one definition and one definition alone to

the Cross of Christ Jesus. His cross IS the POWER TO FORGIVE!
The word power is very important. We hear the words, "He forgave us of our sins." We do not hear the words, "power to forgive was unleashed." Do we not know that when we carry our cross, that same power at His cross will define our life?

This book is a story about the fullness of Christian action. Jesus knew we would be tempted by self-pity and pride. He meant every word He spoke!

What will you do now? What does it mean to you to be born again every day? Is it the gift of grace, our absolute freedom from baggage? When you read this book, measure what has been given to you. **Never read** *From the Bush to the Roots*, **and walk away thinking you already know this. KNOWING IT ALL IS OUR GREATEST BAGGAGE OF ALL!!!**

Your daily freedom without baggage will give you life. You will be life giving. You will, indeed, be a lifetime Samaritan!

CHAPTER 33

In Memory of HEROES OF THE FAITH

I wrote to John Oundo in Kenya in 1993.
I carried two very hard things, John: the message and the labor. The hours in the stretching of my soul continued to be long, painful, and so often full of the sorrows over the chosen weakness of my fellow man. Here, people do not understand, but among you, my heart is content that you do. People here want joy without a cross, but when I looked into your face, you accepted the cross to be your joy.
February 5, 1992, Read in Kenya at the Memorial Service for Jenipher Oduor. Written by Mama Bettie:
Father in Heaven, Your mercy astounds us. We stand here with you today, and with our beloved sister, Jenipher. The Lord Jesus and all of the saints stand with us. Thank you, Father, for this day. Thank you for the mercy you have given us, and your friendship that cannot be broken by distance or by death. Today, we stand before heaven in the Name of our Lord Jesus, Amen.
As I look out on the sea of your faces today, I stand with you. There is strength in our standing together that no one can defeat. No one can ever take this day away from us. This day is one of the greatest days in the history of Good Samaritan Ministries—Kenya. The whole ministry around the world stands with you. There is nothing that can take away from this day. No spirit can harm us. It is the strength of the Lord Jesus Himself that has brought us to this day, and the strength of His mercy will keep us together in His eternal time.
Jenipher Oduor was one of the few people in this world that could make me laugh in the face of all the misery I saw. She could bring out laughter, joy, and peace in this world. I pray in the years ahead, she continues to make us all laugh when things seem too difficult.
Let us remember the infectious light of Jenipher. Her quick little run, her dash to do the work and to be a servant, and her eagerness to go down the road with many. Let us remember the strength of her arms to work, to embrace her children, and to lift her hands to God in praise and joy. Where is Jenipher? We know

where she is. She is face to face with God, the Father of the Lord Jesus, reconciled to him, close to him, a real daughter. She is about her Father's business in intercession, praying for this work, praying for our souls, and begging in such a way for all of us.

Jenipher is not just near Jesus, she is WITH Jesus. All of us have a lot to learn in order to stand WITH Jesus. We don't need to say goodbye to Jenipher today, for indeed, she has not left. She is more alive and more aware of all of us than ever before.

I come to stand beside James Opiyo. I ask your mercy for him, for Jenipher kept James and Mama Bettie in fasting and prayer that we might do the Lord's work and not fail. We are going to turn to you now to continue that work of fasting and prayer for us. Whatever we are able to do, we are going to accomplish it as a team, as a body, and a group of people. Wherever we are, we are going to be together. I stand beside James, and I stand beside the children that God allowed to come into life through Jenipher and her husband. They are children given to water and bless the earth.

May the women of this ministry, the widows, influence the ministry for many years to come. There is much shaping that must be done to all of our characters; that people might look into our faces and know that we are the Sisters of the Lord Jesus Christ.

At this funeral, I have to stand for a moment beside each person that is here because we are friends in ways that are too deep for words. I don't believe that anyone will utter a single word at this funeral that will mean nearly as much as the fact that we stood here today. We bow our heads together, before our God. He has brought us to an understanding of the Kingdom of God that is nearly unknown in the whole earth. I want to stand awhile with you, and touch your hands. I want to stoop down and wipe the tears from the children's faces. We pray the fear out of their eyes. I want to look into the faces of my beautiful sisters and I want to touch your eyes with Jenipher's faith in Jesus Christ.

Jenipher and I exchanged many letters. Often, we wrote a letter each month. I knew her secrets and she knew mine. We held nothing back from each other, but gave each other our best in friendship. We shared a gift of trustworthiness. Every person in this ministry knows that Jenipher's soul was trustworthy. We could whisper our secrets and our pain into her heart and she could be trusted with those things. She would get down on her knees and deliver those things up to her Lord. I know He heard her. Our prayers were answered and our needs were met. Let us be chosen to keep the gift of wise counsel and ears to hear our neighbor. We will continue to be Samaritans in our daily lives.

In a little while, we will all leave this grave. The coffin will go in the ground. There will remain among us her beautiful face. The life that was in that face will smile down from heaven upon the earth. She will be an encouragement to the souls of men for many generations to come. When we go home from this place, we will be quiet. It is my earnest prayer that we will all be different.

Jenipher was a parable given by the Lord Jesus in our midst. From this parable, we can learn what it is to be a counselor, a friend, a servant. We can learn what it means to live a life of prayer. When we go home today, let us look at our children. Let us seek them, cherish them, and keep them. Let us sit with our children for a little while. Let us take pity on our own children and improve the way we take care of them. Let us sit with each other and realize that we have more time to improve the way we do things, but also realize that the time is short in preparation for the work that is ahead when we stand before the throne of Grace.

Today, let us go home together, inseparable as a body, sharing a ministry that is to be poured out for the whole world. Let us understand that this group of people here learned to give in their houses and along the road. We have learned how to give the things that Jesus gave and to live the way He lived. Let us go home, with Jenipher's nine children as reminders to all of us, that our day is coming, reminders to all of us that children must never be forgotten. Let us work harder together to educate the children of Kenya and Africa. We are to bring a hope and a praise on this earth.

Humbly, this day, Lord, we all bow our heads to you and we submit to your glory, for it is truly among us. May the Name of

God be upon this house and this place now and forever more. Amen.

My Sister, Arabelle, tells the following story:

In *1990, Jenipher, while we traveled together in Kenya, had her clothes stolen. We were in the van and a thief grabbed them. She was in a bad place. She asked Arabelle if she could have a dress and a pair of shoes. Of course, Arabelle was glad to share and give it.*

In 1999, Arabelle went back to Kenya. Jenipher's daughter met with her at Nakuru. She said, "I'm wearing the dress you gave Mama and the shoes."

Eulogy for Old Lucy, July 31, 1996

To all our wonderful friends and fellow Samaritans at Uranga, all surrounding villages and towns from Mama Bettie:

Old Lucy has died, and gone to be with Jenipher Oduor, Grandfather William, Rhoda Abungu, Flora Mutaka , and many other very special saints of Good Samaritan Ministries. She is with little children who really love her, and old friends. She is making a new and very special friendship face to face with Jesus.

In our world, Old Lucy became an institution. The issue of the elderly care was settled in Africa. The seniors would be kept, honored, and drawn upon for their wisdom and spiritual courage. They will be washed by Africa. They will be fed by Africa, and they will be housed by an Africa that embraces them. They will not die alone. They will be known in this world as the old ones who are kept.

For the sake of Old Lucy, who lay paralyzed on the floor of her hut for 20 years, I want to personally thank everyone who took care of her: washed her blankets, rubbed her back, patted her hand, cleaned her up, and drew upon the strength of her prayers. I want to thank those of you who were willing to make that long walk to Lucy's house for prayer, or just a good old visit.

There were two special heroes in Lucy's life. One, was James Opiyo, the other was Rose Alloush. We all at Good Samaritan want to thank these two friends, these special heroes of the faith that gave birth to a new vision for the communities of your nation, the communities of Africa, the communities of this world.

We all love you, Lucy. We will see you soon. Above all things today, we know you and Jesus see us very clearly.

Grieve Africa, and rejoice. Your daughter has gone home. She can walk with the Lord.

Your fellow Samaritans salute all of you in Kenya, friends, neighbors, precious ones. Our prayers are with you who have lost body strength from the accident. We are with you always and forever by the power of the Name of Jesus.

James Opiyo reported that Lucy's funeral was an International funeral. 500 people came, many elders and seniors. Nicholas Okungu conducted the funeral and the GSM Choir sang. The first eulogy was from overseas.

We had a wonderful Memorial Service for Old Lucy here in Beaverton, Oregon. Everyone cherished the memories of Old Lucy.

July 15, 1993, I wrote a letter of encouragement to Rose Alloush. She was the faithful caregiver of Lucy and she too passed away early in life. We educated her three children.

In that letter, I said:

Some days it is almost impossible for me to stay off the airplane. I want to decide to come to Kenya and visit. You are incredibly important to us and the reality of our relationship is something that nobody can stop, change, or throw away.

I particularly want you to know that I appreciated you spending the 24 hours of the International Day of Prayer staying in the Good Samaritan building, struggling and suffering in your prayers with all of those who prayed with you. I appreciate the fact that you sold out to Christ totally, 100% just like Mama Jenipher. I want you to know that your work with Lucy and the things you have been able to do for your community had a great effect on many lives. You brought more respect from all in the use of your life as a woman of God!

You know, Rose, if I hadn't come and been a woman, you would probably be nowhere in this world, but because God sent a woman to Uranga, gradually, the men recognized your spiritual work for the Kingdom of God.

B.K. Kirya, Kampala, Uganda, August 15, 1994:
On Wednesday, August 10th, we at Good Samaritan Ministries in Beaverton, Oregon, spent the entire day remembering the life, the teachings, and the example of B.K. to us and to his fellow man. We showed slides and the video of the speech and testimony he gave us while he was here in Oregon. We showed the video of the opening of the water project at Kisinji. We talked about our memories and the things that B.K. did at our house. We listened and will cherish the words "moral fiber," words that he stood for, by example. It was a very special day. Can you imagine clients coming for counseling were asked instead to participate in this event? I believe it was the only such day, in honor of B.K., in the United States. It was fitting and proper that it was here among people that he really loved and respected. We are people he took the time to know well, and we had taken cherished time to know him well.

Osborn said the funeral was wonderful. The testimonies were great. The tears of President Museveni and all of the people were profound. Osborn talked about the silence in Uganda, the day of quiet. "Surely, in the history of Uganda, there has never been such a day," he said. I believe he is right, Grace, because seldom, in all of political history in the entire world, has there ever been such a man. There was never a doubt in my mind that Jesus did call his name and that Jesus chose to use him to teach many. He carried his mantle well!

May 18, 1995, I wrote to Grace Kirya:
I still miss B.K., perhaps not as much as you do. He was a habit at your house, but I miss him in deep and profound ways. You are going to see in this newsletter, that I am going to teach two series on B.K.'s life and what he said to all of us: moral fiber is the essence. I am going to show the video of his life. I will teach the children in a series, and then I'm going to teach the adults in a series. In this way, I am preparing to come to Uganda and meet with you. We must continue his search for the essence of what moral fiber is as revealed by our dear and precious Savior, Jesus Christ.

Charlene Franzen, suffering from cancer, Republic of South Africa.

March 29, 2005, I wrote to Charlene Franzen:

Do you know how it is when a Mama carries a child? Well, the mama does most of the work, and a child just wiggles. You are now a child being carried by many. We are all fellow warriors.

May 18, 2005,
Dear Charlene and Vic,
In your overwhelming weakness, he is profoundly strong. The saints will carry you. Struggle not for life, life is yours. Fight for nothing, the battle is won. Your will is being conformed to the will of God. Your beauty is being transformed into His beauty.

Mr. Vic, in the day-to-day level of things, men have too much on their plate no matter what. You take as many pieces off your plate as you want to give up, but one thing you can never do is stand alone. We stand as a team, formidable before a living God who is fair, just and extremely interested in the outcome of each of our lives.

Vic, sing hymns and praises to God. Do not allow feelings to come and touch your faith nor any realm of your body. It is your assignment to sing unto the Lord.

September 23, 2005. Pastor Willie Booysen wrote:
Charlene was so willing to do our bidding, if she was convinced that something we challenged her with was the Lord's will. Most of the time for her, it just simply became His will. She had a servant's spirit, and put everything into that service: her house, her children, her money, her husband, her time, her talents, and above all, her love. She loved God, not in a gushing way, but she loved Him with everything she had in her. She made everything serve that purpose.

Mama Robinah, Kampala, Uganda:
Mama Robinah was the mother of Stanley Muwanga, the founder of GSM, Uganda. Although Stanley had a severe breakdown, he went on to be a Samaritan and to be more well in

his years that lay ahead. His mother was a great spirit. She never lost sight of what was important.

Osborn shared with us, Mama Robinah never missed a Good Samaritan Ministries meeting or a time of fasting and prayer. She was attentive to the needs that were everywhere. She raised her children in the fear of the Lord. She was respected by her whole community. She was profoundly respected by Bettie P. Mitchell, International Executive Director of Good Samaritan Ministries.

Letter I wrote to Osborn Muyanga upon the death of Mama Robinah, May 20, 2003:

Mama Robinah was born with the heart of a Samaritan. She comes from a time of unprecedented courage when Mamas of Uganda had to be all things for all people for the sake of the gospel. She lived that lesson daily.

In the last 13 years I have known Robinah, I have often found her name in my spirit. When I have gone to pray, it has been strange how her name tumbled out of my mouth almost first: Robinah, Robinah, Robinah. Dear God, remember Mama Robinah. I feel that we were bonded in the spirit in ways beyond our understanding. As we continue to intercede, there will be blessings for the children all over Uganda.

I want to say to the children of Mama Robinah, you have a heritage, but you must fulfill your own integrity. You must not only stand up and walk in the Name of Jesus by words, but also by your actions toward others. May we all be fellow Samaritans and great friends in the time to come, remembering Christ Jesus is among us all.

Osborn, I greet all in the ministry, and ask for comfort over those who have had a loss. You must reach out and appoint many to take Mama Robinah's place.

January 4, 2005, letter I wrote to be read at the funeral of James Kabvalo:

James Opiyo, Continental Director of Africa and myself, as the founder and International Executive Director of Good Samaritan Ministries, wish to proclaim to friends and fellow Samaritans in Malawi that James Kabvalo served the Lord well.

He always kept his priorities to ministry. He was honorable as a husband and a father. But above all things, he was honorable to Christ Jesus his Lord. We are fully aware James Kabvalo suffered much in recent months, but his suffering dates back many years when crowds came to push him, manipulate him, and the whisperers of unfair accusations. Let them all be confounded this day. Christ has prevailed in James Kabvalo's life! He never compromised the assignments given to him by the Holy Spirit.

As a ministry, we wish to comfort and uphold James' family, particularly his wife, Nancy, and their children. To the staff of Good Samaritan Ministries and workers throughout Malawi, we hope the best for you. We lift you up. We embrace you as beloved in Jesus Christ and fellow Samaritans.

As James Opiyo and James Kabvalo agreed upon the appointment of Samson Meleka as Good Samaritan Ministries Director in Malawi, let everyone come together in agreement that these decisions were made. Let there be no divisions, but only great rejoicing.

May the Lord be glorified in his funeral service and in the days ahead.

As I was just finishing up this book, another great hero of the faith, Nicholas Okungu died in November 2013. We had a memorial service for him at Good Samaritan Ministries on December 8, 2013. He gave birth to Good Samaritan Ministries local centers all over Kenya. I am very proud of Nicholas. After a long illness, he finished well!

December 1, 2013
Dear James and all of Uranga:
I know this is one of your times of deepest grief. You must keep your eye on your brother's healing. He has gone home and we will join him soon. Our longing must always be for the Kingdom of God.

I can imagine that the last months have been very painful and difficult to watch the depth of suffering and fear in another soul. I know now you sit and ponder what is required of you. I can honestly say you must remember what was required in Malawi. As Nicholas' life is with the saints, you are called to focus on the work that lays ahead for new leadership. James Kabvalo chose a great man, and the ministry prospered. I call you and challenge your faith to now do the same. I will be in a ton of prayer for you James. This must never be an emotional decision. Remember the Holy Spirit in Nick. Let your country be strengthened by Good Samaritan Ministries. Let living water flow over all of the people. We battle in the Name of Jesus and this will not come to an end, even in our passing over to His full Kingdom!

You know I love you James. You remain a friend of the heart and the Spirit. Catch the vision that the Lord will freely give you at this time. He is the Great Comforter.

I will be at the memorial for Nicholas here. April and Arabelle will come also, and of course Papa Jerry. I know we will all meet on that great road the Holy Spirit is preparing for us!!!

In Memory of Nicholas Okungu (1960-2013)
Letter to be read in Kenya at the funeral service of Nicholas Okungu:

We have been on a great journey together all these many years. At this time we are flooded with new and powerful memories. Nick has always been a servant. I am sure in heaven he will continue to serve His Lord and Savior. You will see great spiritual breakthroughs as he joins in the prayers of the Saints.

It is the privilege of Mama Bettie, Papa Jerry, and April to stand with you at our home in Uranga. We can feel the absolute presence of all of us gathered together, and the presence of those who died in Christ before our brother and faithful friend, Nicholas. The Comforter is present for each of you. He is especially present for his widow, Monica, and all of the family members.

This is not the time of the end of life. It is the time of new life. Illness and sorrow flee before the intimate presence of the Lord. He stands with all of us here today, to honor and remember Nicholas. Christ has a profound understanding of burial and resurrection. Today we are all in the presence of resurrection!

There were very special divine attributes given to Nicholas. He had endurance and compassion full measure and running over. April will always remember the years that Nicholas kept special and faithful intercession for her life. She will remember his kindness and protection that was personal and steadfast.

I will always remember the many journeys we made together. I can see Nick riding up the road on his bicycle to the center, across Kenya, but most of all, Nicholas went to the people. I know of his long hours in prayer, and his pure intentions toward each of us.

We did not share this end time, but we share all time.

I will always remember Nicholas making the trip to Pakistan with Joe Cooke. It was the longing of his heart to go to Pakistan. It was a time of wonder and joy! Healings and Salvations came to many.

My greatest and funniest time with Nicholas was when I was teaching at Uranga, and Nick was translating. He always made every motion I made. His translations were filled with the miracles of the spirit among us. Now on this particulate day, I fainted, and I was truly sick in front of many of you. When I fainted, Nicholas fainted with me, thinking I was probably slain in the Spirit. Everyone watched us while we lay on the cement floor. Then I came to, and Nick helped me up. I went right on teaching and Nick went right on translating.

I know many have come a long distance to be here today. Remember what a gifted teacher this man was. He made words come to life, and thus, many found understanding. I pray James Osewe is with us today. His life was totally changed forever by one small lesson Nicholas gave him.

It is our joy to know that you have all done well. How hard you prayed over the months. God heard them all. He gave an eternal answer. His answer strengthens all of us.

Nick made several trips to Oregon, and started many GSM centers in Kenya. He upheld us all! Now, you must continue to uphold one another! Let this very day bring healing to many of you. All over the world fellow Samaritans join you to honor our brother, Nicholas Okungu.

With great love and respect,
Mama Bettie and Papa Jerry

This book is filled with many stories. Some of these stories have impacted you deeply. Review the lives you've met. Think back to the life that truly impacted you and left you changed. Each of these stories is of faithful Samaritans along the hard road that leads to life for many.

I want you to name the ones you chose. Find the story again. Why did you choose that one? What was it that was speaking so deeply into your own soul? What will be your legacy?

My fellow Samaritans be at peace with one another and live for the purpose of good for all.

MALAWI

The Water Truck
By Vonda Winkle

A little boy covered with dirt,
he has no shoes.
Thirsty, very thirsty, but there is no water!
The rivers are dry, the water turned off.

A little boy waiting for the water truck.
It is the only source of water.
The little boy so thirsty and dry
waits for the water truck.

A little boy sees the water truck come.
Excitement arises, and people start coming.
Buckets in hand and on their heads,
the water has come.

But where is the little boy?
A woman screams and begins to wail.
The little boy was hit by the truck.
The water truck is here to quench the thirst.

Was the little boy's thirst quenched?
What is thirst? Can it be quenched?
Here's my cup, Lord. I lift it up, Lord.
Come and quench the thirst in my soul.

A little boy dies running for water.
Running for water to quench his thirst.
Jesus, meet him to quench the thirst of his soul.
Fill my cup, Lord, fill it up, and make me whole.

About the Author

 Bettie Mitchell lives every day as a Samaritan. She is the founder of Good Samaritan Ministries, and a mother of three daughters, and one adopted son, while married to Jerry for more than 60 years. Her life story will challenge and encourage you. In 1976, at the age of 42, she was standing on the walls of ancient Nineveh at Mosul, Iraq, when she heard the call. This call would change thousands of lives during the next 35 years as she sacrificed comfort to respond to the suffering of others in her neighborhood and in Africa. With a team of Samaritans, led by the Lord, people were healed across cultural, religious and geographic barriers.

An impossible assignment has become the only thing that is possible for a woman who deeply believes the shocking, radical words of Jesus recorded in the Bible. Bettie taught Bible classes at Portland Community College, as well as working for 18 years as a substitute teacher in public schools. During her life, she began traveling with her mother and now has traveled to 55 countries, including 24 times to the Middle East.

In 1976, she heard the call while traveling in Iraq, (as described in her book, *Something Worth Saving*). Bettie was standing on the wall in the ancient city of Nineveh. She saw children playing. Suddenly her thoughts were interrupted. The Lord asked her, "Do you see the children?" She said, "Yes, Lord." He said, "Here are the children, where are the teachers? I want you to go home and quit your teaching job, and teach nothing but my Kingdom."

This call was confirmed three days later in a town called Irbil. Then in Ur she received the message from the Lord, "Every thought in your brain is negative and judgmental." So the instruction from the Lord came: "I want you to take each thought and bring it to me...and I will change your mind." She agreed and did it.

Born in Colorado and raised in Oregon, Bettie began the ministry in her home in Beaverton, Oregon. Read more about her life story in her book, *Something Worth Saving*. In 1986, Bettie was surprised when an African came to her office to meet her. In Bettie's sixth book, *From the Bush to the Roots,* find out how thousands of adults and children in Africa continue to be touched by non-judgmental Samaritan love.

Books by this author:

- *From the Bush to the Roots, The Story of Good Samaritan Ministries in Africa* (2014)
- *Something Worth Saving* (2012)
- *Shall We Walk On By?* Co-authored with Alan R. Gasso (2013)
- *The Power of Conflict and Sacrifice: A Therapy Manual for Christian Marriage* (1995)
- *A Need for Understanding: A Handbook for Basic Counseling Information* (1992)
- *Who Is My Neighbor? A Parable*; Edited and Illustrated by 'Tucker' Mitchell (1988)

Learn more about Samaritan training and outreach—and see the link to the one-hour You Tube video Love Breaks Through & Mission to Africa at the GSM website:

www.GoodSamaritanMinistries.org

Made in the USA
Middletown, DE
16 May 2021